ANALECTA BIBLICA

INVESTIGATIONES SCIENTIFICAE IN RES BIBLICAS

172

HENRY PATTARUMADATHIL, S.J.

YOUR FATHER IN HEAVEN

DISCIPLESHIP IN MATTHEW AS A PROCESS OF BECOMING CHILDREN OF GOD

EDITRICE PONTIFICIO ISTITUTO BIBLICO - ROMA 2008

Vidimus et approbamus ad normam Statutorum Universitatis

Romae, ex Pontificia Universitate Gregoriana
die 06 mensis iunii anni 2007

R.P. Prof. KLEMENS STOCK, S.J.
Prof. MASSIMO GRILLI

ISBN 978-88-7653-172-9

EDITRICE PONTIFICIO ISTITUTO BIBLICO
Piazza della Pilotta, 35 - 00187 Roma, Italia

PREFACE

This book is a revised version of my doctoral dissertation defended at the Faculty of Theology of the Pontifical Gregorian University, Rome, on 19 May 2007.

I dedicate this work to the loving memory of Fr. Philip Kalarickal S.J., who inspired me to join the Society of Jesus, and initiated me into the Jesuit way of life. Fr. Philip used to tell us, pre-novices, that "authenticity" is one of the important characteristics expected of a disciple of Jesus. Eighteen years later when I set out for my doctoral studies, I thought of taking this expected quality of the disciples as the theme for my dissertation. In Matt 6,1-18, I could trace a powerful presentation of this theme. Hence I chose this textual unit for my study and proposed the following title for the consideration of my director: "Jesus' call for authenticity in Matt 6,1-18".

Fr. Klemens Stock S.J., my director, welcomed the suggestion and encouraged me to begin the study of the chosen unit. However, he called my attention to the fact that the word authenticity is a non-biblical word, and he asked me to keep my eyes and ears open while I studied the text, so that I might discover a biblical phrase or a word which would explicate the theme.

After a few days of study the repetitive use of the term "your Father" in this section caught my attention, in fact, it intrigued me. I felt as if somebody was telling me, "this term is special", "this term is the key". With this inspiration when I reread the gospel, I found twenty-one such terms in Matthew, used by Jesus, presenting God as the Father of the disciples. It was also quite exciting to learn that God is portrayed very rarely as the Father of the disciples in the other gospels. This finding prompted me to expand my study to all the "your Father" passages in Matthew; as a result, I changed the title to, "Disciples in Matthew as the children of God". My director was happy with this new turn in my research, but still he reminded me to continue studying the text attentively.

Further, the study of the verse Matt 5,45, especially the clause "so that you may become sons of your Father", raised some new questions. Are the disciples not already children? If they are already children what does it mean to say "become sons of your Father"? If they are not children why does Jesus present God as their Father so frequently? These questions and my discussions with Fr. Stock eventually led me to the thesis that I propound in this work, namely, discipleship is viewed in Matthew as a process of becoming children of God.

The story of the evolution of my thesis reflects also the way my director Fr. Stock accompanied me in this academic pilgrimage. I remember, in one of our first meetings he told me that writing a doctoral dissertation is an academic formation. I have been fortunate to have him as my formator. With scholarly precision and fraternal affection he guided me through the process. My heart leaps with immense joy and gratitude when I think of Fr. Stock and our journey together.

Inexpressible is my indebtedness to my professors and the library staff at the Pontifical Biblical Institute and companions in the Biblicum community for the guidance, love and encouragement I have received throughout the period of my licentiate and doctoral studies.

I am grateful to Prof. Massimo Grilli, the second reader of my thesis, for his insightful and constructive comments on my work. My sincere thanks are due to Frs. Robert Althann S.J., Dean Béchard S.J., Joseph Nalpathilchira, Joseph Kottukapally S.J. and Thomas Panikulam S.J. who read the draft attentively and made some valuable suggestions for improvement. With gratitude I acknowledge the influence of my companions Paul Béré S.J. and Sunny Kokkaravalayil S.J. on the formulation and articulation of my thesis. I thank Fr. James Swetnam S.J. and Mrs Penelope Watson who kindly helped me to amend the text for publication.

I wish to express my sincere gratitude to Fr. Pietro Bovati S.J., the director of *Analecta Biblica*, for graciously accepting to publish my work in this series, and to Fr. Roman J. Lebiedziuk C.R., Mr. Carlo Valentino and Mr. Vincenzo Tocci for all their technical assistance.

Many more are my Jesuit brethren to whom I am deeply indebted: the Provincial and members of Kerala province, the Delegate for the International Houses in Rome and his team, the Regional Assistant and members of the South Asian Assistancy in Rome, the staff and students of the Jesuit Regional Theology Centre (Kalady), the Missionsprokur of Jesuitenmission (Germany). They sustained me throughout my study with fraternal love and care providing me with everything I needed for the completion of my work.

I thank the Lord for my friends and relatives who stood with me in my joys and sorrows during these years of study, strengthening me with their love and prayers.

TABLE OF CONTENTS

GENERAL INTRODUCTION

1. The Thesis

The concept of discipleship in Matthew has been explained in several ways using different "identity defining terms" from the gospel such as "one who does the will of God", "one who practises the greater righteousness", "one who becomes like a child", "one who carries the cross" etc. The present study identifies the extensively but selectively used relational appellation πατήρ for God in the gospel as the most important key for understanding the identity of the disciples. By examining all the passages where this appellation is used to refer to God as the Father of the disciples, this study will show that discipleship is viewed in Matthew as a process of becoming children of God.[1]

2. State of the Question and Focus of the Study

A number of studies have dealt with the theme of disciples and discipleship in Matthew, especially in the last sixty years. The Matthean concept of discipleship has generally been explored in two ways: 1. based on the actual portrayal of the disciples; 2. based on the ideal of discipleship reflected in the teachings of Jesus.

2.1 *On the Actual Portrayal of the Disciples*

Studies on the actual portrayal of the disciples in Matthew often attempt to answer questions regarding the presentation of the character or the behavioural pattern of the disciples and its function in the gospel. How do the

[1] In Matthew God is presented as the Father of the disciples twenty-one times, in Mark once, in Luke four times, and in John once.

disciples respond to the person of Jesus and his teachings? Do they understand him or not? What message has been communicated to the reader through their understanding or misunderstanding?

Those who study the portrayal of the disciples in Matthew with the help of redaction criticism, comparing Matthew's presentation of the disciples with that of Mark, usually come to the conclusion that in Matthew, unlike Mark, the disciples are portrayed as the ones who understand the teachings of Jesus.[2] In contrast, those who study the text using narrative criticism, analyzing the presentation of the disciples in Matthew's plot, come up with a negative view of the disciples as the ones who are "men of little faith" who do not understand Jesus and his message.[3]

Regarding the function of the portrayal of character, reflections are often made on three different levels: its function in the textual world, in the concrete world and in the symbolic world.[4] While the redaction critics in general consider the character of the disciples presented in the gospel as a "reflection" of the Matthean community and a model for the church and its leaders,[5] the

---

[2] Cf. G. BARTH, "Matthew's Understanding of the Law", 106-107; G. STRECKER, *Der Weg der Gerechtigkeit*, 191-198; U. LUZ, "The Disciples in the Gospel", 102-104 (Luz makes a clarification of his view on the understanding of the disciples: "[...] the disciples receive far more frequent special instructions in Matthew than in any other gospel [...]. It means that the disciples often fail to understand, but that they come to understand through Jesus' explanation [13:51]. For Matthew it is important that the disciples do finally – after Jesus' instruction – understand" [pp. 102-103]); M. J. WILKINS, *The Concept of Disciple*, 165, holds the same view as Luz: "It is because of Jesus that the disciples move to understanding"; ID., "Named and Unnamed Disciples", 422. See M. SHERIDAN, "Disciples and Discipleship", 244-246 and J.A. OVERMAN, *Matthew's Gospel*, 127-129, for a very positive view of the understanding of the Matthean disciples.

[3] Cf. J.D. KINGSBURY, *Matthew as Story*, 129.130.138. Referring to Jesus' conflict with the disciples narrated on different occasions in the gospel, Kingsbury interprets this conflict as the disciples' "imperceptiveness, and at times resistance, to the notion that servanthood is the essence of discipleship" (p. 130). R.A. EDWARDS, "Uncertain Faith", 52-59, describes the disciples as "inconsistent followers" who never live up to Jesus' expectations of them; ID., *Matthew's Narrative Portrait*, 38-39.76-77.124-125. 139-140. See also D.B. HOWELL, *Matthew's Inclusive Story*, 148; W. CARTER, *Matthew: Storyteller*, 217-225; T.L. DONALDSON, "Guiding Readers – Making Disciples", 36. More recently, J.K. Brown in her narrative study of Matt 16,21–20,28, comes to the conclusion: "In Matthew, the disciples are consistently portrayed as misunderstanding Jesus' mission and message, as exhibiting inadequate faith, and as falling short of the significant role intended for them as Jesus' disciples." J.K. BROWN, *The Disciples in Narrative Perspective*, 119.

[4] This system of three levels on which to read the gospel of Matthew is suggested by K. SYREENI, "Separation and Identity", 522-541.

[5] Cf. G. BARTH, "Matthew's Understanding of the Law", 110-111; W. TRILLING, *Das wahre Israel*, 159.213; U. LUZ, "The Disciples in the Gospel", 103; (however, according to Luz

narrative critics resist attributing such functions to the portrayal.[6] According to them, the disciples in the narrative function as a teaching tool, at times a negative example – a foil – of discipleship for the readers.[7] From the disciples' incomprehension of the authority and teaching of Jesus the reader learns to avoid such a response and to grow in proper understanding and faith.[8]

The focus of the present study is not so much on the actual portrayal of the disciples or its function as on the ideal of discipleship as it has been presented in Matthew.

2.2 *On the Ideal of Discipleship*

In general, studies and reflections on the ideal of discipleship in Matthew are based on the teachings of Jesus, especially in the Great Discourses. Perhaps, D. Bonhoeffer's, *Nachfolge* (1937) can be considered as one of the first works in the last century dealing with this theme. As the title of its English translation indicates, this book discusses in detail the elements of the call to discipleship and the cost one has to pay for that call.[9] Though Bonhoeffer treats in this book the concept of discipleship in the gospels in general, most of his reflections are based on the gospel of Matthew, especially on the Sermon on the Mount. According to him, discipleship means adherence to Christ; it is primarily a faith-surrender to him as the mediator of God.[10] One's life as a disciple is a growth in faith, which makes one take up the challenges of this call courageously and bear the cost gladly. Bonhoeffer has repeatedly underscored the imperative of fulfilling the ethical demands that

---

the disciples' understanding in Matthew is not intended to idealize them, but to authorize them for the mission given in 28,20); M. SHERIDAN, "Disciples and Discipleship", 255; H. FRANKEMÖLLE, *Jahwebund und Kirche Christi*, 150-158; J. ZUMSTEIN, *La Condition du croyant*, 41-42; P.S. MINEAR, "The Disciples and the Crowds", 31-32; M. J. WILKINS, *The Concept of Disciple*, 171-172; J.A. OVERMAN, *Matthew's Gospel*, 135-136.

[6] Analysing eleven episodes, which he calls "character-shaping incidents", from the gospel, R.A. EDWARDS, *Matthew's Narrative Portrait*, 143, concludes that "a disciple [...] is not an ideal individual who meets Jesus' expectations, but one who recognizes Jesus and who will follow him, in a limited fashion, under most conditions." Similarly, T.L. DONALDSON, "Guiding Readers – Making Disciples", 36: "In their relationship with Jesus, while some positive factors are mentioned, for the most part the emphasis in Matthew's gospel falls on the slowness of the disciples to understand (15:12-20; 16:5-12), on their fear (14:26,30), and on their lack of faith."

[7] D.J. VERSEPUT, "The Faith of the Reader", 21.

[8] D.B. HOWELL, *Matthew's Inclusive Story*, 247.

[9] The title of the English translation is *The Cost of Discipleship*.

[10] D. BONHOEFFER, *The Cost of Discipleship*, 59.

have been required of the disciples. A single-minded obedience to Jesus, an unconditional submission to his law which is the law of the cross, doing the will of the Father revealed through him, following his righteousness – these are some of the essential characteristics of a disciple highlighted in this work.

In later years, too, most of the discussions on the concept of discipleship in Matthew have been centred on the "way of life" or the "proper response" expected of the disciples in Jesus' teachings. Thus, scholars have explained discipleship in the first gospel mainly in two ways: as "a life of submission and obedience" both to the will of God and to the authority of Jesus,[11] and as "imitation of Jesus".[12] In fact, they are two interrelated aspects of discipleship and are not distinct from each other. Whether discipleship is understood as submission to the will of God or to the authority of Jesus, or as imitation of Jesus, the focus of these explanations is on the action, on the ethical practice, of the person.

This common scholarly view of discipleship as an ethical practice has been summarized very well by D. Patte in his study *Discipleship according to the Sermon on the Mount*.[13] He examines in this study the interpretations of six authors, including his own, on the concept of discipleship according to Matt 4,18-22 and the Sermon on the Mount.[14] Patte has carefully analysed

---

[11] G. BARTH, "Matthew's Understanding of the Law", 102: "Since for Matthew the condition of being a disciple is determined by belonging to the διδάσκαλος and κύριος (10.24f.), that means doing the will of God is the entire essence and meaning of being a disciple." See W. TRILLING, *Das wahre Israel*, 187-211; U. LUZ, "The Disciples in the Gospel", 109: "Disciples are those who hear and understand the commands and teachings of Jesus, and do God's will"; R. MOHRLANG, *Matthew and Paul*, 75: "Discipleship means radical submission to the will of God"; see also A. WOUTERS, *„...wer den Willen*, 161-296. Wouters highlights doing the will of the Father and living a greater righteousness following the model of Jesus as the essence of discipleship in Matthew.

[12] G. BORNKAMM, "End-Expectation", 30: "Readiness to suffer (10.17ff.; 16.24ff.), poverty (19.23ff.; 6.19ff.), lowliness (18.1ff.), love (25.31ff. and often), renunciation of worldly honour (23.7ff.) and service (20.20ff.), these are the marks of discipleship." See G. BARTH, "Matthew's Understanding of the Law", 102-105. Consider the following statement from the preface of the commentary of M.H. FRANZMANN, *Follow Me*, vi: "God is known by His works, and the Christ is known by the disciples whom He by His call creates, and by His communion with them shapes in His own image." According to J.D. KINGSBURY, *Matthew as Story*, 140, servanthood on the model of Jesus is the essence of discipleship. U. LUZ, "Discipleship: a Matthean Manifesto", 154-159, specifies imitation of the poverty of the Son of Man and his sufferings as constitutive marks of discipleship; ID., *The Theology*, 80: "Discipleship means conforming to the life of Christ and emulating his model."

[13] D. PATTE, *Discipleship*.

[14] He analyses the works of the following six authors in this study: G. STRECKER, *Der Weg der Gerechtigkeit*; ID., *The Sermon on the Mount*; J.D. KINGSBURY, "The Verb *Akoluthein*", 56-

each one's method of interpretation, their conclusions about what the text is and says, and their conclusions about the teaching of the text for a specific audience. He has also made an attempt to deduce the value judgements emerging from these interpretations and to apply them to situations in real life. Identifying the views of all these authors on discipleship as ethical practice, he groups them into two categories: "discipleship as doing the will of God" and "discipleship as imitation".[15] In his later work, *The Challenge of Discipleship*, following more or less the same method of comparative study, he summarizes the interpretations of seven different authors on the concept of discipleship in four categories: "as doing God's will", "as imitating Christ", "as struggling for the kingdom and God's justice", and "as fulfilling the Scripture".[16] All these designations conceive discipleship basically as an ethical practice.

There have been a few attempts in recent years to look at Matthean discipleship from new angles. S. Grasso in his dissertation, studying all the passages where Jesus speaks about his brothers, presents discipleship as the brotherhood of Jesus.[17] S.C. Barton in his sociological study of Matthean discipleship discusses in great detail the subordination of family and household ties to the call of Jesus and his kingdom.[18] Similarly, C. Landmesser, studying the episode of the call of Matthew and Jesus' dinner with the tax collectors and sinners and the consequent controversy with the Pharisees (Matt 9,9-13), accentuates the soteriological dimension of

---

73; ID., *Matthew as Story*; U. LUZ, "The Disciples in the Gospel", 98-128; ID., *Matthew 1–7*; ID., *The Theology*; W.D. DAVIES – D.C. ALLISON, *Matthew,* I-II; R.A. EDWARDS, *Matthew's Story of Jesus*; ID., "Uncertain Faith", 47-61; D. PATTE, *The Gospel according to Matthew.*

[15] According to Patte's classification the works of Strecker, Kingsbury and Edwards conceive discipleship as "doing the will of God" whereas the works of Luz, Davies–Allison and Patte regard discipleship as imitation. See D. PATTE, *Discipleship*, 267.

[16] D. PATTE, *The Challenge of Discipleship*. Besides the works of the six authors he compares in *Discipleship* (see n. 14), he examines the concept of discipleship reflected in the article by C.B. GALLARDO, "Matthew: Good News for the Persecuted Poor", 173-192, also in this book.

[17] S. GRASSO, *Gesù e i suoi fratelli*, 239-240.

[18] "Following Jesus involves participation in mission to all nations to proclaim the in-breaking of the kingdom of heaven and the soon-coming of the Son of Man. It involves also participation in the new covenant community inaugurated by Jesus. On both scores, family and household ties are relativized strongly. Likewise, and not surprisingly, resistance and hostility from members' own hometown and kinship groups is to be expected." S.C. BARTON, *Discipleship and Family Ties*, 218. See also the study by W. CARTER, *Households and Disciples*.

discipleship in his work.[19] L. Sánchez Navarro, in his study of Matt 11,28-30 and related texts, defines discipleship in Matthew as communion with Jesus which requires a vital apprenticeship (learning from Jesus). Through this communion the disciples participate in the Sonship of Jesus and find rest for the soul. This study regards discipleship as the basis for "ethic" – "the knowledge about happiness and doing good" – in Matthew's gospel.[20]

2.3 *Originality and Limits of the Present Study*

The present study views the life of the disciples in two stages: their life in the present (the earthly stage), and in the future (the kingdom stage). By hearing the message of Jesus and responding to it positively, they receive the grace to enter the family of Jesus in the world and thus are initiated into the process of becoming children of God. In fact, already in the world they are considered children of God by Jesus. That is why he presents God as their Father. But this filial identity in the present stage is not unalterable. They are in an "already" but "not yet" state. There are various inimical forces in this world – both internal and external – which tempt the children to break their relationship with the Father. Those who complete the process successfully here, overcoming enemies, will enter the kingdom stage where they will dwell as the children of the Father for ever.[21]

By presenting discipleship as a process, the present study also underlines the importance of ethical practice in the life of the disciples. To progress in their journey the disciples have to do the will of the Father, which has been revealed through the life and teachings of Jesus; they have to listen to Jesus' words and put them into practice and teach others to obey them. However,

---

[19] C. LANDMESSER, *Jüngerberufung und Zuwendung zu Gott*. The subtitle of his work clearly indicates the focus of the study: "Ein exegetischer Beitrag zum Konzept der matthäischen Soteriologie im Anschluß an Mt 9,9-13."

[20] L. SÁNCHEZ NAVARRO, *"Venid a mí" (Mt 11,28-30)*, 365.

[21] J. GNILKA, *Matthäusevangelium*, I, 193-194, has mentioned this two-stage process of discipleship: "Wir haben die Gotteskindschaft als etwas Dynamisches anzusehen. Gott hat die Jünger bereits angenommen, aber so lange sie in dieser Welt leben, stehen sie unter Bewährung. Erst am Ende werden sie unwiderruflich seine Kinder sein." W. CARTER, in his work *Households and Disciples* presents this process in a different way. Employing Victor Turner's model of liminality (see V. TURNER, *The Ritual Process*), Carter describes discipleship in Matthew as a "liminal existence". "The transition process begins with the separation [call] and ends with reaggregation, with the liminal phase being in-between" (p. 52); Carter identifies the end point of discipleship as the parousia (pp. 53.205); see also ID., *Matthew: Storyteller*, 226.

their "ethical practices" are not the ultimate goal of their discipleship, but a means to arrive at its real goal: becoming children of God.

The present study substantiates its thesis – discipleship as a process of becoming children of God – by showing how this process has been spelled out in the πατήρ passages which refer to God as the Father of the disciples in Matthew. These passages explicitly state the paternity of God and consequently the "filiality" of the disciples.[22] Following the observations of R.L. Mowery on the selective use of the appellation πατήρ for God in Matthew, we show in this study that in the gospel of Matthew the Father-children relationship is a privilege of the disciples of Jesus, the Son.[23]

Several studies on Matthew have highlighted the filial identity of the disciples so intensely presented in the gospel. For example, H. Frankemölle in his book, *Jahwebund und Kirche Christi*, by referring to the "Father passages" and the "son(s) passages" in the gospel, argues that the Father-children relationship between God and the disciples is the basis of membership in the new community, the Church.[24] Similarly, J.D. Kingsbury, *Matthew: Structure, Christology, Kingdom*, in the context of his explanation of Jesus' identity as the Son of God, presents the disciples as the ones called by the Son

---

[22] There has been an ongoing discussion about the nature of the paternity of God mentioned in the gospels. Is his Fatherhood universal or particular? In 1950, W. Bennett, in his article "The Sons of the Father", analysing the passages where Jesus addresses God as the Father in the Synoptic gospels, proposed the following view: "The old and much debated argument of the universal Fatherhood of God and sonship of all men should come to an end. God is supremely and uniquely the Father of Jesus, who reveals him as one whose fatherly love is offered to all men, who must themselves choose either to respond to him as loyal sons or reject him as lost sons, dead in self-determinism" (p. 23). In this article Bennett has reflected upon the disciples' filial relationship with the Father, and has noted how one can grow in this relationship. See W. BENNETT, "The Sons of the Father", 13-23. H.F.D. Sparks, in 1955, examining all the Father passages from the gospels where God is presented as the Father of human beings with the help of redaction criticism, argued that God's paternity mentioned in the gospels is universal. See H.F.D. SPARKS, "The Doctrine of the Divine Fatherhood", 241-262. In the following year, H.W. Montefiore reaffirmed Sparks's conclusion in his article "God as Father in the Synoptic Gospels", 31-46. Several monographs and articles written in subsequent years continued the discussion, examining various aspects of the Fatherhood of God in the OT and in the NT. To mention a few, J. JEREMIAS, *The Prayers of Jesus*, 11-65; R. HAMERTON-KELLY, *God the Father*; D. ZELLER, "God as Father", 117-129; J. BARR, "Abba Isn't 'Daddy'", 28-47; A. STROTMANN, *"Mein Vater bist du!" (Sir 51,10)*; M.M. THOMPSON, *The Promise of the Father*; B. WITHERINGTON III – L.M. ICE, *The Shadow of the Almighty*, 19-65.

[23] R.L. MOWERY, "God, Lord, and Father", 24-36.

[24] H. FRANKEMÖLLE, *Jahwebund und Kirche Christi*, 159-177.

of God to become sons of God through him.[25] More recently, E. Manicardi in his article "Dio Padre nella prospettiva del vangelo secondo Matteo" has underscored the filial identity of the disciples through which the paternity of God is manifested in the world.[26] Likewise, B. Charette,[27] M. Dumais,[28] T. Roh,[29] and U. Vanni[30] have also noted the Matthean presentation of the disciples as the children of God in their respective studies.[31] Since the filial identity of the disciples is not the centre point of their studies, this theme has not been elaborated in their works. Similarly, to our knowledge, no treatise has been written on those πατήρ passages which express the disciples' filial identity, and show discipleship in Matthew as a process of becoming children of God

Five different dimensions of discipleship – christological, ecclesiological, missiological, eschatological, and ethical – are integrated in the present study. Discipleship is a process of becoming children of God: through Jesus, the Son, one can become a child of God (christological); by responding affirmatively to Jesus and to his message one enters the earthly family of God and continues his/her journey with other brothers and sisters (ecclesiological); through their life witness and teachings the disciples attract and invite other people to join them in their process of becoming children of God (missiological); one becomes irrevocably a child of God only in the kingdom (eschatological); to reach this state one should do the will of God and practise the greater righteousness (ethical).

3. **Methodology**

The method of interpretation used in this dissertation is founded on the Christian view that the evangelist is sharing his faith experience and convictions with his readers through the gospel so that they also may enter

---

[25] J.D. KINGSBURY, *Matthew: Structure,* 55-56. In support of his affirmation, Kingsbury refers to the πατήρ passages where God is presented as the Father of the disciples, to the υἱοί passages where disciples are presented as the sons of God, and to the ἀδελφοί passages where they are presented as the brothers of Jesus.

[26] E. MANICARDI, "Dio Padre", 81-106. In this article the author surveys all the Father passages in Matthew and lays emphasis on the Matthean accent on the paternity of God. See also ID., "La paternità di Dio", 101-118.

[27] B. CHARETTE, *The Theme of Recompense*, 93-94.

[28] M. DUMAIS, *Le Sermon sur la Montagne*, 224-226.

[29] T. ROH, *Die familia dei*, 164-225.

[30] U. VANNI, *Con Gesù verso il Padre*, 181-234.

[31] See also M. VELLANICKAL, *The Divine Sonship of Christians*, 53-61; ID., "The Christian Righteousness", 106-121.

into and grow in that faith.[32] Throughout this study we read the gospel and interpret it while keeping in mind this faith-purpose of the evangelist.[33]

In our interpretation of the text we often refer to the OT and sometimes to other Jewish writings. This is on the assumption that these sources have influenced the author in forming his faith convictions and their articulation.

Wherever it is pertinent we point out the distinctiveness of the Matthean text comparing it with the other two Synoptic gospels; however, redactional hypotheses and conclusions are avoided.

Following a synchronic approach, we seek to substantiate our thesis with a textual study of the chosen passages from Matthew in its final form. In each case the text is interpreted considering its grammatical, syntactic and semantic particularities. Reading the text intra-textually and inter-textually we look into the contextual and theological significance of each passage under consideration.

4. **Itinerary of the Study**

This dissertation is organized in four chapters. As the enunciation of the thesis indicates, our study is based on the passages where God is referred to as the Father (πατήρ) of the disciples in Matthew. There are twenty-one such references and they are studied in the first three chapters of this treatise.

Sixteen out of the twenty-one references are in the Sermon on the Mount (SM), in which ten of them are found in 6,1-18, at the centre of the Sermon. Such a concentrated use of this term at the centre of the SM, the first Great Discourse in Matthew, indicates its significance for the whole SM, if not for the whole gospel. In the first chapter we study this unit and show how discipleship is viewed as a process of becoming children of God. With the support of a comparative statistical survey the uniqueness of the use of the term πατήρ for God in Matthew and its theological implications are verified at the outset of this chapter. This is followed by a detailed study of Jesus' teaching on the righteousness of the disciples and three ways of putting it into practice – almsgiving, prayer, fasting – given in this unit. This chapter discusses also the "heavenly reward" that awaits the children at the end of the process.

---

[32] One of the faith convictions of the evangelist we underscore in this study is that Jesus is the Son of God, sent into the world, to make others children of God; those who listen to Jesus' words and live accordingly will become God's children.

[33] See VATICAN COUNCIL II, *Dei Verbum* § 8.17.19; THE PONTIFICAL BIBLICAL COMMISSION, *The Interpretation of the Bible*, 91-92.107-108.

In the second chapter we analyse the remaining πατήρ verses from the SM (5,16.45.48; 6,26.32; 7,11) together with their immediate contexts and highlight various stages of the process reflected in them. Besides the above mentioned sixteen references, there is only one more reference to God as the πατήρ in the SM, and it is in 7,21 where, for the first time in the gospel, Jesus presents God as his Father. Considering the exceptional significance of this verse and its context for our thesis, we also study this verse in the second chapter.

The rest of the πατήρ passages which are distributed in the other Great Discourses in Matthew are examined in chapter three. We identify five of them: two in the Mission Discourse (10,20.29); one in the Parable Discourse (13,43); one in the Community Discourse (18,14); one in the Final Discourse (23,9).

In our study of the πατήρ passages, we come across various guidelines that Jesus gives his disciples to be practised in their lives so that they may complete the process successfully and be received as God's children in the kingdom. Now, throughout the gospel the evangelist presents Jesus as the ideal Son who fulfils all the requirements that he demands from the disciples. It is only through him and following his example that the disciples can become children of God. In the fourth chapter of our study we discuss briefly Matthew's presentation of Jesus' mediatory role in the disciples becoming children of God. We highlight here some passages from the gospel which demonstrate the identity of the Son, those which narrate his calling and forming the disciples, and those which present his exemplary lifestyle.

In the general conclusion, after presenting a summary of the different aspects of the process of discipleship discussed in this study, a brief reflection is made on the dynamics of discipleship today.

CHAPTER I

The Father and Children at the Centre of the Sermon on the Mount

The Sermon on the Mount (SM), the first Great Discourse of Jesus in the gospel of Matthew, can be considered as the manifesto of discipleship. To an audience, which comprises his newly-called four disciples and a crowd who followed him, Jesus explains in detail what it means to be a disciple.[1] Various issues concerning the disciples' identity and lifestyle – their relationship with God, with Jesus, with their brothers and sisters, and with the material world – are discussed at great length in the SM.[2]

---

[1] The reason for Jesus' going up on the mountain is given at the beginning of the SM as his "seeing the crowd" (5,1). It is occasionally interpreted that Jesus went up on the mountain to escape the crowd. Cf. W.D. DAVIES – D.C. ALLISON, *Matthew,* I, 421; D.A. HAGNER, *Matthew 1–13*, 86. But the reaction of the crowd mentioned at the end of the SM (7,28) shows that the crowd also heard Jesus. Therefore, Jesus' climbing up on the mountain may be better interpreted as an act of choosing a suitable place for addressing a large number of people (see 9,36) than as a means of avoiding the crowd (as in 8,18). See P.S. MINEAR, "The Disciples and the Crowds", 32-33; G. STRECKER, *The Sermon on the Mount*, 25-26; G. KEERANKERI, "Matthew's Gospel", 114-115; J. NOLLAND, *Matthew*, 191.

[2] The term "disciples" (μαθηταί) occurs in 5,1 for the first time in the gospel, and the disciples' presence in the scene is specifically emphasized using the word προσέρχομαι (coming near). Matthew uses this word προσέρχομαι fifty-one times in the gospel, of which ten refer to the disciples' coming near to Jesus for various reasons: with a question (13,10.36; 17,19; 18,1; 24,3), with an observation (15,12; 24,1) or with a proposal (14,15; 15,23). In all the above texts προσέρχομαι appears with another supplementary verb. But in 5,1 προσέρχομαι stands alone and the disciples come near to Jesus not to ask him or to propose anything, but to be near to him. See K. STOCK, *Discorso della Montagna*, 13-16. So from the use of

The divine appellation πατήρ occurs seventeen times in the SM, ten of them standing at its structural centre, 6,1-18. Referring to their relationship with the Father, Jesus instructs the disciples in this unit on how they, in contrast to hypocrites and Gentiles, should practise righteous deeds and thus become worthy of the divine reward. The "Our Father", the model prayer Jesus taught, which reflects different aspects of the filial relationship of the disciples with God, appears at the centre of this unit.

In this chapter after a brief presentation of the structure of the SM, which will show the central position of the unit 6,1-18 and its theological importance, we will offer an exegetical study of the unit examining the concept of discipleship expressed here.

1. **The Father-children Relationship, the Focal Point of the SM**

The structural arrangement of the SM clearly shows the central position of 6,1-18 in this discourse. Considering the distribution of the term πατήρ, we can also call it the theological centre of the SM. An examination of the structural and theological centrality of this unit will lead us to the conclusion that the Father-children relationship between God and the disciples, which is the basis of the teachings in this unit, is also the focal point of the whole Sermon.

1.1 *The Central Position of 6,1-18 in the Structure of the SM*

Having considered its context, literary style, form, content, and theology, a number of scholars have suggested a concentric structure of the SM, in which 6,1-18, especially the Lord's Prayer, comes at the centre.[3] Drawing

---

προσέρχομαι which emphasizes the physical proximity of the disciples to Jesus, we may assume that the disciples formed a primary group closer to Jesus, and the crowd sat just behind them forming an "outer circle". See G. KEERANKERI, "Matthew's Gospel", 116-118. We may also consider the crowd here as the crowd who had been following (ἀκολουθέω) Jesus as he was preaching, teaching and healing in Galilee (4,23-25); later some of them might have even followed him permanently. In this study, we use the term "disciples" to refer to both the actual disciples and the "would-be disciples" or the future disciples of Jesus. See J. LAMBRECHT, *The Sermon on the Mount,* 30; D. PATTE, *Matthew*, 63.

[3] See G. BORNKAMM, "Der Aufbau der Bergpredigt", 419-432; J. LAMBRECHT, *The Sermon on the Mount,* 28; U. LUZ, *Matthew 1–7*, 211-213; J.D. KINGSBURY, "The Place, Structure, and Meaning", 136; K. STOCK, *Discorso della Montagna*, 6-8; K. SYREENI, *The Making of the Sermon,* 168-184. However, there are several others who do not consider 6,1-18 as the centre of the SM. For a summary of different proposals regarding the structure of the SM, see the following works: J. DUPONT, *Les Béatitudes*, I, 180-181; D.C. ALLISON, Jr, "The Structure of the Sermon", 424-425; J.S. SIBINGA, "Exploring the Composition of Matthew 5–7", 176-179.

from the observations of some of these authors, we may propose the following structure:[4]

A 5,1-2 the setting
B 5,3-16 general introduction
C 5,17-20 introduction of the particular norms
D 5,21-48 relationship with one's neighbour
E 6,1-18 relationship with God
D[1] 6,19–7,11 relationship with material things
C[1] 7,12 conclusion of the particular norms
B[1] 7,13-27 general conclusion
A[1] 7,28–8,1 the setting

The above structure does not claim that there is an exact and equal correspondence between all the parallel parts. However, a great degree of correlation can be observed. The narrative texts in 5,1-2 and 7,28–8,1 form the framework of the Sermon.[5] The words ὄχλοι and διδάσκω are present in both places; climbing up to the mountain (ἀνέβη εἰς τὸ ὄρος) in 5,1 matches with coming down from the mountain (καταβάντος .... ἀπὸ τοῦ ὄρους) in 8,1. Similarly "he opened his mouth" (ἀνοίξας τὸ στόμα αὐτοῦ) in 5,2 has its counterpart in 7,28 – "when Jesus finished these sayings" (ὅτε ἐτέλεσεν ὁ Ἰησοῦς τοὺς λόγους τούτους).

In 5,3-16 the nature of the teaching is very general in comparison with the teaching on particular issues in 5,21–7,11. The same can be said of 7,13-27. These two sections function as general introduction ("leading in") and conclusion ("leading out") to the main part.[6] The teaching in 5,3-10 is given

---

[4] The structure given below is taken basically from U. LUZ, *Matthew 1–7*, 211-213 and K. STOCK, *Discorso della Montagna*, 6-8.

[5] Allison presents 4,23–5,2 as the introduction of the SM suggesting one more correspondence between 4,25 and 8,1 (great crowds followed him). This extension has two problems: 1. Matt 4,23-24 is a summary of Jesus' mission – teaching, preaching and healing – and SM deals with only one aspect of that mission, i.e. teaching. 2. The crowd mentioned in 4,25 is specific – from Galilee, Decapolis, Jerusalem, Judea and from beyond Jordan. But the crowd in 8,1 is not specific, rather general – "great crowds". See D.C. ALLISON, Jr, "The Structure of the Sermon", 429.

[6] Treating 5,3-16 as one unit and as the general introduction to the SM is not without problems. Such a division does not give enough emphasis to the formal aspects of the beatitudes (e.g. the nine fold repetition of the word μακάριοι); it also ignores the differences between 5,3-10/12 and 5,13-16. Allison avoids this problem by presenting 5,13-16 as a "transitional" summary; D.C. ALLISON, Jr, "The Structure of the Sermon", 431. See the

in the impersonal third person, and it corresponds to the teaching in 7,21-27.[7] Moreover, the same phrase βασιλεία τῶν οὐρανῶν occurs in 5,3.10 and 7,21.

A reference to the Law and the prophets (ὁ νόμος καὶ οἱ προφῆται) is given in 5,17-20 as well as in 7,12. Whereas 5,17-20 clarifies Jesus' approach towards the teaching of the Law and the prophets, which is then demonstrated in the subsequent teachings, 7,12 gives a summary of the new teaching of Jesus relating it to the teaching of the Law and the prophets. Thus 5,17-20 functions as the introduction and 7,12 as the conclusion of the particular norms specified in 5,21–7,11.

As mentioned above, 5,21–7,11 in general deals with various particular issues, and this is the central part of the SM. Following the thematic and formal indications, we can divide this part into three sections:

The first section, 5,21-48, generally known as "antitheses", treats six issues that one may encounter in one's relationship with the other. Every time, after referring to the traditional teaching on a particular issue, Jesus gives his new teaching. This section is formally demarcated by the introductory formula ἠκούσατε ὅτι ἐρρέθη τοῖς ἀρχαίοις or its variants, and the formula, ἐγὼ δὲ λέγω ὑμῖν, which introduces Jesus' teaching in all the six antitheses.

Our pericope 6,1-18 appears as the second or middle section of this central part and it deals with the mode of practising righteousness which has been illustrated by three expressions of traditional Jewish piety: almsgiving, prayer and fasting – issues pertaining to one's relationship with God. The Lord's Prayer (6,9-13) comes as part of the second illustration and it functions as the core of the whole Sermon.[8]

Though 6,19–7,11, the third section, is generally considered as teaching concerned with material things, it also deals with one's relationship with the other (on judging, 7,1-5) and with God (on asking 7,7-11). So thematically it is not a homogeneous unit, nor does it betray any formal peculiarities;

---

proposals of A. Farrer and M. Goulder for a completely different approach. They view the beatitudes as the structural base of the Sermon on the Mount. A. FARRER, *St. Matthew and St. Mark*, 176; M. GOULDER, *Midrash and Lection in Matthew*, 269.

[7] On the other hand if one takes the word μακάριοι as the unifying element of the beatitudes, one may treat, as Allison does, 5,3-12 as one unit. Thus Allison observes nine blessings (3x3) in 5,3-12, which find their an "antithetical correspondence" in three warnings (1x3) in 7,13-27. While his triadic division is justifiable, his claim for correspondence seems strained. See D.C. ALLISON, Jr, "The Structure of the Sermon", 431.

[8] The literary and thematic structure of this unit is discussed in detail below.

however as Luz observes, this section has a certain correspondence in length with 5,21-48.[9]

The above given structural arrangement of the SM verifies that 6,1-18 is the centre of the SM. Now let us examine the distribution of the term πατήρ in this structure.

1.2 *The Distribution of the Term πατήρ for God in the SM*

The term πατήρ for God appears seventeen times in the SM and it is distributed as follows:

A ----
B 5,16
C ----
D 5,45.48
E 6,1.4.6². 8.9.14.15.18².
D¹ 6,26.32; 7,11
C¹ ----
B¹ 7,21
A¹ ----

The way the word πατήρ for God is distributed in the above structure also points to the centrality of 6,1-18 in the SM. The concentrated appearance of the word πατήρ for God in this unit emphasizes the theological centrality of the unit; they all refer to God as the Father of the disciples. The Lord's Prayer (6,9-13), which appears in the middle of this section, illuminates various aspects of this Father-children relationship and could be considered as the kernel of the SM.

2. **God as the Father of the Disciples and Their Identity as the Children**

The basic reason for taking this unit as the first chapter of our study is the repeated use of the divine appellation πατήρ in it. Since this is also the key term on which our thesis is founded, we examine at the outset how unique is its usage in Matthew in comparison with the OT and the other NT writings. There then follows a reflection on its particular function in 6,1-18.

---

[9] Both 5,21-48 and 6,19–7,11 have been presented using 59 lines in the *Novum Testamentum Graece*. U. LUZ, *Matthew 1–7*, 212; see K. STOCK, *Discorso della Montagna*, 7.

2.1 *Matthew's Extensive Use of the Term πατήρ for God*

The divine appellation πατήρ for God, especially as the Father of human beings, occurs with great frequency in Matthew.[10] This needs to be appraised in comparison with the use of this term in the OT.

Studies on the use of the term πατήρ have shown how rarely God was addressed as the Father of individual human persons in the OT.[11] The word πατήρ appears in the LXX (אב in Hebrew) "almost exclusively" in a secular sense.[12] Out of its approximately 1250 occurrences, only twenty-one or twenty-three refer to God as the Father.[13] Wherever it refers to the fatherhood of God, it is to show God's relationship – soteriological and not biological – with the people of Israel or with her kings.[14] No individual is found addressing God as "my Father".[15] However, personal names which contain אב as a theophorous element are quite common in the Hebrew Bible.[16]

---

[10] "Father" referring to God in Matthew: 5,16.45.48; 6,1.4.6^{2}.8.9.14.15.18^{2}.26.32; 7,11.21; 10,20.29.32.33; 11,25.26.27^{3}; 12,50; 13,43; 15,13; 16,17.27; 18,10.14.19.35; 20,23; 23,9; 24,36; 25,34; 26,29.39.42.53; 28,19. "Father" used in a secular sense in Matthew: 2,22; 3,9; 4,21.22; 8,21; 10,21.35.37; 15,4.5.6; 19,5.19.29; 21,31; 23,9.30.32.

[11] The following studies discuss in detail the usage of the divine appellation Father for God in the OT: W. MARCHEL, *Abba, Père!*, 9-52; J. JEREMIAS, *The Prayers of Jesus*, 11-65; R. HAMERTON-KELLY, *God the Father*, 20-51; D.R. TASKER, *Ancient Near Eastern Literature*, 79-200; D.G. CHEN, *God as Father in Luke-Acts*, 73-111.

[12] O. HOFIUS, "Father", *NIDNT*, I, 614.

[13] Cf. J. JEREMIAS, *The Prayers of Jesus*, 12.15; Jeremias identifies fifteen occurrences in the Hebrew canon (Deut 32,6; 2Sam 7,14; 1Chr 17,13; 22,10; 28,6; Pss 68,5 [LXX 67,6]; 89,26 [LXX 88,27]; Isa 63,16^{2}; 64,8; Jer 3,4.19; 31,9 [LXX 38,9]; Mal 1,6; 2,10) and five in the Deuterocanonical [for him Apocrypha] books (Tob 13,4; Wis 2,16; 11,10; 14,3; Sir 51,10); Sir 23,1.4 are presented as doubtful. D.R. Tasker adds 1Chr 29,10 to Jeremias' list. Treating Ps 103,13 and Prov 3,12 where God is compared with the earthly fathers also as passages explicitly referring to God as the Father, he assigns the Father references in the Hebrew scriptures to three groups: "Five of these refer to God as the Father of David and his dynasty, eleven to him being the father of his people, and two compare his relationship with humanity to that of a human father and child." D.R. TASKER, *Ancient Near Eastern Literature*, 6. In a recent study, D.G. CHEN, *God as Father in Luke-Acts*, 79.107, includes Isa 45,10-11 also in this group.

[14] O. HOFIUS, "Father", *NIDNT*, I, 618.

[15] In the Hebrew Bible "my Father" as a vocative is found only in Jer 3,4.19. But here it is not any individual but the community as a whole that addresses God as "my Father"; see O. HOFIUS, "Father", *NIDNT*, I, 618. Perhaps, the debated texts Sir 23,1.4; 51,10 could be considered as exceptions. Cf. J. JEREMIAS, *The Prayers of Jesus*, 12.15; D. ZELLER, "God as Father", 124; J. FITZMYER, "Abba and Jesus' Relation to God", 25.

[16] We have given here the statistical data of the use of the term Father for God in the OT alone. Much discussion is going on in scholarly circles exploring and analysing its use in the literature of Second Temple Judaism, the Greco-Roman world and in the Rabbinical Teachings.

This very restricted use of the divine appellation "Father" for God in the OT, especially the resistance to addressing him as the Father of individual human beings, could be seen as related to Israel's theology and religious culture where the people looked at God with awe and reverence and preferred to worship him from a distance.[17] In that context, Jesus' designation of God as his Father and the Father of the disciples was something extraordinary.

The NT, in contrast to the LXX, uses the word πατήρ more in a religious sense (265 times) than in a secular sense (148 times).[18] Jesus alone calls God πατήρ 174 times in the gospels. Among the NT writers John is the one who uses this divine appellation most (Matt 44x; Mark 4x; Luke 17x; John 109x). However, Matthew exceeds the other evangelists in presenting God as the Father of the disciples.[19] Out of fifty references to God as the Father of human beings in the NT, twenty-one are in Matthew (Mark 1x; Luke 4x; John 3x; Paul 19x; the rest 2x). We will see later in this study that in all these twenty-one occurrences God is referred to specifically as the Father of the disciples.[20]

2.2 *Matthew's Relational and Selective Use of the Term πατήρ for God*

The term πατήρ with reference to God is used exclusively by Jesus in Matthew. He talks about the Father mostly in relational terms. This aspect of relationship has been brought out using various pronouns with πατήρ: "your Father" in the plural (πατὴρ ὑμῶν) is repeated thirteen times (Mark 1x; Luke 3x) and in the singular (πατήρ σου) five times (Mark 0x; Luke 0x), "our Father" (πατὴρ ἡμῶν) and "their Father" (πατὴρ αὐτῶν) once each (Mark 0x;

See A. STROTMANN, *"Mein Vater bist du!" (Sir 51,10)*, 24-377; M.R. D'ANGELO, "Abba and 'Father'", 617-627; B. CHILTON, "God as Father in the Targumim", 39-74; A. GOSHEN-GOTTSTEIN, "God the Father in Rabbinic Judaism and Christianity", 470-504; D.G. CHEN, *God as Father in Luke-Acts*, 17-72.113-143. Pointing out various references within this literature, the authors have shown that the appellation "Father" for God was in use even before Jesus. However, they also agree that in comparison with the NT the presentation of God as the Father of human beings is slender in these writings.

[17] Or as J.D.W. WATTS, "God the Father", *TISBE*, II, 510, puts it: "The OT concept of God as Father is thin and underdeveloped, perhaps deliberately so in order to avoid association with pagan divine fatherhood in the sense of procreation."

[18] O. HOFIUS, "Father", *NIDNT*, I, 618. On the paternity of God in the NT, see W. MARCHEL, *Abba, Père!*, 101-243; R. PENNA, "La Paternità di Dio", 7-39.

[19] See J. SHEFFIELD, "The Father in the Gospel of Matthew", 53-55 for a statistical presentation of Matthew's unique and exclusive use of the term πατήρ for God in comparison with Mark and Luke.

[20] God as the Father of the disciples in Matthew: 5,16.45.48; 6,1.4.6².8.9.14.15.18².26.32; 7,11; 10,20.29; 13,43; 18,14; 23,9.

Luke 0x) – all referring to God as the Father of the disciples; Jesus calls God "my Father" (πατήρ μου) sixteen times (Mark 0x; Luke 4x).[21] These possessive pronouns indicate the kind of relationship that exists between God and Jesus, between God and the disciples, as well as between Jesus and the disciples.

Another significant factor that affirms the relational implication of this divine appellation is its selective use in the gospel. It is important to note that Jesus in Matthew speaks about the Father only to his disciples and to the people who follow him. When Jesus speaks about God to other people he uses the divine appellations θεός (God) and κύριος (Lord). An enquiry into the use of different divine appellations in the gospel will show us how careful the evangelist is in using the term πατήρ for God. For example, Matthew employs the words θεός or κύριος but not πατήρ in the following situations:[22]

i) OT quotations and allusions (e.g. 1,23; 4,7.10; 22,37).

ii) References to the God who spoke and speaks through the OT (e.g. 1,22; 2,15).

iii) Jesus' words addressed to the devil, and to his opponents (e.g. 4,4.7.10; 15,4; 19,6; 22,21.31).

iv) The words of other speakers (e.g. 8,29; 22,16; 26,63).

v) The words of the narrator (e.g. 1,20.24; 2,13.19; 28,2).

The possible theological implications of this selective use of the term πατήρ for God in Matthew can be summarised as follows:

---

[21] The term πατήρ for God with different pronouns in the Synoptic gospels:

	Matt	Mark	Luke
πατήρ	63	18	56
πατήρ for God	44	4	17
πατὴρ ὑμῶν	13	1	3
πατήρ σου	5	0	0
πατήρ μου	16	0	4
πατὴρ ἡμῶν	1	0	0
πατὴρ αὐτῶν	1	0	0
πατὴρ αὐτοῦ	1	1	0
πατήρ (without pronoun)	7	2	10

[22] These observations are taken from R.L. MOWERY, "God, Lord, and Father", 24, and J. SHEFFIELD, "The Father in the Gospel of Matthew", 57.

i) While the OT, the Jewish religion and the Jewish people normally present God as θεός and κύριος, Jesus reveals a different face of God – as Father – to his disciples. Thus, by being a disciple of Jesus they too come to know God as the Father.

ii) Though not very frequent, the image of God as Father is not unknown to the OT or to Judaism. But nobody other than Jesus utters that word for God in the gospel. Not even the narrator! Jesus is the only one who reveals the Father (11,27).

iii) There is only one true Father for all human beings (23,9), but all human beings are not automatically included in the Father-children relationship with God. It is exclusive and conditional. Jesus' opponents are not worthy even to be told of this divine appellation.[23]

iv) The Father-children relationship is reserved as a privilege of those who follow Jesus. So Jesus speaks about the Father only to them. His frequent reference to God as the Father of the disciples shows that Jesus is treating his disciples as the children of the Father.

Matthew presents the Father often as the "Father in heaven" or as the "heavenly Father".[24] These qualifications of the Father are unique to Matthew. Thus the evangelist combines the personal "Father" with the transcendental element "in heaven".[25] Considering Jesus' extensive and exclusive use of the term πατήρ for God in Matthew's gospel we may conclude that this divine appellation is used in Matthew to underscore the specific Father-child relationship between God and Jesus as well as between God and the disciples. This implies, as the identity of Jesus is presented as the

---

[23] Probably 12,50 may be an exception to this. According to the text the Pharisees and teachers of the Law (12,38) might be within the crowd of 12,46 to whom Jesus speaks about his familial relationships. In 26,53, though, Jesus uses this term in the presence of his betrayer and the armed crowd who come to arrest him; it is to one of his disciples that his words are addressed.

[24] "Father in heaven:" Matt 5,16.45; 6,1.9; 7,11.21; 10,32.33; 11,25; 12,50; 16,17, 18,10.14.19; 23,9; 24,36; "heavenly Father:" Matt 5,48; 6,14.26.32; 15,13; 18,35. Only two of these references have parallels (Matt 6,14//Mark 11,25 and Matt 7,11//Luke 11,13).

[25] See D.A. HAGNER, *Matthew 1–13*, 101. In 11,25 Jesus addresses the Father as the "Lord of heaven and earth". Such a presentation of the "Father" as the Lord of heaven and earth corresponds to the OT image of God as the "God of heaven and earth" (see Gen 21,17; 24,3; Deut 4,39; Josh 2,11; 2Chr 20,6; 36,23; Pss 115,3; 136,26; Lam 3,41; Dan 2,18.19.28.37; Jonah 1,9).

Son of God, that the identity of the disciples is conceived in this gospel as the children of God.[26]

2.3 *God as the Father of the Disciples in 6,1-18*

We have already discussed above how Jesus in Matthew regards his disciples as the children of the Father. The SM in general and the pericope 6,1-18 in particular display this "Father-children relationship" very intensely. Though Matthew uses θεός and κύριος for God in Chapters 1–4 , he never uses πατήρ before 5,16.[27] So in the gospel of Matthew, it is at the SM that Jesus reveals God as the Father for the first time.[28] In 6,1-18, the centre of the SM, the term πατήρ for God appears ten times.[29] Nine times it is used with the second person possessive pronoun "your" (ὑμῶν 4x, σου 5x) and once with the first person plural "our" (ἡμῶν).[30] Thus all these occurrences, which present a concentrated use of personal possessive pronouns representing the disciples and the potential disciples together with πατήρ, assert their identity as the children of the Father repeatedly in this section. In addition, the Father

---

[26] This may raise a theological question. Are Jesus and the disciples children on the same level? The early Church seems to have been aware of this question, which may be why Paul makes a distinction between the "sonship" of Jesus and the "sonship" of Christians by using the terms "the firstborn" (Rom 8,29; Col 1,15-17; also Heb 1,6) and "the children of adoption" (see Rom 8,5.23; 9,4; Gal 4,5; also Eph 1,5) etc. Matthew, however, does not use such distinctions. Instead he presents Jesus as the Son of God in essence and existence (1,18; 2,15; 3,17; 4,3.6; ...27,54), who lived here on the earth as an authentic Son fulfilling the will of his Father. It is Jesus who reveals the Father, and it is through him that others enter into a filial relationship with the Father (11,27). Those who accept his call, believe in him, and follow him in words and deeds become the children of the Father. Moreover, though God is presented as the Father of Jesus and of the disciples on various occasions in the gospel, it is to be noted that Matthew never once uses a common possessive pronoun to name God as the Father of Jesus and the disciples together. Thus the evangelist clearly presents the sonship of Jesus as distinct from that of the disciples.

[27] Worthy of note is the following statistical distribution of these terms in the first seven chapters in the gospel. See R.L. MOWERY, "God, Lord and Father", 24-36.

Terms for God in Matthew	Chs. 1–4	Chs. 5–7
κύριος	9	1
θεός	8	6
πατήρ	0	17

[28] But the Son has already been revealed previously (see 2,15; 3,17; 4,3.6)

[29] 22.73% of its total appearances in Matthew; 6,1.4.6^2.8.9.14.15.18^2.

[30] "Our Father" for God appears nowhere else in the gospels.

passages in 6,1-18 reflect various aspects of the relationship between the Father and the children: The Father gives the reward to his children (6,1.4.6.8); he sees in secret the good works of the children done in secret (6,4.6.18); he knows the needs of the children (6,8); he forgives the sins of the forgiving children (6,14).

However, the disciples' privileged filial identity is not without conditions. The instructions given to them clearly indicate that they will enjoy this relationship if and only if they live as the authentic children of the Father. We shall discuss below what is the right mode of living suggested to the disciples in 6,1-18 that they may live as the children of the Father.

3. **The Right Way to be Followed, the Wrong Way to be Avoided**

We have shown above that the identity of the disciples is presented in Matthew as the children of the Father. Is it their actual identity or assumed identity? In other words, does Jesus in Matthew consider them already as the children of God when he refers to God as their Father, or is it a status that they are yet to reach? Matthew's response to this question is unambiguous. By responding affirmatively to the call of Jesus the disciples have received the grace to become the children of the Father. But it is their way of life in this world that will to be the decisive criterion by which they will be judged as children or as non-children. Therefore, it is not an already attained status but a future state which will be given at the end of the process which has been already initiated. Every time that Jesus reminds the disciples of their identity as the children he also gives them specific directions on how to go about this process here and now.[31]

In 6,1-18 this process is spelt out, calling attention to the disciples' way of practising righteousness (δικαιοσύνη). The main theme of the unit is introduced in v.1. Jesus, warning the disciples against ostentation, instructs them in the appropriate manner of doing righteous deeds so that they may become worthy of the "reward with the Father".[32]

Three concrete practices of religious piety – almsgiving (6,2-4), prayer (6,5-15), and fasting (6,16-18) – are discussed within the same thematic frame

---

[31] It is not clear why Jesus uses sometimes the second person plural (6,1.2e.5.8.14.15.16) and sometimes the second person singular (6,2ab.3.4.6.17.18) in this unit to address the disciples.

[32] For an explanation of why the reward is mentioned here as "with" the Father, and not "from" the Father, see below 3.1.3.

in the subsequent verses.[33] The disciples are repeatedly exhorted to avoid following the example of the hypocrites who perform pious deeds to impress people and to get their attention and praise. These three sections are thematically interconnected; at the same time each of them functions in itself as a separate subunit with its own structural unity and accentuates one aspect in particular.[34] Thus together they function like a collage reiterating the same theme from different angles, and v.1 functions as their unifying title.[35] We shall study this unit section by section exploring the significance of the teaching given here for the life of the disciples.

3.1 *On the Children's Mode of Practising Righteousness, their Reward (6,1)*

Matt 6,1 begins with a warning to the disciples. The warning has two parts: in the first part Jesus asks them to be careful not to practise their righteousness before men to be seen by them; in the second part he gives the rationale of this warning – "the reward with the Father". And these two parts are coordinated by a combination of conditional-contrastive-prohibitive-

---

[33] As M. VELLANICKAL, "The Christian Righteousness", 106, notes, these three acts of righteousness have special importance with regard to the lifestyle of the disciples. "The lifestyle of Jesus' disciples implies a specific relationship and attitudes towards God, Man and oneself. The three acts of piety of which Jesus speaks in this passage are related to this threefold relationship and help to create healthy attitudes in those relationships. If almsgiving regulates our relationship with others, prayer regulates our relationship with God, and fasting regulates our relationship with ourselves."

[34] 6,1-18 is thematically, syntactically, and semantically a well-knit unit. The most repeated divine appellation πατήρ is the key unifying factor here. The verses 2-4, 5-6 and 16-18 share various structural similarities: all of them present the particular issue with an introductory ὅταν with a subjunctive and followed by a prohibition (with μή or οὐκ), a comparative clause (with ὥσπερ or ὡς), which points out the wrong mode of action of the hypocrites, and a purpose clause (ὅπως) which shows the wrong intention of the hypocrites. The formula, ἀμὴν λέγω ὑμῖν, ἀπέχουσιν τὸν μισθὸν αὐτῶν, which speaks about the outcome of such action, occurs verbatim in all three. Then follows an adversative clause (always beginning with σὺ δέ), which describes the right mode of action, and a purpose clause (ὅπως, missing in the teaching on prayer see 6,6). The formula καὶ ὁ πατήρ σου ὁ βλέπων ἐν τῷ κρυπτῷ ἀποδώσει σοι, which refers to the reward of the Father, is also repeated word for word in all three sections except for a slight variation in the third situation as the word κρυφαίῳ instead of κρυπτῷ is used there.

[35] Verse 1's function as the unifying title of this pericope can be shown also syntactically and semantically. The three subunits are bound with 6,1 using the linking conjunctions ὅταν οὖν (6,2), καὶ ὅταν (6,5) and ὅταν δέ (6,16) as introductory phrases. The key words "πατήρ" and "μισθός" introduced in v.1 appear in all three subsections, as does the word "ἄνθρωπος". See R.A. GUELICH, *The Sermon on the Mount*, 301-302; K. SYREENI, "Separation and Identity", 538.

emphatic conjunctions εἰ δὲ μή γε. The conjunctive particle δέ links this unit with the previous verse (5,48), where Jesus, concluding the antitheses, exhorts his audience to be perfect as their heavenly Father is perfect.[36]

3.1.1 Righteousness: Way of Life Demanded in the Process

The noun δικαιοσύνη (righteousness) occurs seven times in Matthew, five of these being in the SM.[37] It is a favoured term in Matthew and a key concept in the Sermon.[38] The evangelist seems to have specific motives for choosing and using it in the gospel.

Though Jesus is the only one who uses this word in Matthew,[39] it conveys varied shades of meaning depending on the context.[40] It is found in different

---

[36] Since the textual evidence is divided, a decision regarding the occurrence of the conjunction δέ in the original reading is difficult (while B D W 0250 f^{13} 𝔐 lat sy^{c} mae bo^{mss} omit it, ℵ L Z Θ f^{1} 33. 892. 1241. 1424 al g^{1} sy$^{p.h}$ bo have it). Nonetheless, considering the thematic similarity between 5,21-48 and 6,1-18, its occurrence should be favoured.

[37] Matt 3,15; 5,6.10.20; 6,1.33; 21,32. Since this word has more occurrences in Matthew than in other gospels (Mark 0x; Luke 1x; John 2x; NT 92x, mostly in Paul), and since it is not found in the Lukan parallels of the Matthean passages where it appears (see Matt 5,6 // Luke 6,21; Matt 6,33 // Luke 12,31), several scholars consider it as a Matthean redaction. Cf. G. STRECKER, *Der Weg der Gerechtigkeit*, 153; B. PRZYBYLSKI, *Righteousness in Matthew,* 79; R.H. GUNDRY, *Matthew: Mixed Church*, 70.

[38] This term δικαιοσύνη is unique to the SM and it is not found in any other discourse. It is distributed so well in the SM that it appears in the significant positions. It is found at the close of the first and the second part of the beatitudes (5,6.10). In 5,20, which can be considered as an introduction to the section called antitheses, where the right relationship with one's neighbour is spelled out (5,21-48), Jesus presents δικαιοσύνη as the indispensable condition for entry into the kingdom. The fourth occurrence is in 6,1, where Jesus explains the right mode of behaviour that would give the disciples a reward from their Father in heaven; this verse also introduces the teaching on the right relationship with God (6,2-18). The last occurrence of δικαιοσύνη is in 6,33 and it has a conclusive function. Having spoken about the right relationship with material things in 6,19-32, Jesus declares the absolute priority of the kingdom of the Father and his righteousness.

[39] Cf. Luke 1,75.

[40] Several attempts have been made to explain the meaning of righteousness in Matthew. In general, the authors hold one of the following three positions: 1. In Matthew, righteousness refers to a divine gift, God's saving activity (M.J. FIEDLER, "Gerechtigkeit im Matthäus-Evangelium", 63-73; H. GIESEN, *Christliches Handeln,* 237-241). 2. It refers to a divine demand upon human beings (G. STRECKER, *Der Weg der Gerechtigkeit*, 153-158.179-181.187; D. HILL, *Greek Words with Hebrew Meanings*, 124-128; J. DUPONT, *Les Béatitudes*, III, 211-305; B. PRZYBYLSKI, *Righteousness in Matthew*, 99; U. LUZ, *Matthew 1–7*, 177-178; W.D. DAVIES – D.C. ALLISON, *Matthew,* I, 327; K. STOCK, *Discorso della Montagna*, 75-82; A. WOUTERS, *„...wer den Willen*, 205-272; J.D. CHARLES, "Garnishing with the 'Greater Righteousness'", 5). 3. Righteousness could refer to both a divine gift and/or a demand; so the

expressions like "fulfil all righteousness" (3,15), "hunger and thirst for righteousness" (5,6), "persecuted for righteousness' sake" (5,10), "unless your righteousness exceeds" (5,20), "perform righteous deeds" (6,1), "his kingdom [God's] and his righteousness" (6,33), and "in the way of righteousness" (21,32).[41]

Most scholars interpret δικαιοσύνη[42] in Matt 6,1 as a divine demand upon man.[43] This is a valid interpretation, since in 6,1 δικαιοσύνη is linked with an

---

specific meaning of each occurrence should be discerned from the particular context (G. BORNKAMM, "End-Expectation", 31; J.A. ZIESLER, *The Meaning of Righteousness*, 130-136; J.P. MEIER, *Law and History*, 77-78; J. REUMANN, *Righteousness in the New Testament* 126-135; R.A. GUELICH, *The Sermon on the Mount*, 84-87; R.H. GUNDRY, *Matthew: Mixed Church* 70; D.A. HAGNER, "Righteousness in Matthew's Theology", 107-120).

[41] The LXX translates the Hebrew root צדק with δικαιο- words in most cases (In a few contexts צדק is translated also with ἐλεημοσύνη [9 times] or ἔλεος [3 times] in the LXX). In the Hebrew OT צדק appears 523 times with a wide semantic range (statistics taken from, J.J. SCULLION, "Righteousness", *ABD*, *V*, 725). It has been used to refer both to the activities of human beings and of God (Cf. J. REUMANN, *Righteousness in the New Testament,* 14-15, for a summary of the usage of this term in both senses in the OT). As activity or behaviour of human beings it is used with various connotations like legal activity, ethical uprightness, covenant loyalty, obedience to the Torah and forensic righteousness. Similarly, as God's activity it is used to refer to his legal, moral, salvific, vindicating or forensic righteousness; see J.A. ZIESLER, *The Meaning of Righteousness*, 23-32; B. PRZYBYLSKI, *Righteousness in Matthew*, 9; J. REUMANN, *Righteousness in the New Testament,* 14. Przybylski, in his study on righteousness in the Dead Sea Scrolls, notes the following distinction found between God's righteousness and Man's righteousness in the Scrolls: God's righteousness is primarily understood in terms of God's ordinances which were revealed to the community and Man's righteousness is understood in terms of the ideal of perfect adherence to God's ordinances. So as a human ideal, righteousness was conceived as the symbolic expression for everything that was right in the sight of God (B. PRZYBYLSKI, *Righteousness in Matthew*, 35). In the Tannaitic literature (A.D 10 – A.D. 200) righteousness is understood as a norm, "strictly the demand of God upon man". Przybylski summarises the general principle of the Tannaitic literature: "By living according to the norm of righteousness (*tsedeq*) the righteous one (*tsaddiq*) demonstrates that he wants to remain in a relationship with God culminating with life in the world to come" (B. PRZYBYLSKI, *Righteousness in Matthew,* 76).

[42] Some late manuscripts (L W Z Θ f^{13} $sy^{p.h}$) have the Greek word ἐλεημοσύνη instead of δικαιοσύνη which would make Matt 6,1 refer specifically to almsgiving, the theme discussed in 6,2-4. But more ancient manuscripts ($א^{*.2}$ B D 0250 f^{1} 892 *pc* lat) have the word δικαιοσύνη which renders the meaning of 6,1 in general terms, establishing the principle to be applied to all acts of righteousness referred to in 6,2-18. Textual support is evidently strong for δικαιοσύνη making v.1 an introductory statement. Different versions translate the word δικαιοσύνη in different ways in this context: e.g. alms (KJV), righteous deeds (NAB), acts of righteousness (NIV), piety (NRS). In this study the word δικαιοσύνη is translated as "righteousness" as in other contexts of Matthew. See W.D. DAVIES – D.C. ALLISON, *Matthew,* I, 577; L. MORRIS, *Matthew*, 136; J. NOLLAND, *Matthew*, 272.

action verb, ποιέω, an adverbial phrase, ἔμπροσθεν τῶν ἀνθρώπων, and a purpose clause, πρὸς τὸ θεαθῆναι αὐτοῖς. The combination of this verb and these phrases gives us a clear hint that the righteousness referred to here is something objective that can be done and seen here and now. Similarly, the use of the pronoun ὑμῶν together with δικαιοσύνη in 6,1 makes explicit that the demand is placed directly on the disciples of Jesus. The same pronoun ὑμῶν is used in 5,20 where it also refers to the righteousness of the disciples. In 5,20 the demand is much more obvious as Jesus compares the righteousness of the disciples with that of the scribes and Pharisees. So in these two contexts (5,20; 6,1) δικαιοσύνη refers evidently to a divine demand upon human beings as something they should live and practise in their life. Or in other words, it refers to a way of life required of the disciples during their life in this world.

Matt 7,21-28 gives us some clear indications about the nature of this divine demand. As in 6,1, the verb ποιέω appears in 7,21 referring to doing the will of Jesus' Father (τὸ θέλημα τοῦ πατρός μου), and also in 7,24 in reference to doing Jesus' words (μου τοὺς λόγους). In 7,21 Jesus insists on the necessity of doing the will of the Father for entrance into the kingdom. In 7,24-27, concluding his teaching, Jesus reminds his audience that it is not enough to listen to his words, but it is absolutely necessary to put them into practice. The three expressions, "to do righteousness", "to do the will of my Father" and "to do my words" designate the same human action which is necessary for entering into the kingdom of heaven. They express three essential aspects of the conduct of an authentic disciple: he/she should live according to the right norms (practising righteousness), which are determined by the Father (doing the will of the Father) and communicated authoritatively by Jesus (acting in accordance with Jesus' words).[44]

In 5,20 Jesus says that the δικαιοσύνη of the disciples should exceed that of the scribes and Pharisees. Let us see the implications of this demand.

a) Righteousness as "Exceeding Righteousness"

---

[43] J.P. MEIER, *Law and History*, 77; B. PRZYBYLSKI, *Righteousness in Matthew*, 88; J. REUMANN, *Righteousness in the New Testament*, 129; R.A. GUELICH, *The Sermon on the Mount*, 84; W.D. DAVIES – D.C. ALLISON, *Matthew*, I, 577; K. STOCK, *Discorso della Montagna*, 78; D.A. HAGNER, *Matthew 1–13*, 138.

[44] See K. STOCK, *Discorso della Montagna*, 78-79; A. WOUTERS, *„...wer den Willen*, 270-272.

The special characteristic of the righteousness Jesus demands from the disciples is defined in 5,20. Referring to the "righteousness" of the scribes and Pharisees, in 5,20 Jesus tells the disciples that if their righteousness does not surpass (περισσεύω) the righteousness of the scribes and Pharisees, they will not enter the kingdom of heaven. Jesus' reference to the δικαιοσύνη of the scribes and Pharisees shows that they also had either lived or practised righteousness to a certain extent. The point here is that their way of "practising righteousness" is not enough for the disciples of Jesus.[45]

We can assume that when Jesus spoke about the righteousness of the disciples he meant something more than the commonplace understanding of the term, as it had been conceived and practised by the scribes and Pharisees of his time. The context of 5,20 explains one of such possible commonplace understandings. In Matt 5,17 Jesus declares that he has come not to destroy the Law or the prophets but to fulfil them. A solemn affirmation of the validity of the Law and an exhortation to obey and teach the commandments follow (5,18-19). But in the antitheses, 5,21-48, revealing his great authority, Jesus gives his new interpretation of the concept of "fulfilling of the Law". Now 5,20, which comes in between these two sections, can be considered either as a conclusion of 5,17-19, or as an introduction to 5,21-48, or as a link between these two. In either case 5,20's connection with the Law and its fulfilment is quite apparent. Therefore, in 5,20, when Jesus refers to the righteousness of the scribes and Pharisees, he is, most probably, hinting at their way of observing the Law and the prophets.[46]

It is true that, Jesus does not say anything specific about the higher or exceeding righteousness that is demanded of the disciples in 5,20. We need to interpret it in the light of the "new way" Jesus elaborates in the antitheses (5,21-48). Six examples from the Law are treated in the antitheses. Every time, after quoting a commandment from the OT, Jesus gives his teaching with respect to that commandment, framed with the formula "but I tell you". Three of these, the teachings on murder (5,21-22), adultery (5,27-28) and love for neighbour (5,43-44), basically follow the precepts of the Mosaic Law but extend or deepen the demands. But the teachings on the other three – on divorce (5,31-32), oaths (5,33-37) and retaliation (5,38-39) – seem to reject

---

[45] See J. KALLIKUZHUPPIL, "The Greater Righteousness", 94-95.

[46] This conclusion is plausible, since "observing the Law and the prophets" was one of the commonplace meanings of righteousness in the OT and in Jewish literature. See Ezek 18,19.21. Various accounts of his conflict with the Jewish authorities concerning the observance of the Law also show that Jesus did not accept everything they did under the pretence of the Law and tradition (cf. Matt 9,12-13; 12,1-14; 15,1-9.10-20).

Mosaic precepts as a standard of conduct for the disciples. These teachings show clearly the contrast between what the Mosaic Law requires and what the Law as modified and reinterpreted by Jesus demands.[47] The righteousness Jesus wants his followers to pursue is not a mere performance of the Law like that of the scribes and Pharisees but a genuine living that flows from their relationship with the Father, a matter of the heart, as Jesus taught and fulfilled in his own life.

The call for a genuine living before the Father in Matt 6,1-18 continues the spirit of 5,20-48. Besides the coordinating conjunction δέ in 6,1, the reference to the heavenly Father in 5,48 and 6,1 (and in more verses later) keeps these units syntactically connected. In 5,20 the disciples are warned that they will not enter the kingdom of heaven if their δικαιοσύνη doesn't exceed that of the scribes and Pharisees. Similarly, in 6,1 the disciples are warned that they will not have any reward with the Father in heaven if they do not achieve δικαιοσύνη properly, and later in vv.2-18 the hypocrites are presented as contrary models in parallel with the scribes and Pharisees of 5,20. The fact that in both the verses δικαιοσύνη is oriented towards a future recompense is an additional reason to infer that δικαιοσύνη in 6,1, which refers to the behaviour of the disciples, indicates the same demand of an exceeding righteousness as that of 5,20. Moreover, it is logical to conclude that the righteousness expected of the disciples in 6,1 cannot refer to the righteousness that is said to be inadequate in 5,20-48, but it too refers to the "exceeding righteousness", the "new way" that Jesus demands of the disciples.

We have seen that righteousness in 6,1 and 5,20 refers to the right way of living shown by Jesus. There are three more references to righteousness in the SM (5,6.10; 6,33), and all of them share the same shade of meaning, emphasizing the unceasing desire and zeal with which the disciples should follow this new way. A brief reflection on these passages is given below.

b) To be Sought Passionately and Joyfully (5,6.10; 6,33).

In Matt 5,6, Jesus says: "Blessed are those who hunger and thirst for righteousness, for they shall be satisfied." "Hunger and thirst" is a metaphor connected with human life. It means that righteousness, for the people who

---

[47] For example, the people who followed the Mosaic Law might not have committed murder or adultery, they might not have divorced without the proper document, they might have told the truth under oath, and they might have also loved their neighbour, but that alone does not meet the demands of Jesus' exceeding righteousness. See D.O. VIA, *Self-Deception and Wholeness*, 89.

hunger and thirst for it, is like food and drink which maintain their very existence.[48] In other words, righteousness is the prime concern of their life, and they passionately desire it at every moment.[49] Following our explanation of righteousness as the divine demand upon human beings, we can understand this "hunger and thirst" as the disciples' deep desire to fulfil all that God demands from them. Or more concretely, it is their total commitment to the "righteousness" they witness and experience in the life and ministry of Jesus.[50] In this context, the second part of the beatitude, "they shall be satisfied", can be understood as Jesus' promise to them, that they will be given what they are seeking (see the divine passive, χορτασθήσονται); it is also an assurance that they will successfully complete the process into which they are initiated.[51]

In Matt 5,10 δικαιοσύνη is presented as a possible cause for "blessed persecution" which would enable one to inherit the kingdom. Here the meaning of δικαιοσύνη appears to be plainer as it is linked with the perfect passive participle of the verb διώκω. The same verb is repeated again in 5,11 and 12 associating the fate of these "blessed ones" with that of the prophets. This indicates that these persecuted ones are like the prophets who strove for the fulfilment of the will of God, lived it, and taught others to follow it.[52] The prophets were persecuted because often their message and way of life were a

---

[48] In this context, it is proper to remember Jesus' words in John 4,34: "My food is to do the will of him who sent me, and to accomplish his work."

[49] The present tense of the participles (οἱ πεινῶντες καὶ διψῶντες) shows the habitual nature of the desire.

[50] According to some scholars, "righteousness" in 5,6 refers to God's eschatological vindication: e.g. J.P. MEIER, *Law and History*, 77; J. REUMANN, *Righteousness in the New Testament* 128; R.A. GUELICH, *The Sermon on the Mount*, 84-87; R.H. GUNDRY, *Matthew: Mixed Church,*70; D.A. HAGNER, "Righteousness in Matthew's Theology", 112. Though this interpretation is plausible considering the tone of eschatological expectation present in the other beatitudes (5,4-9; see 6,10; 16,27; 24,36.44; 25,31.34; 26,29), it does not go along with the meaning this term conveys elsewhere in the gospel. Our interpretation corresponds to the positions of D. HILL, *Matthew*, 112; U. LUZ, *Matthew 1–7*, 237; W.D. DAVIES – D.C. ALLISON, *Matthew,* I, 453; K. STOCK, *Discorso della Montagna*, 83; D.A. CARSON, *Matthew 1–12*, 134; A. WOUTERS, *„...wer den Willen*, 268-269.

[51] The difference between Matthew and Luke is significant. In the Lukan parallel it is the hungry who are blessed and who will be satisfied (6,21). By focusing on hunger and thirst for δικαιοσύνη Matthew gives completely a different thrust to this beatitude.

[52] The phrase "the prophets before you" might imply that Jesus regards his disciples as the ones standing in succession to the prophets. See A. SAND, *Das Gesetz und die Propheten*, 171-173; G.R. BEASLEY-MURRAY, *Jesus and the Kingdom of God*, 168; B. CHARETTE, *The Theme of Recompense*, 89.

threat to those who resisted God's ways.[53] Similarly, the righteousness for which these μακάριοι are persecuted can be interpreted as their way of life, similar to that of the prophets, which is lived in accordance with the will of God and his rule.[54]

The theme of persecution is continued in 5,11-12 applying it directly to the disciples of Jesus.[55] The cause for persecution is specified as "for my sake" (ἕνεκεν ἐμοῦ) in 5,11. Thus persecution for righteousness sake (5,10) is qualified as persecution for Jesus' sake. Elsewhere in the gospel this expression "for my sake" describes a response motivated by one's following of Jesus (10,18.39; 16,25; 19,29). Those who are persecuted for the sake of righteousness are in fact persecuted for the sake of Jesus himself, because it is he who taught them this new way which they followed in their life. The followers of Jesus who practise righteousness cannot expect to be preserved from persecution and sufferings, but in the midst of their torments they can be absolutely confident that their Father is with them in their sufferings, and they are already counted as the heirs of the kingdom.[56]

In 6,33 δικαιοσύνη is qualified with the possessive pronoun αὐτοῦ, which stands for the Father; "his righteousness" is linked together with "his kingdom".[57] Referring to human anxiety over food, drink and clothing, in 6,25-32 Jesus says these are not the things the disciples should seek in their life, but the Father's kingdom and his righteousness (6,33). The reference to material needs in 6,25-32 can be contrasted with the "hunger and thirst for righteousness" in 5,6. Verse 33 which functions as a conclusion to 6,25-32 presents "seeking the Father's kingdom and his righteousness" as the true purpose of the disciples' life. So, what the disciples "hunger and thirst for" in 5,6 could be this righteousness of the Father – the righteousness that the Father requires, which is the law of his kingdom.[58] Now, in the context of Jesus' demand for exceeding righteousness, the Father's righteousness that the

---

[53] See 1Kgs 18,4; 19,14; 2Chr 16,10; Jer 20,1-2; 26,8-11.20-23; 37,11-16; 38,6; Jesus' reference to the persecution of the prophets: Matt 13,57; 23,29-31.34.37.

[54] See Wis 2,10-22.

[55] See the change from third person (5,10) to second person (5,11ff.).

[56] See K. STOCK, "Giusto e Ingiusto", 141-142.

[57] See Ch. II,3.3.2.

[58] G. STRECKER, *Der Weg der Gerechtigkeit*, 155; W. TRILLING, *Das wahre Israel*, 146-147; J. DUPONT, *Les Béatitudes*, III, 302-303; U. LUZ, *Matthew 1–7*, 407; R.T. FRANCE, *Matthew*, 141; W.D. DAVIES – D.C. ALLISON, *Matthew*, I, 661; K. STOCK, *Discorso della Montagna*, 79; J. NOLLAND, *Matthew*, 315; Against, J. SCHNIEWIND, *Matthäus*, 94; R.H. GUNDRY, *Matthew: Mixed Church*, 118, who interpret righteousness here as God's activity, his eschatological vindication.

disciples should seek could be interpreted also as the upper limit of this exceeding righteousness. This answers the question: how exceeding should be the righteousness of the disciples? It is to be as exceeding as that of the Father. This interpretation recalls 5,48 where Jesus, concluding the antitheses, says "be perfect as your heavenly Father is perfect."[59]

We have seen all the five references of δικαιοσύνη in the SM. In all these passages δικαιοσύνη refers to the right action that is required of the disciples in their process of becoming children of the Father. Two aspects are particularly important: 1. it is the righteousness shown by Jesus (exceeding righteousness) that they have to pursue in the process; 2. only this righteousness will make them worthy of entering the kingdom of the Father (i.e. successful completion of the process). Both these aspects are put together explicitly in 5,20: "unless your righteousness exceeds that of the scribes and Pharisees, you will never enter the kingdom of heaven."[60]

c) Jesus and John: Two Models to be Imitated

Outside the SM there are only two δικαιοσύνη passages found elsewhere in the gospel (3,15; 21,32). Both of them are connected with John the Baptist

---

[59] Przybylski rightly argues that 5,48 and 6,33 perform similar function in the SM. "In both verses the disciples are urged to imitate God. Seeking God's righteousness (6,33) is essentially the same as being perfect as God is perfect (5,48)." B. PRZYBYLSKI, *Righteousness in Matthew*, 90.

[60] In the distribution of δικαιοσύνη in the SM 5,20 comes at the centre, functioning as the focal point of this teaching. Verses 5,6 and 6,33, the first and the last occurrences of the term δικαιοσύνη in the SM, require an earnest desire for righteousness, namely to hunger and thirst for it (5,6) or to seek it as one's basic priority in life (6,33). In 6,33, righteousness is connected with the kingdom of God which underlines that the desire and attempt for righteousness is, in fact, the desire and attempt for the kingdom. Those who are persecuted for righteousness are proclaimed as blessed ones in 5,10. Their practising righteousness cannot be stopped by human threats, or insults or persecutions. In 6,1 Jesus instructs his disciples that their doing righteousness should not be motivated by the desire for praise and admiration by people. Framed concentrically by these four occurrences, 5,20 comes at the centre establishing the principle that the entry into the kingdom depends on the practice of the superior righteousness that is taught by Jesus. We can summarize these observations as follows (adapted from K. STOCK, *Discorso della Montagna*, 80):

5,6 Passionate commitment to seeking righteousness
  5,10 Practice without considering the reaction of others
    5,20 Absolute necessity of "exceeding righteousness"
  6,1 Practice without considering the reactions of others
6,33 Passionate commitment to seeking righteousness.

and his mission. Jesus and John are presented as models of righteousness in these passages.

In Matt 3,15, responding to John the Baptist who shows resistance to baptising him, Jesus says, "Let it be so now; for it is proper for us in this way to fulfil all righteousness."[61] Linked with the verb πληρόω ("fulfil"), δικαιοσύνη refers in 3,15 to something that is to be fulfilled. In the formula quotations in Matthew, πληρόω indicates the fulfilment of the OT prophecies (1,22; 2,15.17.23; 4,14…).[62] In Matt 5,17 πληρῶσαι (same form as in 3,15) is used to make reference to the fulfilment of the Law and the prophets who communicate the will of God.[63] In the same way, the phrase "fulfil all righteousness" in 3,15, can be interpreted as referring to the fulfilment of the OT prophecies or/and the Law[64] in and through the lives of both Jesus and John.[65] This conclusion is reasonable since John's baptism had real continuity with the teaching of the Law and the prophets. Both the Law and the prophets had insisted on repentance, confession of sin, and conversion (turning away from sin) as basic requirements for having fellowship with God (see Lev 5,5; 26,40-42; Num 5,5-6; Isa 1,16-17; 30,15; Hos 14,1-2; Joel 2,12-13). As Son of God (see 3,17), Jesus was sinless and had no need of conversion; still he joined the sinners and stood before John to be baptised as "he felt impelled to do so by God";[66] thus he embraced the will of God communicated through John's ministry (see 27,19).

To the chief priests and the elders of the people who came to question his authority, Jesus said "John came to you in the way of righteousness, but you

---

[61] John's objection to Jesus and Jesus' response to John are seen only in Matthew among the Synoptics. Unlike Luke who is hesitant to say that Jesus was baptised by John, Matthew presents Jesus as the one who received baptism from John, together with other sinners. Matthew alone mentions the presence of Pharisees and Sadducees there. The evangelist seems to be aware of the ignominy of the situation. Still he may want to show that Jesus' counting himself with the sinners and submitting to the authority of John were part of his "new way", his exceeding righteousness, and were nothing ignominious.

[62] Of its sixteen appearances in the gospel the verb πληρόω is used twelve times in the fulfilment formula texts.

[63] See K. STOCK, *Discorso della Montagna*, 76.

[64] For a summary of the different interpretations of this passage see W.D. DAVIES – D.C. ALLISON, *Matthew,* I, 325-327.

[65] As G. KEERANKERI, "Fulfilling all Righteousness", 150, observes, "For Matthew Jesus' ministry, his passion and death, are the fulfilment of all righteousness, the righteousness of the Kingdom. In the light of this presentation of Jesus, the event of his baptism seen in the light of Jesus' own comment on its justification (3:15) seems to function in Matthew as a proleptic metaphor of the meaning of his ministry, death and vindication."

[66] J. NOLLAND, "In Such a Manner", 73.

did not believe him, but the tax collectors and the prostitutes believed him" (21,32). According to the context, believing John when he came in the way of righteousness would mean recognizing him as a prophet sent by God and accepting his teaching as communication of the will of God (see 21,24-26).[67] Moreover, John himself was an example for those who live up to the righteousness demanded by the Law and the prophets. Matt 14,4 presents John as an advocate of the Law (see Lev 18,16). His adherence to the Law of God and his courage to rebuke the lawlessness of the king brought him persecution and death (4,2; 14,3-10). Therefore, the "way of righteousness" (21,32) in which John came can be interpreted also as the way of living according to the Law.[68] John's identity as a prophet (11,13; 21,26) and the fulfilment of prophecies in his mission (3,3; 11,10) confirm this interpretation. At the same time, his righteousness was not like that of the Jewish leaders (5,20). If it were so, he would not have rebuked them for running away from the wrath of God (3,7) and they would not have rejected his way (21,32); rather they too would have regarded him as a prophet (21,26). The "way of righteousness" in which John came was a way which demanded the sacrifice of his own life. He could be counted with "οἱ μακάριοι" who are persecuted for righteousness (5,10).

d) The Righteous: the Worthy Children

We shall conclude our study of the term δικαιοσύνη in Matthew by giving a brief summary of the use of the adjective δίκαιος with reference to the people who really lived the righteousness shown by Jesus. They too are models for the disciples in their process.

The adjective "righteous" (δίκαιος) occurs seventeen times in Matthew.[69] We mention here only seven of them (10,41^3; 13,43.49; 25,37.46), which are important for our study.[70] In these texts δίκαιος seems to refer to the people who follow the way of the "exceeding righteousness" taught by Jesus. Concluding the Mission Discourse, Jesus tells the disciples that whoever

---

[67] See K. STOCK, *Discorso della Montagna*, 76.

[68] This interpretation resonates with the use of "way of righteousness" in Proverbs where it refers to the way of life determined by the Law (Prov 8,20; 12,28; 16,17.31; 17,23).

[69] Mark 2x; Luke 11x; John 3x; Paul 17x; NT 79x.

[70] In fact, we could add to this group 1,19, the first occurrence of δίκαιος in the gospel, which refers to the character of Joseph. Joseph's righteousness could be understood as his faithfulness to the Law. However his decision to divorce his wife in secret shows the "exceeding" nature of his righteousness. If he had wanted, he could have submitted her to a public humiliation (see Deut 22,20-21).

receives them receives him and whoever receives him receives the one who sent him (10,40). Continuing the same line of thought, in 10,41 Jesus says that anyone who receives a prophet because he is a prophet will receive a prophet's reward, and that anyone who receives a righteous man because he is a righteous man will receive a righteous man's reward. Unlike 13,17 and 23,29, where prophets and righteous refer to OT persons, here these titles refer to the ones sent by Jesus (see 23,34). Here and in 13,43.49; 25,37.46 δίκαιος is mentioned in the context of an eschatological judgement.[71] While the wicked will be condemned to punishment (13,50; 25,46) the righteous will "receive a reward" (10,41), will "shine forth as the sun in the kingdom of their Father" (13,43), will "enter into eternal life" (25,46). Reading these passages in the light of Jesus' teaching in 5,20, we can say that these are the ones who live an exceeding righteousness and become worthy of entering the kingdom.

We have seen above how different texts that refer to δικαιοσύνη and δίκαιος and their contexts convey the nuance of an exceeding righteousness that is demanded by Jesus. Nowhere in the gospel is this "exceeding righteousness" defined specifically. Doing the will of the Father as it has been communicated by Jesus can be regarded as the sum and substance of this demand. The following characteristics of it are given in the gospel: its fulfilment was part of the vocation of John and Jesus (3,15; 21,32); Jesus promises that those who passionately long for it will be satisfied (5,6); it may bring persecution and suffering for those who seek it (5,10); it is a different way of life compared to that of the scribes and Pharisees (5,20); it would make one eligible for a reward from the Father in heaven (5,10; 6,1; see 10,41); it is a condition for the entry into the kingdom (5,20; see 25,46); the upper limit of this exceeding righteousness is the righteousness of the Father itself (6,33); and the righteous ones (οἱ δίκαιοι) will shine forth like the sun in the kingdom of their Father (13,43). What is important for our study is the dynamic nature of this demand and the promise of reward aligned with it. It is not an already acquired – once and for all – characteristic of the disciples. It is something they should seek (5,10), practise (5,20; 6,1) and grow into (6,33). It

[71] Therefore, the principal verbs in all these verses are in the future tense. The indicative mood of these verbs shows that this judgement is definite.

is an ongoing process, and only those who can endure the pain of living it can rejoice and be glad and have the Father's reward (5,12).[72]

3.1.2 The Prohibited Mode of Doing Righteousness

As mentioned above, the main purpose of this unit is to instruct the disciples in practising the exceeding righteousness befitting their identity as the children of the Father. In other words, the instructions in this unit show the disciples the proper way to reach their goal. We can divide these instructions into two general categories: the path the disciples should not pursue, and the one they should pursue as they do good works. Jesus explains the wrong manner in 6,1 with a general prohibition on public show, which is reiterated in the subsequent teachings on almsgiving, prayer and fasting, with the example of the bad model of the hypocrites. In the instruction on prayer Jesus presents a second bad model, the Gentiles, whose mode of prayer the disciples should not imitate. All through the unit, reference to these bad models and to their wrong manner of acting is followed by a teaching on the right manner that the children of the Father should follow.[73]

In 6,1 the warning is introduced with a plural present imperative of προσέχω. The present tense of the verb calls for a constant and ongoing vigilance against the thing warned against here. The same imperative is used in four other places in the gospel always to warn the disciples about the obstacles they would face during their journey to the Father: in 7,15 against the false prophets, in 10,17 against the persecutors, in 16,6.11 against the leaven of the Pharisees and Sadducees. The warning in 6,1 is linked with 5,48 with the conjunctive particle δέ. This reinforces the necessity of heeding this warning if they want to become the perfect children of their heavenly Father.[74]

The prohibitory-infinitive clause (beginning with μὴ ποιεῖν) which functions as an object to the verb προσέχω states the warning very specifically,

---

[72] As J.D. KINGSBURY, "The Place, Structure, and Meaning", 137, summarizes, "The greater [the exceeding] righteousness is that style of life intended to be the mark of the disciples of Jesus [...]. It is a behaviour that comports itself with living in the sphere of God's kingdom."

[73] In 6,1-18, there are four warnings against affectation (6,1.2.5.16). Though in 6,1 it is given as a general principle, without referring to any particular group, it clearly corresponds to the behaviour of the hypocrites forbidden in 6,2.5.16.

[74] Probably, the reward with the Father in 6,1 refers to the same status of being the children of the Father (see below).

using an adverbial phrase ἔμπροσθεν τῶν ἀνθρώπων[75] and a purpose clause πρὸς τὸ θεαθῆναι αὐτοῖς. The present tense of the infinitive (ποιεῖν) in the prohibition underscores the lasting validity of the prohibition.[76] But the infinitive in the purpose clause is in the aorist (θεαθῆναι). This change of tense may be to emphasize the transient dimension of the attention one could receive from such a public show.[77] Similarly, no specific indication is given of the agent who might see their deeds; the simple dative αὐτοῖς shows the impersonal means by which the verbal action is carried out.[78] Thus the people to whom one may exhibit one's righteousness are presented as an insignificant crowd. Consequently, one could imagine the nature and quality of the praise one could obtain from these people. The triviality of such transient human rewards and the foolishness of the people who go after them can be understood only in comparison with the "reward" (μισθός) one could have with the Father.[79]

What will be the consequence if the disciples do not heed the warning? The second part of 6,1, introduced by the consequential clause, εἰ δὲ μή γε, ("otherwise"), gives the rationale of the warning: they will have no reward with the Father, as they already have it from men. The indicative mood in the

---

[75] Five out of six appearances of this phrase ἔμπροσθεν τῶν ἀνθρώπων in the NT are in Matthew (5,16; 6,1; 10,32.33; 23,13); the remaining one is in Luke 12,8.

[76] See M. ZERWICK, *Biblical Greek*, § 243, 79.

[77] Normally the aorist tense is used in Greek to show the action as a whole while the present tense shows the ongoing or habitual dimension of the action. See D.B. WALLACE, *Greek Grammar,* 751.

[78] See D.B. WALLACE, *Greek Grammar,* 434.

[79] This first part of 6,1, where Jesus warns the disciples not to perform their δικαιοσύνη before others, may appear at first glance to contradict 5,16 where the believers are called to manifest their light before others (the same adverbial phrase ἔμπροσθεν τῶν ἀνθρώπων is used in both verses). In fact, they are not contradictory; rather both texts reveal the same truth: through their good deeds the disciples should seek the glory of their Father (δοξάσωσιν τὸν πατέρα ὑμῶν) and not their own glory. In 5,16 it is given affirmatively, but in 6,1 negatively. In effect, 6,1 complements 5,16, by pointing out the need to avoid the possibility of seeking one's self glorification, rather than the Father's glory, by means of one's good works or through the performance of righteousness. The purpose clause, πρὸς τὸ θεαθῆναι in 6,1, makes this dimension more explicit. The same purpose clause is found in 23,5 where the covetousness of the scribes and Pharisees for honour and recognition is mentioned. Evidently, what is denounced in 6,1 is not the good deeds (δικαιοσύνη) but their wrong intention. See AUGUSTINE, *Sermon on the Mount*, II, 1:2, 111; T.W. MANSON, *The sayings of Jesus*, 164; W. HENDRIKSEN, *Matthew*, 319; R.T. FRANCE, *Matthew*, 130-131; R.H. MOUNCE, *Matthew*, 53; C.L. BLOMBERG, *Matthew*, 116; D.A. CARSON, *Matthew 1–12*, 162; K. SYREENI, "Separation and Identity", 538. For a different view cf. H.D. BETZ, *Sermon on the Mount*, 346-347. Betz sees this difference as the result of the assimilation of different sources.

negation, οὐκ ἔχετε, underlines the certainty of the speaker regarding the thing negated. The prepositional phrase παρὰ τῷ πατρὶ ὑμῶν could be translated as "with your Father" as παρά with the dative normally expresses nearness.[80] Positively, it could mean that δικαιοσύνη done in a proper manner would acquire a reward for the disciples with their Father in heaven.

The general prohibition against affectation in 6,1 introduces three important themes that refer to two stages of the disciples' life and their identity, which are discussed in detail in the subsequent verses 6,2-18: 1. Presenting God as their Father, it underscores their present identity as God's children. 2. Warning them against public displays of righteousness, it shows them the right manner of living their divine filial identity. 3. Referring to their reward with the Father, it points to their possible future status as the children of God. We have already discussed the first two themes above; now let us see what this "reward with the Father" means in Matthew.

3.1.3 The Reward with the Father

The concept of a fair recompense, immediate or distant, for people who obey God and lead a righteous life is greatly emphasized in the teachings of the OT. One may recall the frequent promises of blessing for the virtuous and threats of punishment for the wicked resounding in all the three sections of the OT. In general, a divine reward is described in the OT as a blessing with material prosperity like land, good yield of crops, long life etc. (see Exod 20,12; Deut 11,13-15.21; 15,10; 28,1-15).[81] The word μισθός (the noun used four times in Matt 6,1-18, referring to reward) appears seventy-six times in the LXX, and often it carries a secular meaning, "wages", "recompense", or "payment".[82] In some passages it is used in promising a divine reward to the deserving human person, especially to the righteous and godly. The exact content or nature of this reward is not quite explicit; often it is presented as "this worldly reward", a mysterious, unexplainable intervention or protection

---

[80] Several English versions translate it as "from the Father" interpreting Father as the "source" of the reward (e.g. NAB, NIV, NJB, NRSV). When referring to the "source", the preposition παρά is normally used with the genitive of the noun (e.g. 2,16; 18,19; 21,42). See D.A. HAGNER, *Matthew 1–13*, 139; D.B. WALLACE, *Greek Grammar*, 378.

[81] See B. CHARETTE, *The Theme of Recompense*, 21-62, for a detailed discussion on the theme of recompense in the OT. According to him, "A very convincing schema, and indeed the fundamental recompense schema of the Old Testament, is that which is centred on the land. The promised land along with the blessings associated with it became, in effect, the reward for the people of Israel" (p. 61).

[82] See H. PREISKER, "μισθός", *TDNT*, IV, 697.

on the part of God in a person's life, present and future, together with earthly prosperity.[83] Nonetheless, allusions to a reward in the afterlife also can be found in some texts, especially in the later writings.[84]

The nature of the divine reward promised in Matthew is more eschatological than imminent. Besides the noun μισθός[85] and the verb ἀποδίδωμι, various phrases, symbols and metaphors alluding to a future reward are used in the gospel: e.g. "enter the kingdom" (5,20; 7,21; 18,3; 19,23-24; 21,31), "life/eternal life" (7,14; 16,26; 18,8.9; 19,16.17.29; 25,46), "be saved" (10,22; 19,25; 24,13.22), "treasure in heaven" (6,20; 19,21), "banquet/feast" (8,11; 22,2-9; 25,10).[86] A study of the divine recompense motif in Matthew will show us that this eschatological reward refers to the final, eternal and irrevocable reception of those disciples of Jesus who successfully complete their journey in this world into their Father's family as his children.

a) The Recipients of the Reward

---

[83] For example, in Gen 15,1 God promises Abram a "great reward". As Abram wants to know immediately what God is giving him, God makes a covenant with Abram in which he swears that he will provide progeny and property to Abram and his descendants (Gen 15,4-6.18-21). In Ruth 2,12, appreciating all that Ruth has done for her mother-in-law, Boaz, Ruth's mother-in-law's kinsman, blesses her saying: "May the Lord reward you for your deeds, and may you have a full reward from the Lord, the God of Israel, under whose wings you have come for refuge." The happy ending of the story of Ruth, who became the great grandmother of king David, whose name Matthew included in the genealogy of the Messiah (Matt 1,5), could be read as a manifestation of this reward. Comforting the people of Israel, the prophet Isaiah writes about the coming of God: "See, the Lord comes with might, and his arm rules for him; his reward is with him, and his recompense before him" (Isa 40,10; see Isa 62,11).

[84] Proverbs 11,18 and 21 speak of a faithful reward that the righteous will receive. In Prov 11,21, as in Matt 6,1, the words μισθός and δικαιοσύνη appear together. In Wis 5,15, it is written, "The righteous live for ever, and their reward is with the Lord." The author explains it further: "Therefore they will receive a glorious crown and beautiful diadem from the hand of the Lord, because with his right hand he will cover them, and with his arm he will shield them" (Wis 5,16). The author of Sirach identifies the "blessing of the Lord" as the reward of the godly (Sir 11,22), and he ends the book with the saying: "Do your work before the appointed time, and in God's time he will give you your reward" (Sir 51,30).

[85] The word means simply "pay", "wages", "recompense" (see Matt 20,8). C.J. CADOUX, *The Historic Mission of Jesus*, 209-210, has noted that both μισθός and ἀποδίδωμι are commercial terms belonging to the sphere of paid labour.

[86] We may also add to this list the following verses, which directly or indirectly refer to a future reward, also to this list: 5,3-12; 7,1-5.7-11; 11,28-30; 12,50; 13,12; 19,30; 20,16; 22,14; 23,12; 25,29. See C.J. CADOUX, *The Historic Mission of Jesus*, 208-245.

The noun μισθός occurs ten times in Matthew,[87] and six of them refer to a divine reward (5,12.46; 6,1; 10,41^{2}.42).[88] The verb ἀποδίδωμι with a sense of divine repayment appears four times (6,4.6.18; 16,27). Though the fundamental nature of the reward is not given explicitly in any of these texts, certain characteristics of it can be observed: it is a heavenly reward (5,12), which will be with the heavenly Father (6,1) and given by him (6,4.6.18); it cannot be attained by doing ordinary things which even "publicans" do in their life, but it demands an "extraordinary" way of living (5,46); it is different from human rewards, and those who practise righteousness with the intention of attracting human attention and praise will not be given this reward (6,1, in contrast with 6,2.5.16); those who are persecuted and reviled on account of Jesus will receive it in great measure (5,11-12); each will receive it according to his/her worth (10,41-42).[89] The above characteristics point out two facts concerning the conferral of the reward: 1. it will not be given to all, but to a chosen few; 2. to become worthy of it one has to fulfil certain conditions during one's life in the world.

Even a cursory reading of the above passages would show that the recipients of the reward intended here are the disciples of Jesus, because the demands required here for the reward are the same as those required of the disciples. In 5,12, where the word μισθός appears for the first time in the gospel, the persecuted ones are encouraged to rejoice and be glad over the persecution, for they will have a great reward in heaven. In the previous verse it has been clearly stated that it is for Jesus' sake (ἕνεκεν ἐμοῦ) they are persecuted.[90] It is obvious that it is their uncompromising life as the disciples of Jesus that brings them persecution and death. The reward promised in 16,27 also is directed to the people who willingly commit their lives to the cause of Jesus. In 16,24 Jesus declares: "If any man would come after me, let him take up his cross and follow me." By responding to this call one may even risk losing one's life (16,25). But the authentic disciples know that this is not a loss but, in fact, a real profit (16,26). So they can rejoice and be glad over everything they have to suffer for his sake.

---

[87] Matt 5,12.46; 6,1.2.5.16; 10,41^{2}.42; 20,8; (Mark 1x; Luke 3x; John 1x; Acts 1x; NT 29x).

[88] Matt 6,2.5.16; 20,8 (?) refer to human rewards.

[89] We have mentioned only the passages where the words μισθός and ἀποδίδωμι occur. As mentioned above, Matthew has used many other words and metaphors to signify the divine recompense. We shall discuss some of them below.

[90] As B. CHARETTE, *The Theme of Recompense*, 89, notes, "The phrase 'for my sake' makes it clear that the promise in view does not apply to just any persecution but only to that which is suffered because of the disciples' association with and confession of Jesus."

We have seen above that the disciples of Jesus are called to practise not an ordinary righteousness but an exceeding righteousness. The teachings on reward in 5,46 (see the question τί περισσὸν ποιεῖτε in 5,47), 6,1.4.6.18 make the same demand. Those who love or do pious activities in an ordinary way, as they are done by publicans and hypocrites, are not going to get any reward. But only those who love their enemies following the model of their Father and who practise good things secretly, trusting in their omniscient Father, will be rewarded. The subject "your Father" in 6,4.6.18 clearly indicates the identity of the ones who are going to receive the reward. They are the ones who have already been given the grace to become his children.

The reward promised in 10,41-42 is given not to the twelve disciples of Jesus but to those who receive them in their mission.[91] As mentioned in the Mission Discourse, the disciples who go out for mission will not be received well by all. On the contrary, people will throw them out, persecute them, drag them before kings and rulers, and kill them (10,16-19).[92] If the missionaries are persecuted and killed because of their message, those who welcome them and listen to their words may also be treated in the same way. Thus, it is very likely that these people would know that by receiving the disciples they are inviting problems for their lives. They would not take such a risk, if they were not convinced of the message they hear from them. In fact, their reception of the disciples is an affirmative response to the call of Jesus given through them. Therefore by receiving the disciples, they are actually receiving Jesus and the Father who sent him (10,40). Thus they too become the disciples of Jesus. They represent the generations of disciples who respond to the call of Jesus given through the disciples and their disciples (see 28,19-20).

It is evident from the above overview of the reward passages that the recipients of the reward will be those who respond to the call of Jesus, live according to his words, and take up his cross in their daily life. What is the reward that awaits these disciples? The evangelist has given certain indications about its nature through various symbols and metaphors. We discuss some of them below.

b) Reception of the Children into the Father's Kingdom

The "entry sayings" and the "inheritance sayings" are two important sources in Matthew that give us some idea about the nature of the reward that

---

[91] The prophets and righteous mentioned here correspond to the prophets, wise men and scribes referred to in 23,34. They are Jesus' disciples sent by him.

[92] See Ch. III,1.1

awaits the disciples of Jesus. The first of the entry sayings is given in 5,20: "For I tell you unless your righteousness exceeds that of the scribes and Pharisees you will never enter (εἰσέρχομαι) the kingdom of heaven." The verb εἰσέρχομαι is found again with the object kingdom of heaven in 7,21; 18,3; 19,23 and 23,13.[93] According to these texts the reward is the kingdom.[94] The qualification "heaven" refers to its transcendental realm. We have noted above that Matthew associates the Father also often with heaven – "Father in heaven" or "heavenly Father". Therefore, the kingdom of heaven can be understood as a metaphor referring to the abode of the Father, or a sphere where one can experience the presence of the Father continuously. It is in this heavenly abode that the disciples are asked to store up their "treasures" (6,20; 19,21).

In 18,8-9 and 19,17 (see also 7,13-14) the object of εἰσέρχομαι is τὴν ζωήν (the life). Thus, entering into the life is given as the reward in these texts. In fact, entering into the kingdom and entering into the life refer to the same blissful state.[95] Insofar as one is in the presence of the Father in the kingdom, one really lives. The preposition παρά with dative τῷ πατρί in 6,1 makes good sense in this context. We mentioned above that παρά refers not to the source but to the proximity. Definitely it is the Father who gives the reward, and the reward is the children's dwelling in the kingdom close to and with the Father (see 13,43). This life in the kingdom is irrevocable; therefore the phrase "eternal life" (ζωὴ αἰωνία) is also used in the gospel to portray the reward (19,16.29; 25,46).

All the "entry saying" texts mentioned above somehow speak about the impediments that would prevent one from entering the kingdom. They all underscore the fact that entry into the kingdom is not unconditional; in order to receive it one must follow a certain way of life.[96] In our explanation of righteousness, we summarised the way of life required of the disciples as the

---

[93] See G. SCHWARZ, "Matthäus vii 13a", 230; B. CHARETTE, *The Theme of Recompense*, 80, for the use of εἰσέρχομαι in Matthew as a technical term for the entry sayings. We may add 21,31 also to this group where the verb προάγω instead of εἰσέρχομαι is used to refer to the entry.

[94] "Matthew writes with an eye to the kingdom. For him, the hope of gaining entrance to the kingdom of heaven is of central importance and bears directly upon the whole matter of ethics." R. MOHRLANG, *Matthew and Paul*, 48.

[95] As B. CHARETTE, *The Theme of Recompense*, 80, notes, "The two terms, 'kingdom' and 'life' are effectively synonymous; [...] yet one would wish to make a conceptual distinction between the two terms to the extent that whereas 'kingdom' can frequently connote the sphere of this final state, 'life' describes something of its quality."

[96] See A. WOUTERS, *„...wer den Willen*, 67.

"doing of the will of God", communicated through Jesus (5,20; 7,21.24-25).[97] In 12,50 Jesus acknowledges those who do the will of his Father as his brothers, sisters and mother. Combining 7,21 and 12,50 with all the other entry sayings, we can say that those who fulfil the will of the Father in their life in the world will be rewarded by entry into the kingdom as the children of the Father and the brothers and sisters of Jesus.[98] The reward indicated in 5,45 for loving one's enemies points to the same truth: "so that you may become the sons of your Father" (see the use of the word μισθός in the next verse). Similarly, in 5,9 the peacemakers are promised that they will be called sons of God.[99]

The "inheritance sayings" (5,5; 19,29; 25,34) in the gospel also highlight the filial identity of those who enter the kingdom of the Father. The word κληρονομέω itself suggests this truth. Normally, it is the children who receive the right of inheritance. That is why when the wicked tenants saw the son of the owner of the vineyard coming to them as the envoy of his father, they said among themselves, "This is the heir (κληρονόμος); come let us kill him and have his inheritance (κληρονομία)" (21,38).

In 5,5 the meek (πραΰς) are promised that they will inherit the earth. The earth belongs to God and the real heirs of it are his children. Not the arrogant and the haughty but the humble and the lowly are the children of the Father. Their model is the Son who is meek (πραΰς) and humble (11,29; 21,5). In the present age, they are marginalized and receive very little, but in the coming age there will be a great reversal, and their meekness will be vindicated.[100] According to Psalm 37 "inheriting the earth" would mean their becoming heirs of a peaceful, joyful and eternal life in God's presence (see Ps 37,9.11.22.29.34).[101]

---

[97] Doing the will of the Father is not merely following the stipulations of the Law, but living according to the words of Jesus. The episode of the rich young man (19,16-22) is a typical case. He was confident enough to tell Jesus that he had been observing the requirements of the Law that Jesus mentioned (Exod 20,12-16; Deut 5,16-20; Lev 19,18). But when Jesus asked him to sell his property and give it to the poor he went away sad. It was his treasure, and he was not confident enough to give it up and trust in the heavenly Father. His heart followed the treasure in which it was anchored!

[98] The real life of the disciples is in the family of the Father, enjoying the fraternity of Jesus. Therefore those who save their life in this world will lose it, but those who lose it here for Jesus will truly save it (10.39; 16,25).

[99] See Ch. II,2.2.2.

[100] See B. CHARETTE, *The Theme of Recompense*, 86.

[101] See W.D. DAVIES – D.C. ALLISON, *Matthew*, I, 450-451; K. STOCK, *Discorso della Montagna*, 61.

To Peter's question, "We have left everything and followed you; what will there be for us?" Jesus responds with a double promise (19,27-29). He says that everyone who has abandoned family, kith and kin, and properties for the sake of his name will receive a hundred-fold and will inherit eternal life. It is for Jesus and for his words that they forsook all that they had in the world. By becoming his followers they had already received the grace to become the children of the Father. Now, the "hundred-fold" and eternal life promised to them can be understood as the culmination of that Father-children relationship. The king's invitation to those who are at his right to inherit the kingdom can be seen in the same light (25,34). They are the blessed ones of the Father, because they showed the compassionate face of the Father to the poor and needy. By serving the hungry, thirsty, naked, the stranger and the prisoner, they served Jesus who suffered in them. Thus they lived as the authentic children of the Father, and now as his children they inherit the eternal life with the Father.[102]

Summarizing the above observations, we can say that the reward of the disciples is their final reception as the children of the Father into his family.[103] But to arrive at this final and eternal bliss the disciples have to practise their righteousness in the proper way, giving glory to their Father. If they are doing these good things for their own glory, seeking attention and appreciation from people, that itself is their reward, and they will not have anything more with the Father (6,1). Referring to the hypocrites' way of giving alms, prayer and fasting, Jesus reminds the disciples about this paid-off reward repeatedly in 6,2-18.

3.2 *On Helping the Needy Brethren (6,2-4)*

Jesus presents almsgiving (ἐλεημοσύνη) as the first of the three examples of righteous deeds that he explains in 6,2-18.[104] The noun ἐλεημοσύνη and its

---

[102] G. DE RU, "The Conception of Reward", 217-218, defines this reward as "closer communion with God in Christ through the Holy Spirit".

[103] See M. DUMAIS, *Le Sermon sur la Montagne*, 231. Dumais defines the reward as the Father-children relationship which is both imminent and eternal.

[104] Though the word righteousness is not used again in the remaining part of the unit (6,2-18), the literary structure of the unit shows that the three acts of piety – almsgiving, prayer and fasting – explained here are clear illustrations of the righteousness mentioned in 6,1. These three acts of piety are firmly rooted in the OT and were considered as the concrete expressions of genuine religiosity during Jesus' time. Jesus expects his disciples to practise these pious deeds, not like the hypocrites or the Gentiles, but as the children of the Father. See G.B.

cognates ἐλεέω, ἐλεήμων, and ἔλεος, basically convey a meaning which is closer to "sympathy" or "mercy" or "compassion" to someone who is in need.[105] The meaning of ἐλεημοσύνη could be defined as a "compassionate or merciful activity" (almsgiving) for the needy.

All the three appearances of ἐλεημοσύνη in Matthew are in the present context. In verses 6,2 and 3 it is connected with the verb ποιέω (see Tob 1,3.16; 4,7-8; Acts 9,36; 10,2; 24,27). As mentioned above, the teaching here is not on the necessity of giving alms or helping the poor but on the intention and mode of doing it. However, the importance and necessity of almsgiving are already implied here as almsgiving is linked with "reward".[106] Referring to the hypocrites' conspicuous way of giving alms, Jesus asks the disciples to help the needy in secret in such a way that not even their left hand may know what their right hand is doing.

Though the word ἐλεημοσύνη is not used anywhere else other than in 6,2-4, compassion towards the poor and needy is emphasized greatly in Matthew (9,36; 14,14; 15,32; 20,34). To the young man who wanted to follow him, Jesus said, "If you would be perfect, go, sell what you possess and give to the poor, and you will have treasure in heaven; and come, follow me" (19,21). The only criterion by which the King makes his judgement on the last day, for receiving or refusing the subjects in to his kingdom, is their acts of kindness towards the needy (25,31-46).

3.2.1 Wrong Model to be Avoided

It is not enough that the disciples do righteous acts; their intentions must be pure and their praxis appropriate. Otherwise they will be making use of these acts as means for attaining human praise and honour for themselves.

GINZEL, *Die Bergpredigt*, 80-96; G.W. BUCHANAN, *Matthew*, I, 286-317; C.S. KEENER, *The IVP Bible*, 61-63, for references to parallel texts from the OT and Jewish literature.

[105] ἐλεέω appears twenty-nine times in the NT and in Matthew eight times (Matt 5,7; 9,27; 15,22; 17,15; 18,33^2; 20,30.31); ἐλεήμων appears only twice in the NT, Matt 5,7 and Heb 2,17; ἔλεος NT 27x, Matt 3x (Matt 9,13; 12,7; 23,23).

[106] In the OT, charity shown to the poor is considered as a means of atonement of sins (see Dan 4,27) and a way of attaining divine reward. There are three explicit texts in Proverbs which refers to ἐλεημοσύνη with a consequent blessing from God. In Prov 3,3-4, it is said almsgiving and faithfulness (ἐλεημοσύναι καὶ πίστεις) will secure good reputation before the eyes of God and men. Prov 16,6 (LXX 15,27) speaks about the atoning power of ἐλεημοσύνη. In Prov 21,21 ἐλεημοσύνη is presented together with δικαιοσύνη; and it is said whoever pursues them will find honour and life. See R. BULTMANN, "ἔλεος", *TDNT*, II, 485-486. See also Mark 9,41; Luke 12,33; Acts 10,4; Heb 6,10-11.

Pointing out the ostentatious behaviour of the hypocrites – their hidden motive and false piety – Jesus instructs the disciples on what should be their manner and intention when they practise righteous deeds.

a) The Hypocrites

There are various occasions in Matthew where Jesus confronts the hypocrites or makes a reference to their attitude and conduct.[107] Often it is the scribes and Pharisees who are addressed directly as hypocrites (15,7; 23,13.15.23.25.27.29; disciples of the Pharisees and Herodians in 22,16-18).[108] But in Matt 6,2.5.16; 7,5; 24,51, "hypocrite" is used as a general term and its subject is unspecified. It seems to be not a specific group but the hypocritical conduct that is referred to and criticized in these verses. As a mode of behaviour, hypocrisy is "the complete antithesis" of "exceeding righteousness".[109]

In Classical and Hellenistic Greek, a hypocrite is understood as an actor.[110] The use of the term hypocrite in Matt 6,2.5.16 also shares this nuance. An actor on the stage is only an actor; he has nothing to do with the reality behind the role he plays.[111] The same person can act as a king or a beggar, as a hero or a villain, and once his mask is taken away, he has no association with the role he plays. Similarly for the hypocrites these pious

---

[107] Matt 6,2.5.6; 7,5; 15,7; 22,18; 23,13.15.23.25.27.29; 24,51. See S. VAN TILBORG, *The Jewish Leaders in Matthew*, 8-26, for a detailed discussion on the use of the term hypocrites (ὑποκριταί) in Matthew.

[108] In Luke, people (12,56) and the ruler of the synagogue/opponents of Jesus (13,15) are also called hypocrites.

[109] See I.J.W. OAKLEY, "Hypocrisy in Matthew", 118.

[110] In Classical and Hellenistic Greek the verb ὑποκρίνομαι is used with the meanings "to explain", "to answer" or "to interpret". The noun ὑπόκρισις has the derived meaning "answer". But the agent of the action ὑποκριτής is used normally with the meaning "actor". However in Classical and Hellenistic Greek, no moral connotation has been found attached to the word ὑποκριτής; see U. WILCKENS, "ὑποκρίνομαι", *TDNT*, VIII, 559-562.

[111] See AUGUSTINE, *Sermon on the Mount*, II, 2:5, 113.

practices are like ready-made masks to be worn for a short time and later to be thrown away.

More than an actor, a hypocrite is understood in the LXX as a person who is pretentious and godless, and who has no fear of God.[112] The Matthean description of the performance of righteous deeds by the hypocrites in 6,2.5.16 seems to hold such an understanding of the hypocrite. For their own selfish motive, to receive praise from people, they go on pretending that they practise righteous deeds. Being intoxicated with the desire for such human praise, they fear neither God nor man. That may be the reason why they make use even of religious means for their egotistic gains. The present indicatives ποιοῦσιν (6,2), φιλοῦσιν (6,5) and ἀφανίζουσιν (6,16), which refer to the behaviour of the hypocrites, show the habitual nature of their pretension. That means pretentiousness was not just a weakness but was part of the personality of these people.[113]

b) Hypocrites' Mode and Intention of Giving Alms

Hypocrites give alms in public in order to be seen by people. Referring to their behaviour, Jesus tells the disciples, "[...] when you give alms, sound no trumpet before you, as the hypocrites do in the synagogues and in the streets [...]" (6,2).[114] Blowing a trumpet, especially in the OT, was to attract public attention.[115] By using this metaphor, Jesus figuratively hints at the display-mania of the hypocrites. The location of their charitable acts – "synagogues and streets"[116] – does indicate their desire for a public show.

---

[112] Different from the Classical/Hellenistic authors the LXX uses the term ὑποκρίνομαι with a negative meaning. See U. WILCKENS, "ὑποκρίνομαι", *TDNT*, VIII, 563-564.

[113] "The hypocrites of chapter six appear to be people who are motivated not by the desire to gain God's approval through the obedient fulfilment of his will, but rather by the desire to gain the recognition of onlookers through the fulfilment of a religious action." B. CHARETTE, *The Theme of Recompense*, 96. See also S. VAN TILBORG, *The Jewish Leaders in Matthew*, 11; H. GIESEN, *Christliches Handeln*, 155.

[114] Scholars have given various suggestions for the phrase "sounding the trumpet", e.g. coin box, sound of the coin etc. For a summary, see H.D. BETZ, *Sermon on the Mount*, 355. As Betz rightly comments, these suggestions are only attempts to find a rational explanation for it. He himself explains it as a symbolic phrase. See also G.W. BUCHANAN, *Matthew*, I, 287, for a similar view.

[115] 1Sam 13,3; 2Sam 20,1. See M. VELLANICKAL, "The Christian Righteousness", 110; W.D. DAVIES – D.C. ALLISON, *Matthew*, I, 579.

[116] "The former provides a public religious setting where people are gathered; the latter is a nonreligious public setting where people are present and move by in considerable numbers." J. NOLLAND, *Matthew*, 275.

The hypocrites' intention of giving alms is exposed by the purpose clause "that they may be praised (δοξασθῶσιν) by men". The verb δοξάζω, which refers to the real motive of their almsgiving, reveals the inflated image of the hypocrites. In Matthew δοξάζω occurs in three other contexts (5,16; 9,8; 15,31), always referring to God as the object of praise and glory.[117] In 5,16, Jesus instructs his disciples to shine forth their light before men, so that seeing their good works, people may give glory to their Father in heaven. Jesus is presented in 9,8 and 15,31 as a model for one who gains glory for God; the crowd who witnesses his healing ministry glorifies God with awe and wonder. While 5,16 specifically sets the goal of disciples' good works, 6,2 shows an example that goes against this goal. The disciples' good works are foreseen as Father-centric, while the hypocrites' pseudo-charity is given as egocentric.[118] By attempting to seize the glory, which should be given only to God,[119] the hypocrites make themselves idols – objects of worship – and thus they mislead people by making them naïve adorers of human idols (see 23,7-10).[120]

c) The Paid-off Reward of the Hypocrites

The hypocrites give alms, pray and fast with the intention of being praised by others. They immediately receive what they seek. The ἀπό perfective ἀπέχω, introduced by the emphatic particle ἀμήν together with λέγω, declares this fact.[121] Though the same word μισθός is used in 6,2.5.16 to refer to the reward the hypocrites receive, its significance is different from that of 6,1. The standard meaning of μισθός as "wages" or "payment"[122] for a worker, as it is in 20,8,[123] can be applied to 6,2.5.16. They indicate here the already

---

[117] See Mark 2,2; Luke 5,25f; 7,16; 13,13; 17,15; 18,43; 23,47; Acts 11,18; 21,20; Rom 15,6.9.

[118] This is one of the differences between a child and a "non-child". An authentic child seeks to glorify the Father in and through its life, while a non-child gathers glory for itself.

[119] See Exod 15,1-11; Pss 22,23; 86,9.12; Isa 5,16; 25,1; 49,3; Rom 1,21.

[120] See W.D. DAVIES – D.C. ALLISON, *Matthew*, I, 581-582.

[121] The same formula ἀμὴν λέγω ὑμῖν, ἀπέχουσιν τὸν μισθὸν αὐτῶν is used again in 6,5 and 6,16. Structurally it functions, every time, as the conclusion of the prohibition on imitating the hypocrites in their almsgiving (6,2), prayer (6,5) and fasting (6,16). It explains the basis of the prohibition. It functions also as a reminder to the disciples of the ultimate goal of their good works or pious activities.

[122] See H. PREISKER, "μισθός", *TDNT*, IV, 695.

[123] Though μισθός is used in 20,8 (in the Parable of the Vineyard Owner) with a secular meaning – wages for work – it has a theological significance. The parable emphasizes the absolute freedom of the owner to give his possessions to whomever he chooses. Comparing the

received wage of the hypocrites for their public performance. Thus, while the reward in 6,1 alludes to a heavenly reward that is with the Father, in 6,2.5.16 it refers to human rewards.[124] Jesus abruptly qualifies it as "their reward". The verbs ἔχετε (6,1) and ἀπέχουσιν (6,2.5.16) also highlight the difference in significance. Though both are in the present tense forms, ἔχετε is used here with a future sense[125] and ἀπέχουσιν with a completed sense.[126]

From the context it is evident that the reward they have received is the attention and praise they sought and obtained from other human beings. These verses expose the ignorance or blindness of the hypocrites. Obsessed with momentary human praise, they ignore God's demands and forego a possible eternal reward.[127] In the subsequent verses, as Jesus commands the disciples to do the same acts of righteousness in a different way, he gives them specific directives to overcome such blindness.

3.2.2 Almsgiving of the Children

After presenting the self-glorifying mode of the hypocrites' almsgiving and after mentioning the type of reward they would receive for this, Jesus says to his disciples, "But when you give alms, do not let your left hand know what your right hand is doing."

The emphatic pronoun σοῦ in 6,3, (σύ in 6,6 and 6,17) together with the conjunction δέ marks a contrast between the conduct of the hypocrites and the

---

kingdom of God with the owner in the parable Jesus draws attention to the divine freedom to invite the least and the last to the kingdom.

[124] Unlike in 6,2.5.16, μισθός is used in 6,1 without an article. This could be interpreted in three ways: 1. Since μισθός in 6,1 refers to the reward one may have with the Father and μισθός in 6,2.5.16 refers to the human rewards, the author may be drawing attention to the indefinite or open-ended nature of the divine reward in comparison with the definite or limited nature of the human rewards. 2. The author may be treating μισθός as a monadic noun in 6,1 since it is qualified with παρὰ τῷ πατρί (for an explanation of anarthrous monadic nouns, see D.B. WALLACE, *Greek Grammar,* 248). 3. It may be simply to give an extra emphasis to the negation ("you will have no reward – whatever type – at all from the Father"). However, the first two interpretations can be justified only in the present context. There are other occasions in the NT and in Matthew where μισθός is used with and without an article, which do not follow our conclusion. See Matt 5,12; 10,41; Luke 6,23.35; Acts 1,18.

[125] M. ZERWICK, *Biblical Greek*, § 278, 93-94, comments that this is due to Aramaic influence.

[126] ἀπό compound verbs can convey a *perfective force*; see M. ZERWICK, *Biblical Greek*, § 132, 45. Here the usage seems to be very deliberate: the same verb root, one without ἀπό (6,1) and others with ἀπό (6,2.5.16), demonstrates the difference.

[127] See A. PLUMMER, *Matthew*, 91.

"expected conduct" of the disciples. Moreover, the emphasis on the subject "you" points to the distinctive identity of the disciples in comparison with that of the hypocrites. The disciples are children of the Father (υἱοὶ τοῦ πατρός); so how can they behave like the hypocrites?

The use of the hyperbole, "Do not let your left hand know what your right hand is doing", underscores the intensity and seriousness of this concern.[128] It seems rather absurd to make such a distinction since it is the whole person and not any part of the body that performs an action. But metaphorically, it signals the gravity of the demand.[129] Let nobody else, not even your other side, know about your charitable acts.[130] The hyperbole has been further clarified by the purpose clause, "so that your almsgiving may be in secret".

Whereas the intention of the hypocrites' almsgiving is mentioned specifically as "to be glorified by people", nothing is said about the disciples' intention when they give alms. It is not said because it is known to all, or it is already implied in the suggested mode. As mentioned in 5,16, to give "glory to the heavenly Father" should be the primary intention of the disciples' acts of charity, prayer, fasting or any good deed. The second intention implied here is intrinsic to the very act of almsgiving. Alms are given normally to those who are deprived of their basic needs and are struggling to cope with their miseries. When this is done in secret, the needs of the receiver would be met and his dignity respected. The children of the Father should treat persons in need not as means to acquire glory and praise but as brothers and sisters who are entrusted to their care.[131]

---

[128] Though hand has been used as a symbol of giving in the OT (Deut 15,7; Pss 104,28; 145,16; Prov 31,20), this teaching of Jesus, which has become a proverbial saying today, has no parallel in the OT.

[129] Identifying symbolically the "left hand" with the desire for praise and the "right hand" with the intention of fulfilling the divine precepts, AUGUSTINE, *Sermon on the Mount*, II, 2:8, 117 writes, "[…] when a desire for the praise of men is associated with the good intention of one who gives alms, then it is that his left hand becomes aware of what his right hand is doing."

[130] See O. DA SPINETOLI, *Matteo*, 188; U. LUZ, *Matthew 1–7*, 357.

[131] As M. VELLANICKAL, "The Christian Righteousness", 111, writes, "It is the Father-son relationship that should induce us to give alms. In other words the almsgiving should come out of the heart of a child of God, which pours itself forth in a brotherly love towards his neighbour. Thus almsgiving, when it comes purely out of the love of the children of God, enables us to grow in our divine sonship [...]. it is this growth itself, which is the reward from the Father."

3.2.3 The Father's Seeing in Secret and his Reward

Jesus repeatedly assures the disciples that their Father sees their actions performed in secret and that he will reward them (6,4.6.18). It may be easier to believe in a revealing or manifesting God than to believe in an invisible God. Only a person with deep faith can experience the presence of a God who is in secret (6,4.6.18) and feel confident of the Father's seeing one's good works done in secret. The assurance of the Father's seeing their good works in secret invites the disciples to go beyond their limited sense experiences and grow in that faith which demands an absolute trust in their Father who is omniscient and omnipotent. It is the same trust and confidence that would strengthen the disciples to face persecutions and trials fearlessly (5,10-12; 10,18-20.29-31).[132]

When Jesus refers to the reward of the hypocrites, he does not mention the source from which they receive it. There is no action verb there to indicate the giver. It is evident that the appreciation or the praise they get from people itself is their reward. Different from this human reward, which the hypocrites seek and seize, is the reward offered to the one who does good deeds in secret. Here it is the Father in heaven who rewards his self-restrained children.[133] He alone knows their good works, so it is quite logical that they have a reward with him.

Unlike 6,2.5.16 where the reward of the hypocrites is mentioned using the word μισθός, no substantive is used in 6,4.6.18 to refer to the reward of the Father. Instead, the verb ἀποδίδωμι in the future indicative guarantees the reward. In addition to its use in the present context, the verb ἀποδίδωμι appears also in 16,27 with a meaning of divine recompense.[134] The future tense in all these four instances shows the futuristic dimension of the repayment, and the indicative mood asserts the certainty of it. However, the specific content of the reward is not explicit in any of these texts.

The futuristic dimension of the Father's reward and its unspecific nature also demand a total surrender in faith. While the hypocrites enjoy the praise and approval of the people here and now for their acts of piety, the children,

---

[132] Similarly, at the end of the gospel Jesus promises his everlasting presence with the disciples as he entrusts them with the mission (28,20). Evidently his presence is hidden and only with faith can the disciples experience him further (see also 18,19-20).

[133] To emphasize this point, some later manuscripts (D W f^1 𝔐 h q $sy^{p.h}$) have added αὐτός before the verb ἀποδίδωμι. However, the shorter text is better attested (ℵ B K L Z Θ etc.).

[134] The word ἀποδίδωμι appears eighteen times in Matthew, but in most of the passages it means "to pay back" (see its repeated use in 18,25-34).

in contrast, are to wait patiently and silently for their reward. They need to resist the ongoing temptations to conform to the worldly standards of popularity, fame and name. Often they will be ignored and looked down on by the mainstream heroes. Even their hope in the Father and in his reward may be labelled as irrational and foolish imaginings. The only guarantee they have is the words and deeds of Jesus. If they can trust him and follow his words, they will be able to trust the Father and live like his children and be made worthy of the eternal reward (7,24-27).

The Father-children relationship demands a children-children relationship. In their process of becoming children of the Father, the disciples cannot neglect their brothers and sisters. When a child is in need, it is the duty of other children to support him/her. So giving alms, viewed from the Father-children relationship, is, in fact, more than an act of charity; it is an assertion of fraternity. Those who authentically extend a generous hand to their brothers and sisters in need live out their identity as the children of the Father. God, for his part, will surely reward these children who express their compassionate love in deeds (10,42; 19,21; 25,35.37-40). But the hypocrites make use of the poor as a means to acquire human praise. Their purpose in giving alms is not to help the poor but to put on a "compassionate countenance" before others. In Matt 6,2-4 Jesus denounces such bogus giving and sets a paradigm for his disciples to follow: "When you give alms, do not let your left hand know what your right hand is doing." Only such an authentic giving will be rewarded by the Father in heaven, who sees them in secret.

3.3 *On Praying (6,5-15)*

Having given directions on the proper manner of almsgiving, Jesus speaks about prayer in vv.5-15. Compared to the teaching on almsgiving and fasting, this section on prayer is longer and can be divided into four parts. The first part, vv.5-6, is similar to vv.2-4 and 16-18 in structure and content. Denouncing the false prayer of the hypocrites, which is done to impress others, Jesus asks the disciples to pray in secret to their Father. The Gentiles' false notion and manner of prayer are discussed in the second part (vv.7-8). The disciples are told here about the right attitude they should have when they stand in prayer before their Father. It is followed by the "Our Father", the model prayer Jesus teaches the disciples (vv.9-13). The section on prayer is concluded in the fourth part with a teaching on forgiveness (vv.14-15). As a whole, this section on prayer underscores the disciples' filial relationship with God and portrays prayer as a celebration of this Father-children relationship.

Prayer is presented in Matthew as a privilege of Jesus and the disciples. Different occasions of Jesus' prayer and his teaching on prayer are given in the gospel.[135] Besides the most common verb προσεύχομαι, which appears six times in 6,1-18, and its derivative προσευχή, the evangelist has used also αἰτέω and δέομαι to refer to prayer.[136] In all the references and allusions to prayer, the Father is the focus, and Jesus is the one who prays or teaches the disciples to pray.

The Father-child relationship, the hall-mark of discipleship in Matthew, is also the prerequisite for prayer in the gospel. In 6,9 Jesus teaches the disciples to address their prayers to the Father. At Gethsemane Jesus himself prays to the Father (26,39.42.44), and he exhorts the disciples to pray that they may not enter into temptation (26,41). A deep intimacy between the Father and the Son pervades this setting. Jesus never teaches the "non-children" how to pray as he does not speak about the Father to them. Matt 6,5 is the only place in the whole gospel where the word προσεύχομαι is used to refer to the prayer of the "non-children". But in this context – where the present indicative of the finite verb φιλέω introduced by the subordinating conjunction ὅτι shows the real motive of their "habitual standing at the synagogue and street corners" – the reference to the prayer of the hypocrites, given in an infinitive form (προσεύχεσθαι), sounds more ironical than real.

3.3.1 Prayer of the Hypocrites and of the Children (6,5-6)

Prayer is a channel that connects the children with their heavenly Father. During their earthly life, it helps them to discern the will of the Father and live as his authentic children (26,39.42.44). But if it is done with a motive of impressing people, it cannot be called a prayer but a show. Referring again to the wrong model of the hypocrites, in 6,5-6 Jesus instructs the disciples on what should be the right mode and intention of their prayer. The coordinating conjunction καί, with which 6,5 begins, binds this section with the previous

---

[135] For a survey of the prayer vocabulary in Matthew, see I.H. MARSHALL, "Jesus – Example and Teacher of Prayer", 113; W. NGOWI, *Jesus' Teaching on Prayer*, 7-8.

[136] The verb προσεύχομαι occurs fifteen times: Matt 5,44; $6{,}5^2.6^2$.7.9; 14,23; 19,13; 24,20; 26,36.39.41.42.44 (Mark 10x; Luke 19x; NT 85x); and the noun προσευχή two times: Matt 21,13.22 (Mark 2x; Luke 3x; NT 36x). The verb αἰτέω is used not exclusively for prayer; for its references to prayer see Matt 6,8; 7,7.11; 18,19; 21,22. In the gospel of Matthew δέομαι appears only once: 9,38.

one and thus to the general principle in 6,1.[137] A contrast between the prayer of the hypocrites and that demanded of the disciples and their recompense is given explicitly in this section.[138]

a) Hypocrites' Prayer and their Reward

The prayer of the hypocrites is self-styled. It is an expression not of their relationship with God but of their self-love; they do not surrender to the will of God but sing their own praises; their prayer is an act not of faith but of deception.

As they do when giving alms, the hypocrites choose public places for their prayer (6,2.5).[139] The present indicative of the finite verb φιλέω in 6,5 shows the real motive for their "habitual standing at the synagogue and street corners".[140] The verb φιλέω with the meaning "love" appears four times in Matthew (6,5; 10,37²; 23,6).[141] In all these situations φιλέω conveys the connotation of a personal attachment that the subject shows towards the object. Its use in 23,6, where Jesus refers to the character of the scribes and Pharisees, is similar to that of 6,5. In 10,37 φιλέω is used to refer to human affection towards one's father, mother, son or daughter. There Jesus demands

[137] So the teaching on prayer comes as the second example of the righteousness mentioned in 6,1.

[138] This section also begins with a prohibition. The subordinating conjunction ὅταν with the present subjunctive of προσεύχομαι forms a temporal clause and performs the same function as in 6,2. So the prohibition given here is applicable also for all time. While in 6,2, and 6,16 prohibitions are on doing, like the hypocrites in almsgiving (μὴ σαλπίσῃς ἔμπροσθέν σου ὥσπερ οἱ ὑποκριταὶ ποιοῦσιν) and in fasting (μὴ γίνεσθε ὡς οἱ ὑποκριταὶ σκυθρωποί), in 6,5 it is on being like the hypocrites (οὐκ ἔσεσθε ὡς οἱ ὑποκριταί) in prayer. Being like hypocrites can be more disastrous than acting like them. In that sense Jesus' prohibition in 6,5 is more emphatic than in 6,2 and 6,16. The categorical prohibition, the negative particle οὐκ with the future of εἰμί, clearly expresses this emphasis. This usage, which is common in OT legal language, is very rare in the NT (see Matt 20,26 for another example). See M. ZERWICK, *Biblical Greek*, § 443, 149.

[139] The places mentioned in 6,2 and 6,5 referring to the self-exhibition of the hypocrites are almost identical.

[140] Reference to the synagogues and the standing posture of prayer may cause people to doubt whether Jesus is attacking Jewish prayer here. As many have pointed out, it is not the place or posture of prayer that is criticized, but the hypocrites' ostentation rooted in their avarice for praise and recognition. See O. DA SPINETOLI, *Matteo*, 191; W. HENDRIKSEN, *Matthew*, 322; W.D. DAVIES – D.C. ALLISON, *Matthew,* I, 585; D.A. CARSON, *Matthew 1–12*, 165; F.H. AGNEW, "Almsgiving, Prayer, and Fasting", 241; C.S. KEENER, *Matthew*, 139.

[141] There is a fifth appearance of this word in Matt 26,48. This refers to the deceitful kiss of Judas.

that the disciples have a relationship with him that is more intimate than even their most intimate kinship relations. In 23,6 the object of φιλέω is not human persons, but the hypocrites' desire for places of honour at banquets and places of worship. Similarly in 6,5, the verb φιλέω points out their deep attachment to the immediate outcome of their pious pretence, i.e. the human praise and recognition they expect in return. The hypocrites show themselves praying at the synagogues and the street corners with a well-hidden desire to gain honour for themselves. They never direct their hearts to God in faith, but only to the public in pretence.

Parallel to the purpose clause "that they may be praised (δοξασθῶσιν) by men" of 6,2, "that they may be seen (φανῶσιν) by men" is used in 6,5 and 6,16 to refer to the intention of the hypocrites. It appears that in 6,2 the motivation of the hypocrites is given more specifically than in 6,5 and 6,16. But from the context it is clear that in 6,5 and 6,16, φαίνω is communicating the same point as that of δοξάζω in 6,2. The literal meaning of the verb φαίνω is "to shine" or "to give light"; in the passive it refers to someone or something that "appears" or "becomes visible" or "exposed to view".[142] For example, the angel appeared (1,20; 2,13.19), the star appeared (2,7), lightning shines (24,27) or the Son of Man will appear (24,30). These shining appearances have a conspicuous nature of which one may hardly fail to take notice. The hypocrites manifest themselves in such a way so as not to lose the attraction of others, believing that it would bring them glory and honour among people.[143]

By standing and praying in public places the hypocrites seek to gain the praise and reverence of the people. Jesus repeats his judgement on their performance, "they have already received their reward."

b) Prayer of the Children

Contrasting the ostentatious prayer style of the hypocrites, Jesus tells the disciples, "But when you pray, go into your inner chamber and shut the door and pray to your Father."[144] The images of going to the inner chamber[145] and

---

[142] See BAGD, 851-852.

[143] The shallowness of such a "show" is criticized severely in 23,27-28: "For you are like whitewashed tombs, which on the outside *look beautiful* (φαίνονται ὡραῖοι), but inside they are full of the bones of the dead and of all kinds of filth. So you also on the outside *look righteous* (φαίνεσθε δίκαιοι) to others, but inside you are full of hypocrisy and lawlessness."

[144] The identity of the disciples is emphatically contrasted with that of the hypocrites by the opening phrase σὺ δὲ ὅταν προσεύχῃ of 6,6.

[145] See Isa 26,20.

shutting the door suggest an absolute secrecy in prayer. It need not mean a complete withdrawal. It emphasizes the importance of communion with the Father in prayer rather than its outward expression.[146] Praying in secret has various implications. First of all, it shows the children's conviction of the Father's presence in their life; it manifests their confidence in the Father. More importantly, it confirms their intimate and personal relationship with the Father and their longing to be with him.

The imperative "pray to your Father" (πρόσευξαι τῷ πατρί σου) summarises the mode and intention of the disciples' prayer. It is to their Father the children pray, and nobody else needs to know about it. It is entirely a personal matter, a one-to-one affair between the child and the Father. Only one who shares a filial relationship with the Father can enjoy the beauty of that communion.

The child who enters into communion with the Father in secret expresses his trust and confidence in the Father and experiences the Father's presence in his life. Jesus promises that such a child will surely be rewarded by the Father. In fact, the child's communion with the Father, a grace of faith, which is free from all social pressures and influences, itself is a great reward. Nonetheless, Jesus is promising something more, a future reward that is awaiting the children with the Father.

By praying in public places, hypocrites give people an impression that they are men of God. Thus they invite people's attention and reverence. Prayer, for them, is only a means to gain people's praise and honour. But for the disciples, prayer is a privilege, an expression of their filial relationship with the Father and a celebration of that relationship. It is an act of faith and a total surrender to the Father who is in secret, and who sees in secret. Those who live in this communion with the Father in this world will be rewarded by living with him eternally as his children.

3.3.2 Another Wrong Model to be Avoided in Prayer (6,7-8)

We have seen above how Jesus referring to the bad model of the hypocrites instructs the disciples to live a life worthy of their identity as the

---

[146] Different from 6,4, in verses 6,6 and 6,18 the Father is qualified as one who is in secret (τῷ ἐν τῷ κρυπτῷ; τῷ ἐν τῷ κρυφαίῳ). This may be to harmonize with the phrases that follow (ὁ βλέπων ἐν τῷ κρυπτῷ; ὁ βλέπων ἐν τῷ κρυφαίῳ). However, this qualification gives emphasis to the fact that the Father is also there with the child as he prays or fasts in secret.

children. In 6,7-8 Jesus points out the wrong model of another group, the Gentiles, and their mistaken understanding of prayer. The Gentiles are outsiders, and they do not belong to the family. Their prayer manifests their identity and their distance from the Father. Jesus instructs the disciples to keep away from imitating their manner of prayer.

a) The Gentiles

In addition to in 6,7, the term ἐθνικός for Gentiles appears in two other contexts in Matthew (5,47; 18,17).[147] A derogatory undertone is observable in all these occurrences. Moreover, in all these contexts the Gentiles are portrayed in contrast to the children of the Father. In 5,47, teaching them of the necessity of loving their enemies, Jesus asks the disciples, "If you salute only your brethren, what more are you doing than others? Do not even the Gentiles do the same?" The implication is clear: how can the disciples, the children of the Father, remain at the level of ordinary Gentiles in their dealings with others? In 18,15-17 a series of procedures are suggested for winning back a brother who goes astray. But if he does not abide by any of them, the last (probably the worst) of the treatments is to consider him as a Gentile or a tax collector, because he resists listening even to the church – the communion of the children.

In Matthew the word ἔθνος is also used to denote the Gentiles (see 6,32; 10,5.18; 20,19.25). In 6,32 referring to people's anxiety over food and clothing, Jesus tells the disciples that these are the concerns of the Gentiles, and that the disciples should not worry about them since their heavenly Father knows their needs. This verse parallels 6,7 and presents the Gentiles as people ignorant of the gracious Father. In the early part of the mission instruction, in 10,5, the disciples are forbidden from going to the territory of the Gentiles and the Samaritans; they are told in 10,18 that they will be dragged before the kings and rulers to bear testimony before them and the Gentiles. In 20,19 Jesus predicts that he himself will be handed over to the Gentiles to be mocked, flogged and crucified (see also 24,9).[148] From the above negative

---

[147] See K.L. SCHMIDT, "ἔθνος", *TDNT*, II, 372; N. WALTER, "ἐθνικός", *EDNT*, I, 381.

[148] For a detailed discussion on the anti-Gentile statements in Matthew, see D.C. SIM, "The Gospel of Matthew and the Gentiles", 19-48.

references to the Gentiles in the gospel, we may describe them basically as persons who have no knowledge of the Father[149] and therefore who do not share a filial relationship with him. Consequently, they do not belong to the kingdom family and to the fraternity of Jesus and his disciples.[150]

b) Gentiles' Mistaken Notion and Manner of Prayer

The Gentiles' lack of knowledge and relationship with the Father is expressed in their prayers too. Just as the hypocrites' prayer is rejected because it is insincere and ostentatious, so also the prayer of the Gentiles is censured because it reflects a false understanding of the purpose (δοκοῦσιν γὰρ ὅτι...) and practice (βατταλογέω) of prayer.

The verb βατταλογέω is a *hapax legomenon* in the NT. The word πολυλογίᾳ in the next clause, which is also a *hapax* but whose meaning can be explained etymologically as "many words", helps us to understand the sense of this saying. Most probably, Jesus is referring to the soulless repetition of words, which may be in the form of petitions, by which Gentiles suppose that they could attain the blessing of God.[151] The present indicative of the verb

---

[149] See B.M. NEWMAN – P.C. STEINE, *A Translator's Handbook*, 161; A.J. SALDARINI, *Matthew's Christian-Jewish Community*, 82.

[150] However, the mission of Jesus and the disciples includes bringing the Gentiles to the kingdom family and to the Father-children relationship. Quoting Isaiah at the beginning of the ministry of Jesus, the evangelist gives an orientation to this vision of Jesus' mission: "Land of Zebulun, land of Naphtali, on the road by the sea, across the Jordan, Galilee of the Gentiles – the people who sat in darkness have seen a great light, and for those who sat in the region and shadow of death light has dawned" (4,15-16). In chapter 12, again quoting the prophet, the evangelist presents Jesus as the prophesied hope of the Gentiles: "[...] he shall proclaim justice to the Gentiles. [...] and in his name will the Gentiles hope" (12,18-21). The primary meaning of the Greek word ἔθνος is nation/people, and on various occasions Matthew uses this word with that sense (see 21,43; 24,7.9.14; 25,32; 28,19). Nevertheless, in the Matthean context this meaning could be understood as an enlargement of the concept "Gentiles", i.e. people who do not share in a Father-children relationship, as we discussed above. If this is acceptable, one can see a movement in the gospel where the "Gentiles" become the children. The concluding statement of the parable of the Vineyard and the Tenants in 21,33-43 (see esp. 21,43) and Jesus' commandment to make disciples of all nations (τὰ ἔθνη) in 28,19 could be considered as signs of this movement. See A.J. SALDARINI, *Matthew's Christian-Jewish Community*, 68-83; D. SENIOR, "Between Two Worlds", 14-16; B. BYRNE, "The Messiah in whose Name", 58-68.

[151] See 1Kgs 18,26-29; Isa 1,15; Qoh 5,1; Sir 7,14. Various conjectures have been made on the specific practice behind this verse: Liddell-Scott-Jones compares βατταλογέω with βατταρίζω, which means "to stammer", and attributes the meaning "speak stammeringly or say the same thing again and again" to it (LSJ, I, 311); Betz suggests it as a caricature term which was developed as part of Jewish polemic against "paganism"; H.D. BETZ, *Sermon on the Mount*, 366; According to R.T. FRANCE, *Matthew*, 132, "Prayer in the non-Jewish world was

δοκέω (to think, to believe) shows the customary nature of their supposition. Though there is no negative particle used in this clause, it is clear from the context that their supposition is regarded as false by Jesus. The passive of εἰσακούω can be considered as a divine passive,[152] but the omission of the agent seems to be deliberate.[153] The future tense of εἰσακούω indicates the vain hope of the Gentiles. They suppose that they will be heard for their many words, but they will not be! This prayer model of the Gentiles speaks about their image of God. They believe, "unless called upon in such compelling ways the gods do not care, and unless informed about the person's needs they do not know what to do."[154]

c) The Right Attitude of the Children

Presenting the Gentiles' mode and their false notion of prayer, Jesus tells (μή with the aorist subjunctive) the disciples that their prayer should not be like that of the Gentiles. They should not think that God is ignorant of their needs and that they have to compel him to act in their favour. He is not an unknown deity but their Father, who is actively present in their lives, knowing all their needs and caring for them (see 6,32).[155]

What is expected of the disciples in this section is to realize their real identity as the children of the Father and live trusting in him. The underlying principle of all the prayer references in the gospel is this filial trust (see, 6,9-13.25-32; 7,7-11; 18,19; 21,22; 26,39-44). When they lose this confidence

---

often characterized particularly by formal invocations and magical incantations, in which the correct repetition counted rather than the worshipper's attitude and intention." R.H. GUNDRY, *Matthew: Mixed Church*, 104, suggests, "The verb may denote meaningless or repetitive speech, as in the extensive listing of divine names by pagans. They hoped at least one of the names might prove effective for an answer." see also G. DELLING, "βατταλογέω", *TDNT*, I, 597; D.A. HAGNER, *Matthew 1-13*, 147; C.S. KEENER, *Matthew*, 139-140.

[152] The verb εἰσακούω which is a *hapax* in Matthew appears five times in the NT, three times referring to God's positive response to prayers and supplications (see Luke, 1,13; Acts 10,31; Heb 5,7). It is used often in the LXX to mention God's listening to or attending to the prayers of the people (e.g. Gen 21,17; Pss 4,3; 5,4). See also W. NGOWI, *Jesus' Teaching on Prayer*, 45.

[153] This use of the divine passive, as Betz observes, also makes it possible for the SM to avoid naming the pagan gods; H.D. BETZ, *Sermon on the Mount*, 367.

[154] H.D. BETZ, *Sermon on the Mount*, 367. See also J. GNILKA, *Matthäusevangelium*, I, 210.

[155] The image of an omniscient Father should be seen against the Gentiles' image of God in the previous verse, as one who can be influenced by the many words of people. Betz, basing himself on a creator-creature relationship between God and people, explains this verse as an orthodox teaching on prayer. He seems to miss the point as he ignores the Father-child relationship that pervades Matt 6,1-18; cf. H.D. BETZ, *Sermon on the Mount*, 368-369.

they become like the Gentiles who do not even know the Father. Then, their so-called prayer will remain mere babbling, gabbled in vain.

The Gentiles do not know the Father. While praying they repeat many words thinking that some gods listen to their prattle and bless them. The disciples are not like the Gentiles. They are the children of the Father. Their Father knows them and all their needs. Their prayer should be a celebration of their filial relationship with the Father.

3.3.3 A Model Prayer for the Children (6,9-13)

Having warned the disciples not to imitate the bad models of the hypocrites and the Gentiles in prayer, Jesus teaches them how to pray. This prayer, known as "the Lord's Prayer" or "Our Father", serves as a model prayer for the disciples that helps them to live their filial relationship with the Father and fraternal relationship with one another.[156]

Unlike Luke, who introduces the prayer as a response to the request of the disciples with a brief introductory phrase in reported speech, Matthew presents it directly as an instruction of Jesus using the present imperative of προσεύχομαι. The combination of the adverb οὕτως and the conjunction οὖν in the introductory sentence indicates that this section provides a logical solution to the problems discussed in the previous sections on prayer. The second person plural pronoun ὑμεῖς, used here as an emphatic subject, calls attention to the contrast with the previous subjects οἱ ὑποκριταί (6,5-6) and οἱ ἐθνικοί (6,7-8).[157] The implication is: you have seen how and why the hypocrites and the Gentiles pray, but you (children of the Father) pray like this.

The model prayer instructs the disciples about the real concerns they should have as they are the children of the Father. Once again, their relationship with the Father and with their brothers and sisters functions as the core of these concerns. There are six petitions in this prayer, in which the first

---

[156] A comparatively shorter version of this prayer is given in Luke (11,2-4). But the context in Luke is quite different from that of Matthew. In Luke Jesus teaches the prayer to the disciples following the request of one of them to teach them to pray as John the Baptist taught his disciples to pray. But in Matthew, it is given as a continuation of a discourse on prayer, and it is Jesus who takes the initiative to teach it. An important aspect of the Matthean Our Father is that it is given at the centre of the SM. It is the focal point or the nucleus of the Sermon. A version similar to Matthew's Lord's Prayer is found also in *Didache* (*Did* 8,2).

[157] See BDF § 277:1, 145; R.T. FRANCE, *Matthew*, 133.

three – "you-petitions" – deal with the Father's name, kingdom and will (6,9-10) and the second three – "we-petitions" – focus on the concerns of their life, including their relationship with the other children (6,11-13).[158]

a) Paternity of God and Fraternity of the Children

The model prayer begins with addressing God as the Father of the disciples: "Our Father, who art in heaven". It is a confession of their filial relationship with him, a relationship stressed repeatedly in the previous sections. There are three more occasions in Matthew where πατήρ is used in the vocative. All these three occurrences are in the personal prayers of Jesus (11,25; 26,39.42).[159] But nowhere in the NT is this vocative used with the pronoun ἡμῶν. In the Lukan parallel only πάτερ is used. This, once again, confirms the Matthean emphasis on a personal "Father-children relationship" of the disciples with God.[160]

By instructing the disciples to call God "our Father" Jesus is inviting them to take part in the personal relationship he has with his Father.[161] Consequently, it is also a reminder to them of their real identity as the children, which is distinct from that of the scribes and Pharisees and the Gentiles. If they do not see themselves as his children, they cannot address him as "our Father".[162] The plural ἡμῶν may be due to the didactic nature of this unit. At the same time, it also shows the inter-relationality of the children (see 18,20).[163] By calling God our Father, every child recognizes that he/she belongs to a family of the children of God. This inter-relationality binds them to love each other and take care of each other (see 22,39; 25,31-46).

---

[158] Some authors count the last petition, "do not lead us into temptation but deliver us from evil", as two petitions and thus argue for a total of seven petitions. See T.M. TEHAN – D. ABERNATHY, *An Exegetical Summary*, 116-117, for a list of authors who argue for six, and for seven.

[159] See Luke 10,21; 11,2; 22,42; 23,34.46; John 11,41; 12,27.28; 17,1.5.11.21.24.25.

[160] Betz explains the fatherhood of God in relation with the whole creation. Though he uses the term "father-child relationship" here, he overlooks the fact that the term "Father" for God is a reserved term in the gospel of Matthew – used by Jesus only to his followers. Cf. H.D. BETZ, *Sermon on the Mount*, 387. However Betz is right as he challenges the hypothesis of Joachim Jeremias that Jesus' address of God as "Father" must be interpreted as *abba* (see Mark 14,36). As he rightly says, there is no textual evidence in Matthew for this proposal. Cf. J. JEREMIAS, *The Prayers of Jesus*, 54-57; H.D. BETZ, *Sermon on the Mount*, 374.

[161] See TERTULLIAN, "Prayer", 2:5, 160; CYPRIAN, "The Lord's Prayer", 8, 133-134.

[162] ORIGEN, "Prayer", 22:3, 74.

[163] See CYPRIAN, "The Lord's Prayer", 8, 132-133; J. CHRYSOSTOM, *Homilies*, 19:6, 134.

The Father whom the children are addressing is in "heaven". It shows the glory and transcendence of the Father.[164] This also points out the heavenly identity of the children. Though they are here on earth, their existence is not merely earthly (Phil 3,20). Through the Father their earthly existence is linked with heaven. So as the children of the Father, they are also heirs of heaven.[165]

b) Desire for the Hallowing of the Name

The first thing the children pray for to the Father is that his name may be sanctified.[166] God's name, in the OT, is synonymous with God's person, his presence and his authority (Gen 21,33; Exod 20,7; Lev 24,11; Num 6,27; Deut 12,5, etc.). In Matthew this metaphor of the "name" is used in the same sense relating to the Father (6,9; 28,19; see also, 21,9; 23,39), to Jesus the Son (7,22; 10,22; 12,21; 18,5.20; 19,29; 24,5.9; 28,19) and to the Holy Spirit (28,19).[167]

The verb ἁγιάζω is a derivative of the adjective ἅγιος.[168] As holiness is God's basic nature (Exod 15,11; 1Sam 2,2; Isa 6,3; 40,25; see Rev 15,4), to hallow God's name would mean recognizing and accepting this nature and its demands.[169] So the people of Israel were asked to hallow God's name[170] by revering God acknowledging him as their creator and liberator, by meditating upon his great deeds (Deut 10,20-21; Josh 24,14; 1Sam 12,24; Isa 8,13; 29,23…), and by living a life according to the commandments of God (Lev

---

[164] As several scholars have suggested, the address "our Father" with the qualifier "in heaven" "is a combination of intimacy and immanence as well as of God's transcendence." T.M. TEHAN – D. ABERNATHY, *An Exegetical Summary*, 118; see C.L. BLOMBERG, *Matthew*, 119; D.A. CARSON, *Matthew 1–12*, 169. U. VANNI, *Con Gesù verso il Padre*, 189, summarises both these dimensions beautifully: "Dio è divinamente padre e paternamente Dio."

[165] See ORIGEN, "Prayer", 22:5, 76.

[166] The expression ἁγιασθήτω τὸ ὄνομά σου, occurs nowhere else in the NT, except in the parallel of the model prayer in Luke (Luke 11,2).

[167] See J. SWETNAM, "Hallowed Be Thy Name", 558; R.T. FRANCE, *Matthew*, 134; W.D. DAVIES – D.C. ALLISON, *Matthew*, I, 603.

[168] In the Synoptic gospels the verb ἁγιάζω appears only four times (Matt 6,9; 23,17.19 and Luke 11,2). In Matthew 23,17 and 19, it refers to the gold dedicated (set apart) for the temple rites.

[169] "The hallowing of the Name means the making of the Name holy, i.e., causing God to be acknowledged for the God he is." C.F. EVANS, *The Lord's Prayer*, 28; see also C.W.F. SMITH, "Lord's Prayer", *IDB*, *III*, 155; D. HILL, *Matthew*, 136.

[170] The hallowing of God's name was one of the primary ritual obligations of the Jewish religion (Exod 20,7; Lev 22,32; Isa 29,23). See H.D. BETZ, *Sermon on the Mount*, 390.

22,32).[171] In the book of the prophet Malachi God complains about his priests, "A son honours his father, and servants their master. If then I am a father, where is the honour due me? And if I am a master, where is the respect due me?" (Mal 1,6). The basis of God's demand for honour from the people of Israel was his relationship with them. They were his chosen people, whom he delivered and preserved. The disciples' filial relationship with the Father is evident in the first petition. An authentic child would find joy in honouring the name of its father and giving glory to him (Matt 5,16). By teaching the disciples to pray for the hallowing of the name of their "Father", Jesus is asking them to acknowledge and live out their identity as the authentic children.[172]

Who can sanctify the Father's name? In the OT there are texts which refer to the sanctification of the divine name by God himself (Ezek 36,22-23; 38,23; 39,7) and which speak about the sanctification of the divine name by humans (Exod 20,7; Lev 22,32; Isa 29,23).[173] In Matt 6,9 the verb ἁγιάζω is in the passive, and it can be interpreted as a divine passive.[174] This means it is the Father himself who is requested to sanctify his name (Ezek 36,23). The petition clearly expresses an intense longing of the children for a situation where God is honoured and revered by every reality in the universe. This can happen only when God's kingdom comes into its fullness, i.e. at the eschatological consummation.[175] As the children pray in the next petition, only God, not human beings, can bring his kingdom; hence only God, not

---

[171] Through the often repeated theological refrain "be holy because I am holy" in Leviticus (Lev 11,44.45; 19,2; 20,7.26; 21,8.15; 22,9.16.32) the people of Israel were exhorted to partake in the holiness of God and sanctify his holy name through their lives.

[172] The similarity between the model prayer of Jesus and the Jewish *Kaddish* Prayer is discussed extensively among scholars. References to the sanctification of the name of God, to his will, and to the establishment of his kingship in both the texts evidently presents some striking similarities. However, the differences are also very conspicuous. A parallel expression to Matt 6,9 is found in the *Kaddish* prayer: "May His great name be exalted and sanctified" (see The *Kaddish Prayer*, Trans. by N. SCHERMAN, 49). Both the model prayer and the *Kaddish* prayer use the term "name" for God; but, unlike the *Kaddish* prayer, the model prayer offers it as a direct and intimate address to the Father. If we agree with the claim that the *Kaddish* prayer has influenced the model prayer, then this difference is significant. It could be further proof for Jesus' emphasis on the Father-children relationship of the disciples with God.

[173] See U. LUZ, *Matthew 1–7*, 379 ; M. DUMAIS, *Le Sermon sur la Montagne*, 242 ; J. NOLLAND, *Matthew*, 285-287.

[174] See BDF § 130:1, 72.

[175] W.D. DAVIES – D.C. ALLISON, *Matthew*, I, 603.

human beings, can cause the true sanctification of the name.[176] In fact the petition for sanctification is a confession by the children of their ardent desire as well as their limitation. They ask the Father to hallow his name himself as they themselves are incapable of doing it. Naturally, praying for such a state of affairs includes the children's promise of an unceasing commitment for the same goal. Jesus' call to strive for the Father's kingdom, will and righteousness does indicate such a commitment (5,10; 6,33; 26,39).[177]

The opposite of sanctification is profanity. Repeatedly, the OT warns the people of Israel, who were known to others as the people of God, not to profane God's name through their sins such as idolatry (Lev 18,21; 20,3; Ezek 20,39; 43,6-9), irreverence (Lev 22,2; Ezek 22,26) injustice and wickedness (Jer 34,16; Amos 2,6-7), and blasphemy (Lev 24,16; Isa 52,5).[178] The disciples, as the Father's children, bear the name of the Father before the world. If they are radiating light through their lives, it will lead people to glorify their Father (5,16).[179] But if they are diffusing darkness, it will cause others to stumble and profane the Father's name (18,6). By praying for the sanctification of the name of the Father, the children are implicitly imploring the Father to spare them from everything that might cause others to profane his name, which they bear. Or positively, they are asking for the Father's grace to live a life that will induce others to sanctify his name.

c) Desire for the Kingdom

Having prayed for the hallowing of the name of the Father, the children pray for the coming of the kingdom (βασιλεία) of the Father. In Matthew βασιλεία appears fifty-five times.[180] It is the opening message of John the

---

[176] See O. DA SPINETOLI, *Matteo*, 198. Some authors interpret the petition for the sanctification of the name (other petitions too) as eschatological based on the aorist tense of the verb. Cf. R.E. BROWN, "The Pater Noster", 228; R.A. GUELICH, *The Sermon on the Mount*, 289; against this view, cf. BDF § 337:4, 173; U. LUZ, *Matthew 1–7*, 378.

[177] As R.T. FRANCE, *Matthew*, 134, puts it: "This clause may thus express both a desire to see God truly honoured as God and an eschatological longing for the day when all men acknowledge God as the Lord."

[178] The prophet Jeremiah interpreted the exile as a punishment for Israel's profaning the name of God (Jer 34,16ff; see also Ezek 36,20.21).

[179] See J. CHRYSOSTOM, *Homilies*, 19:7, 134.

[180] Thirty-two referring to the kingdom of heaven, four to the kingdom of God (12,28; 19,24; 21,31.43), five to the Father's kingdom (6,10.33; 13,43; 25,34; 26,29), two to the kingdom of the Son of Man (13,41; 16,28), one to Jesus' kingdom (20,21), six to "the kingdom" (4,23; 8,12; 9,35; 13,19.38; 24,14), one to Satan's kingdom (12,26) and four to other kingdoms. Though in 6,10 and 6,33 it is not directly connected with the term Father, from the

Baptist (3,2) and of Jesus (4,17): "Repent, for the kingdom of heaven is at hand."[181] Similarly, as Jesus sends his apostles for the mission he asks them to proclaim the same message (10,7). In the summary descriptions about Jesus' ministry, proclamation of the good news of the kingdom is presented at the middle together with his teaching and healing ministries (4,23; 9,35). In the Final Discourse, it is said that this good news of the kingdom will be proclaimed throughout the world before the end (24,14). Different parables of the kingdom, like the mustard seed (13,24), the yeast (13,33), the treasure hidden in the field (13,44), the merchant in search of fine pearls (13,45), call attention to the preciousness of this message.

The expressions, the "kingdom of God", or the "kingdom of heaven", do not refer to a political or spatial territory as the term "kingdom" would normally mean.[182] Rather, they refer to God himself, his sovereign authority and dominion. When Jesus announces the kingdom is at hand (ἤγγικεν), it means that God like a king, with all his power and glory, comes to establish his sovereignty over the people.[183] At the same time, the kingdom should not be understood as an abstract quality like omnipotence or omniscience. A king is always a king of his people. In fact, the sphere of God's kingdom is his

---

context it is obvious that the kingdom in these texts refers to the kingdom of the Father. See R.L. MOWERY, "The Matthean References to the Kingdom", 398.

[181] The phrase "kingdom of heaven" is found only in Matthew. The extensive use of this phrase in Matthew instead of the phrase "kingdom of God" (Matt 4x; Mark 14x; Luke 32x) has been traditionally interpreted as the result of the evangelist's attempt to avoid the use of the divine appellation "God". Thus, scholars generally treat these phrases as synonymous. See G. DALMAN, *The Words of Jesus*, 92; Str-B, I, 172; C.J. CADOUX, *The Historic Mission of Jesus*, 110; G. STRECKER, *Der Weg der Gerechtigkeit*, 17.166; W. TRILLING, *Das wahre Israel*, 143; J.D. KINGSBURY, *Matthew: Structure,* 134; K. STOCK, "Die Bergpredigt", 1; G. KEERANKERI, "Matthew's Gospel", 104. However, the fact that Matthew has used also the phrase "kingdom of God" at least four times in the gospel raises a question against this supposition. Though various attempts have been made to solve this problem and to show that Matthew had a definite purpose in using these phrases differently, none has proved convincing. Cf. A. KRETZER, *Die Herrschaft der Himmel*, 21-31; M. PAMMENT, "The Kingdom of Heaven", 211-232; A. WOUTERS, *„...wer den Willen*, 70-103; J.C. THOMAS, "The Kingdom of God", 136-146; R.L. MOWERY, "The Matthean References to the Kingdom", 398-405.

[182] In 1Chr 28,5; 2Chr 13,8 the phrase the kingdom of Yahweh (מלכות יהוה) is used. Otherwise the phrases "kingdom of God" or "kingdom of heaven" do not occur in the OT. But the idea of God as the one who rules over Israel as its king is one of Israel's basic faith proclamations (e.g. Exod 15,18; Deut 33,5; Pss 47,2; 93,1; 96,10; 103,19; 145,10). See J.D. KINGSBURY, *Matthew: Structure,* 134. For a view of the kingdom as a territorial reality, both in the OT and in the NT. see J.C. O'NEILL, "The Kingdom of God", 130-141.

[183] See C.J. CADOUX, *The Historic Mission of Jesus*, 111; K. STOCK, "Die Bergpredigt", 4.

people.[184] The imagery of a king can be compared to a shepherd (see Ezek 34,11-31). Like a shepherd he leads his people and protects them from their enemies.[185] Similarly, God's sovereignty over his people implies that he will defeat all the other powers that rule over his people and redeem them from their slavery and give them life in its fullness. This is the good news (εὐαγγέλιον) Jesus brought (4,23; 9,35), and this is the good news to be proclaimed to all the nations before the end (24,14).

When the children pray for the coming of the kingdom, they are praying for the sovereignty of God over their lives as well as over all the earth.[186] This prayer has a special significance as we consider the life of the disciples in this world as a process of becoming children of God. As long as they are in the world, many anti-God powers attempt to rule over them and distract them from their way to the Father. These powers use different strategies: they may tempt the children offering glory, honour, prosperity and other worldly rewards (see 4,9; 6,1.2.5.16.24; 19,22; 26,15), or choke them with different thorns like anxiety over life, over food and clothing, disease and other calamities (6,25-34; 13,22.25), or threaten them with persecution and death (5,10-12.44; 10,23; 23,34). By praying for the coming of the kingdom of the Father, the children ask the Father for his regal protection in their lives to conquer all these enemies on their journey.[187]

Implicit in the prayer for the coming of the kingdom is a deep desire to be the members of that kingdom. We have seen above that only those who fulfil the will of the Father, manifested through Jesus, can enter the kingdom. In other words, only those who live as the authentic children of God can long for it. This condition has been given already in the announcement of the kingdom by John and Jesus (3,2; 4,17). To receive the kingdom, people have to prepare and change their lifestyle. The word μετανοέω, which appears in the announcement, indicates what sort of a change is needed in their lives, so that they may become citizens of the kingdom. Literally, μετανοέω means "change of one's mind" – normally translated as "to repent" or "to be converted".[188] Therefore the repentance intended here can be understood as a change of attitude, a change of perception, which will lead to a change of lifestyle.

---

[184] See C.F. EVANS, *The Lord's Prayer*, 32.

[185] God's kingship can be seen also as an extension of his fatherhood. As the head of the family, a father takes care of his children; as the head of the nation the king protects and guides his people. In fact, every member of his kingdom is a son or daughter to the king.

[186] See ORIGEN, "Prayer", 25:1, 84-85.

[187] See GREGORY OF NYSSA, "The Lord's Prayer", 3, 51.

[188] See K. STOCK, *Marco*, 33-34.

Certainly, it includes a conversion to a morally upright life,[189] but more importantly, it calls for a change of attitude and perception regarding one's identity. Rebuking the Pharisees and Sadducees who came to him for baptism, John said to them, "Do not presume to say to yourselves, 'We have Abraham as our father', for I tell you, God is able from these stones to raise up children to Abraham" (3,9). Those who think (δοκέω) of anybody else, even of Abraham, other than God as their father cannot welcome the kingdom. They have to turn away from all earthly fathers (and dominations) and turn towards God and become his children to be the members of the kingdom. Then their only concern will be the will of the Father, his kingdom and his righteousness (6,33).[190]

d) Desire for the Realization of the Will of the Father

When the kingdom is established, everything on the earth will be governed according to the will of God. Therefore, the children's third petition for the realization of the will of the Father on earth as in heaven can be

---

[189] In his proclamation of the kingdom, Jesus demanded a different lifestyle – a higher righteousness that exceeds that of the scribes and Pharisees – for any one aspiring to enter into it (5,20). It is not one's origin (8,12), pious words (7,21), opulence (19,23-24), or a superior religious or social status (21,31) that makes one eligible to enter the kingdom. Quite the reverse, Gentile or social outcast, all who fulfil the will of the Father would inherit it (7,21; 21,31.43; 25,34). The kingdom proclamation of Jesus was a call to conversion, to poverty in spirit (5,3), to exceeding righteousness (5,10.20; 6,33; 13,43), to surrendering faith (8,11), to childlikeness (18,4; 19,4), to unconditional forgiveness (18,23), to care for the needy (25,34).

[190] In the model prayer and in most of the other texts in Matthew, the kingdom is presented as an imminent but entirely future reality. At the same time, there are some texts in Matthew which depict the kingdom as a present reality, one which has already arrived (see 11,12; 12,28). Sometimes this difference is viewed as a contradiction, for which scholars have given various explanations (see W.G. KÜMMEL, *Promise and Fulfilment*,19-140; M. PAMMENT, "The Kingdom of Heaven", 211-232; U. LUZ, *Matthew* 8–20, 204). As C.F. EVANS, *The Lord's Prayer*, 36, suggests, it should be seen not as a contradiction but a "fruitful tension". Though the final consummation of the kingdom is an eschatological event, a future reality, with the advent of Jesus it has been already inaugurated. Jesus' teaching with authority, his miracles and healings, especially his casting out demons etc. can be seen as the signs of the kingdom present in this world (see 11,5-6). Beyond doubt, Jesus was the "Champion of the kingdom, Initiator of the kingdom, Mediator of the kingdom, Bearer of the kingdom, Revealer of the kingdom" (G.R. BEASLEY-MURRAY, *Jesus and the Kingdom of God*, 146). The disciples of Jesus have witnessed and experienced it (see 13,16-17). So when they pray for the "coming of the kingdom", they ask the Father to make it possible to have a complete and eternal experience of the kingdom, which they have enjoyed in part, in and through the life of Jesus, his Son. Therefore, it is not a prayer for a utopian, never attainable "pie in the sky", but for a concrete reality, which they have already tasted in some measure.

considered synonymous with their prayer for the coming of the kingdom.[191] Unlike the first two, the third petition has two parts. While the first part, "your will be done", expresses the desire, the second part, "on earth as in heaven", specifies the space in which the children want this will to be done.[192]

The substantive θέλημα occurs six times in Matthew;[193] only Jesus uses this word, and it refers always to the θέλημα of the Father.[194] In Jesus' prayer at Gethsemane (26,42) it is used exactly as in 6,10 together with the same verb and the same pronoun. In 7,21;12,50 and 21,31 θέλημα is given as the object of the verb ποιέω, which shows that the will of the Father is not an abstract concept but a concrete demand which the disciples should "practise" in their lives.

The word θέλημα can mean a desire, a wish, a purpose or something that is willed.[195] It is generally translated as "will" in the English NT versions. When somebody wills something, he/she draws a concrete programme to achieve what is willed; otherwise it remains as a simple wish. Jesus in Matthew seems to be referring to such a willed programme of the Father as he prays to the Father at Gethsemane: "My Father, if this cannot pass, unless I drink it, thy will (θέλημα) be done" (26,42). We know the cup Jesus had to drink was his passion and death (see 20,22; 26,27-28.39). The will of the Father referred to here is the redemption of human persons – forgiveness of their sins (26,28). In 18,14 Jesus says that it is not the will of his Father that any of the "little ones" be lost. In other words, the Father wants all to be saved from the slavery of sin and to become his children in his family.[196] For that purpose, he sent his Son to this world (10,40; 15,24; 21,37) as its saviour (1,21) to serve and give his life as a ransom for many (20,28).[197] The Son was fully aware of this divine mission with which he was sent, and throughout his life he sought to fulfil it (see 9,15; 16,21; 17,22-23; 20,17-19; 26,2.24.29.53-54). Although human pain and suffering shook him for a moment, he

---

[191] The third petition γενηθήτω τὸ θέλημα σού is found only in Matthew. Luke seems to be unaware of this phrase. While Matthew uses the same formula in Jesus' prayer at Gethsemane, Luke uses a different and more elaborate one (see Matt 26,39; Luke 22,42).

[192] In fact, this second part functions also as a conclusion of all the three petitions. It can be read as: hallowed be your name on earth as in heaven; your kingdom come on earth as in heaven; your will be done on earth as in heaven. See ORIGEN, "Prayer", 26:2, 88; R.T. FRANCE, *Matthew*, 135.

[193] Matt 6,10; 7,21; 12,50; 18,14; 21,31; 26,42; (Mark 1x; Luke 4x; John 11x).

[194] See Luke 12,47; 23,25; John 1,13.

[195] See LOUW–NIDA, I, § 25:2, 289.

[196] See 1Tim 2,4.

[197] See John 3,15-17.

triumphed over temptation and surrendered totally to the will of the Father. This meaning of θέλημα as the Father's will for the redemption of human beings (18,14; 26,42) can be applied also to 6,10.[198] The children pray: Father, realize your heavenly redemptive programme upon the earth!

Heaven is the sphere where this redemption is fully experienced as it is the reign of the Father, and there are no counter-forces to push or pull the children into sin.[199] There the redeemed ones will shine like the sun (13,43). Now, the children are praying the Father to bring about that redemption also upon the earth, so that they could live here fully as his children without being disturbed by their enemies.[200] In fact, when this petition is fully realized, the earth – as the children experience it now – will exist no more; it will have been transformed into heaven.[201]

As indicated above, the references to θέλημα in 7,21; 12,50 and 21,31 demand a certain conduct from human persons. In 21,31 this conduct can be identified as obedience to the Father. In the immediate context of 7,21 this conduct is explained as hearing and performing the words of Jesus (see 7,24-27). In 12,50 the specific nature of this conduct is not explicit. In 7,21 it is given as the condition for entering the kingdom and in 12,50 as the condition for entering into the fraternity of Jesus. In either case, it refers to the requirement needed for an eternal filial relationship with the Father. Therefore, the conduct demanded in these texts can be explained in the light of the meaning of θέλημα that we have deduced from 26,42: it is a way of life that will make one worthy of the redemption the Father wills for human beings.[202] If we apply this dimension of θέλημα to the third petition of the

---

[198] See R.E. BROWN, "The Pater Noster", 236-237; M. VELLANICKAL, "The Christian Righteousness", 116.

[199] Heaven is the dwelling place of the Father, the ultimate goal of his children's life (5,20; 7,21; 18,3; 25,34). It is his throne and the abode of the angels (5,34; 18,14; 22,30); evil has no place there. On the other hand, the earth is the present sphere of life and activities of the children. Here, they have to coexist with the "sons of the evil one" (13,25.38), and they are threatened and tempted by various powers (13,19). However, it is not impossible for the children to overcome these hurdles, because their Father is the supreme authority also over the earth, (5,35; 11,25; 28,18); he is the one who takes care of the birds and lilies (6,26.30); he knows even of the fall of a sparrow (10,29), and he is always with his children (6,4.6.18).

[200] See GREGORY OF NYSSA, "The Lord's Prayer", 4, 62. As we have seen in the prayer for the coming of the kingdom, the disciples already had a foretaste of this redemption through their life with Jesus (8,23-27; 14,22-33; see Luke 1,69.71.77; 19,9).

[201] See ORIGEN, "Prayer", 26:6, 91-92.

[202] How does one know about this lifestyle? Through Jesus the Son! From the beginning to the end of the gospel the believer is guided to experience the will of the Father as it has been unfolded in and through the life and mission of Jesus the Son. He submits himself

model prayer we may interpret it as the children's desire to live according to the redemptive will of the Father for them here and now, as it will be done in their future life in heaven. Concretely, they are asking the Father's grace to live as his children, fulfilling his will manifested through his Son, and thus to participate in his redemptive programme for the world.[203]

By praying for the fulfilment of the will of the Father upon earth, the children express also their willingness to surrender their self-will to the will of the Father. Thus they profess that the redemptive programme of their Father is the only thing they want to have in their life. Such a total surrender to the will of the Father can come only when they are confident of their identity as the children of the Father.

e) Request for Bread

The second part of the model prayer, which is dominated by "we petitions", begins with the request for bread. The object of the petition is τὸν ἄρτον, and it is modified with two adjectives: ἡμῶν and ἐπιούσιον. What is this bread the children are asking their Father for? What is the significance of this petition in their process?[204]

The adjective ἐπιούσιος, which alone can explain the precise nature of the bread intended here, is a rare word. No occurrence of this word outside the model prayer has yet been reported.[205] Various suggestions, mainly

---

unconditionally to the will of the Father and fulfils it. Those who hear his words and perform them will be like a wise man who builds his house upon rock (7,24). See Ch. IV.

[203] We have interpreted the "realization of the will of the Father" in the third petition both as an eschatological establishment of God's will upon earth, as well as the children's living according to the will here and now. This goes along with the interpretation of most of the commentators: D. HILL, *Matthew*, 137; U. LUZ, *Matthew 1–7*, 380; R.T. FRANCE, *Matthew*, 134-135; W.D. DAVIES – D.C. ALLISON, *Matthew*, I, 605-606; U. VANNI, "Il Padre Nostro", 351; M. DUMAIS, *Le Sermon sur la Montagne*, 243-244; D.A. CARSON, *Matthew 1–12*, 170-171; W. NGOWI, *Jesus' Teaching on Prayer*, 69; J. NOLLAND, *Matthew*, 288. For a different view cf. R.H. GUNDRY, *Matthew: Mixed Church*, 106, who argues that the petition refers primarily to the obedience of the disciples to the will of the Father and not to the eschatological establishment of God's will. On the contrary, C.F. EVANS, *The Lord's Prayer*, 41-42; R.E. BROWN, "The Pater Noster", 234-238; J.P. MEIER, *Matthew*, 61, accentuate more the eschatological dimension of the petition, without excluding the element of human cooperation with God's plan.

[204] For a detailed treatment of the historical, existential, salvific and sacrificial significance of the bread-petition, see R. MEYNET, "La composition du Notre Père", 158-191.

[205] Scholars frequently refer to an instance found in an upper Egyptian papyrus of the 5th century A.D, but nothing earlier than that. Cf. R.E. BROWN, "The Pater Noster", 239; G. STRECKER, *The Sermon on the Mount*, 117.

etymological, have been made attempting to decipher its meaning, but none has proved conclusive.[206] In general, two types of conclusions regarding the nature of the bread petitioned for stem from these conjectures on the meaning of ἐπιούσιος: 1. bread as "daily bread" or for "the coming day" which is needed for one's sustenance here and now;[207] 2. bread as "eschatological bread" which will be enjoyed in the heavenly banquet.[208] Scholars have given arguments for and against these two possibilities.[209] According to our thesis, both these positions are plausible.[210] While the first option deals with the life of the children during their process in the world, the second one focuses on life at the victorious end of the process.

If an allusion to Exod 16,4 is assumed in this verse, the idea of bread as "daily bread" can be accepted without difficulty. God fed Israel with daily Manna in the wilderness during their journey to the Promised Land. Thus the liberator God acted also as their protector and provider.[211] In the context of the model prayer, where the Father's sovereignty is acknowledged and prayed for in the previous petitions, portraying the Father as the daily bread giver as

---

[206] These suggestions can be summarised in the following four: 1. Derived from ἐπί and οὐσία (from the verb εἰμί,) meaning "for existence", or the "substance" required for survival. (This etymology was first suggested by Origen and followed by several others. He interpreted ἄρτος ἐπιούσιος as the supersubstantial bread – the spiritual bread – which unites with the human substance; see ORIGEN, "Prayer", 27:1-13, 92-102. Following the same line Jerome translated this phrase as *panem nostrum supersubstantialem* in the Vulgate.) 2. Derived from ἐπὶ τὴν οὖσαν ἡμέρα, meaning "for the present day" or "daily". 3. From ἡ ἐπιοῦσα ἡμέρα, meaning "for the coming day" or "for the following day". 4. From ἐπιέναι, (to come) referring to the coming day, whether tomorrow or the eschatological last day. Adapted from T.M. TEHAN – D. ABERNATHY, *An Exegetical Summary*, 122. See also: the critical apparatus of NESTLE–ALAND, *Novum Testamentum Graece*[27] for Matt 6,11; W. FOERSTER, "ἐπιούσιος", *TDNT*, II, 590-599; R.E. BROWN, "The Pater Noster", 239-240; G. STRECKER, *The Sermon on the Mount*, 117-118; U. LUZ, *Matthew 1–7*, 381-382; W.D. DAVIES – D.C. ALLISON, *Matthew*, I, 608-609; H.D. BETZ, *Sermon on the Mount*, 398; M. DUMAIS, *Le Sermon sur la Montagne*, 248-251.

[207] So argue, W. HENDRIKSEN, *Matthew*, 332; R.H. GUNDRY, *Matthew: Mixed Church*, 107-108; E. SCHWEIZER, *Die Bergpredigt*, 66-67; R.A. GUELICH, *The Sermon on the Mount*, 291-292; R.H. MOUNCE, *Matthew*, 57; C.L. BLOMBERG, *Matthew*, 119; U. VANNI, "Il Padre Nostro", 353; D.A. CARSON, *Matthew 1–12*, 171; J. NOLLAND, *Matthew*, 289-290.

[208] J. JEREMIAS, *The Prayers of Jesus*, 101-102; R.E. BROWN, "The Pater Noster", 241-243; P. TRUDINGER, "The 'Our Father' in Matthew", 53; D.A. HAGNER, *Matthew 1–13*, 150.

[209] See D. HILL, "'Our Daily Bread' (Matt 6.11)", 2-10.

[210] See D. HILL, *Matthew*, 137-138.

[211] Like Mark, Matthew has given two episodes of the multiplication of loaves. The words εὐλογέω (14,19) and εὐχαριστέω (15,36) used in the context of the multiplication of the loaves indicate that it is on the authority of his Father in heaven that Jesus provides bread for the hungry.

in the Exodus story is quite appropriate. Thus, in a different way this petition also recognizes the Father's authority over the children. In the Exodus story, daily gathering of the bread was a symbol of people's trust in divine providence (Exod 16,17-20). Likewise, the children's asking for the daily bread expresses their continual trust in God's parental care (Matt 6,34).

In Matthew the word ἄρτος (bread) appears twenty-one times, mostly referring to it as a basic item of the human diet. The first appearance of ἄρτος is in the context of Jesus' temptation (4,3-4). Knowing that Jesus was hungry, the tempter asks Jesus to command the stones to become bread (4,3). Thus he uses Jesus' hunger as a means to tempt him. Hunger is a reality, which can make people feel very fragile and vulnerable (13,22). It can tempt the children to give up their trust in the Father and go after other "masters" who would offer them a temporary relief and make them their slaves (6,24; see 1Tim 6,8-10). Similarly, the threat of hunger might move them to store up treasures for their morrows (6,19). Seen from this existential situation, the children's prayer to the Father for daily bread can be considered as a confession of their human limitation, i.e. a situation without bread might tempt them to leave their way to the Father. So, relying on their filial relationship with the Father, they appeal to him to be their daily bread-donor, so that nobody else makes any claim over their existence.

At least in two contexts in Matthew where Jesus speaks about bread, he alludes to a father-children relationship as the basis of "bread-giving". In 7,9-11 the heavenly Father is compared with a human father who would give bread, not stone, to his son who asks for it. Then Jesus asks the disciples, "If you then, who are evil, know how to give good gifts to your children, how much more will your Father in heaven give good things to those who ask him" (7,11). No doubt, the children can confidently ask their Father for their daily bread. To the Canaanite woman who pleads with Jesus to heal her daughter Jesus says, "It is not fair to take the children's bread and throw it to the dogs" (15,26). Though the meaning of bread is symbolic in this context, by this statement Jesus affirms the fact that the children have a right to their Father's bread. This justifies the children's qualifying the daily bread they ask their Father for as "our" bread in the model prayer.

When interpreted as a request for daily bread, this petition underscores also the children's mutual relationship. They ask for the bread not as individuals but as a family. Similarly they ask for "daily" bread and not for "all-days" bread. Bread is a concern of every child, and every child has a right to receive it. At the same time, no child has a right to accumulate it for his whole life and deprive other children of their daily sustenance.[212] All children will be asked at the end to give an account of how they shared their Father's bread with each other before they will be welcomed to or rejected from the Father's kingdom (25,35.42).

As mentioned above, in view of our thesis, the request for bread in the model prayer can be understood also as a request for "eschatological bread". In that case, the bread mentioned here needs to be understood as a symbol of the eschatological banquet itself (see Luke 14,15). In Matt 8,11 and 26,29 Jesus refers to such a banquet that will take place in the kingdom. Similarly, the Parable of the Wedding Feast in 22,1-14 and the wise virgins' entering with the bridegroom for the marriage in 25,10 also allude to this banquet (see Rev 19,7-9).

Jesus' reference to the banquet at the Last Supper (26,29) is particularly significant for our study. After the blessing of the cup, Jesus tells his disciples that he will not drink the fruit of the vine until that day when he drinks it anew with them (μεθ' ὑμῶν) in the kingdom of his Father.[213] Thus, he indirectly promises the disciples that they will join him in the imminent banquet in the kingdom.[214] Now, this is a future situation which will be realised only at the end of their process. Before arriving at this blissful state, the disciples have to traverse a long way in this world. As in the earlier petitions, by asking the Father to give that day's bread today, the children may be expressing their overwhelming desire to experience that final consummation where everything will be ruled by God and his will, where they will sit at the table with the Patriarchs (8,11) and the Son in the Father's kingdom as his children.[215]

f) Request for Forgiveness

The fifth petition has two parts. In the first part the children ask the Father to forgive their debts, and in the second part they confess the indispensable condition for receiving the Father's forgiveness: their willingness to forgive

---

[212] See G. GIAVINI, *Ma io vi dico*, 128.

[213] This μεθ' ὑμῶν is not found in the Markan parallel (Mark 14,25). In the Lukan text, Jesus seems to refer to his banquet with the disciples in the kingdom, but this is not as explicit as in Matthew (Luke 22,15-16).

[214] It is important to note that this promise is made only after foretelling the betrayal of Judas and the woe that would befall him (26,24-25; see John 17,12; Acts 1,25). Judas is an example of those persons who initially respond to the call of Jesus and thus receive the grace to become children of God, but abandon it by turning away from Jesus and turning against him.

[215] The aorist of the verb δίδωμι supports the eschatological nature of the petition – "once-and-for-all" giving of the bread (compare with the present tense in Luke 11,3).

their brothers and sisters. Thus the children admit that they are aware of the fact that their debts will not be forgiven unless they forgive the debts of others. The same theme is treated again in Jesus' teaching on forgiveness in 6,14-15 (immediately after the model prayer) and in the parable of the Unforgiving Servant in 18,23-35.

The verb ἀφίημι used in the aorist imperative in the first part and in the aorist indicative in the second part of this petition means "to forgive" or "to pardon" in this context (see also 6,14.15; 9,2.5.6; 12,31.32; 18,21.35; 26,28).[216] The substantives ὀφείλημα (translated as "debt") and ὀφειλέτης (translated as "debtor") are derivatives of the Greek verb ὀφείλω, which means "owe to" or "have an obligation to" or "be indebted to" (see 18,28.30.34; 23,16.18).[217] The debt for which the children are asking remission here is generally understood as the sins they have committed in their life.[218] Lukan use of the term ἁμαρτία (sin) instead of ὀφείλημα in the model prayer (Luke 11,4) and the appearance of the word ἁμαρτία together with ἀφίημι in Matt 9,6 and 18,21 further substantiate this interpretation.

Whether ὀφείλημα means sin or debt, the focus of the fifth petition is obviously the theme of "forgiveness". An implicit acceptance of human nature echoes in this prayer. Even though one shares a filial relationship with the Father, the possibility of sin cannot be negated. The Father knows the limitation of his children, and forgiveness of their sins is a major agenda of his divine programme for which he has sent Jesus, his Son (1,21; 9,2.5.6; 26,28). So the children can fearlessly ask for forgiveness. At the same time, the Father demands the same from the children that they should forgive the

---

[216] The verb ἀφίημι appears forty-seven times in Matthew with a wide semantic range, e.g. "to allow" (3,15), "to leave behind" (4,20), "to dismiss" (14,15), "to depart from" (18,12), "to leave in a place" (24,2) etc. See R. BULTMANN, "ἀφίημι", *TDNT*, I, 509-512 for various meanings of this verb.

[217] See LOUW–NIDA, I, § 57:221-222, 582.

[218] See TERTULLIAN, "Prayer", 7:2, 165. In Aramaic the root חוב is used both for debt and sin. See M. BLACK, *An Aramaic Approach to the Gospels and Acts*, 140; D. HILL, *Matthew*, 138; R.T. FRANCE, *Matthew*, 136; W.D. DAVIES – D.C. ALLISON, *Matthew,* I, 611; D.A. HAGNER, *Matthew 1–13*, 150; D.A. CARSON, *Matthew 1–12*, 172; H.D. BETZ, *Sermon on the Mount*, 400; J. NOLLAND, *Matthew*, 290. Against van Tilborg who interprets the debts here as real monetary debts, Betz rightly observes that this language of debt and obligation taken from commercial language has been used here metaphorically for sins. Cf. S. VAN TILBORG, *The Sermon on the Mount,* 114. More literally, S.T. LACHS, "On Matthew vi. 12", 6-8, argues that the debt in the fifth petition is dealing not with sins but with loans made in the sixth year, one year before the Jubilee.

sins not only of their brothers and sisters (18,21-22) but also of every one (see the phrase ἀφῆτε τοῖς ἀνθρώποις in 6,14-15).

It is important to note that in the model prayer it is the children themselves who tell the Father that they forgive (have forgiven) their debtors.[219] More than a claim for the Father's forgiveness, an affirmation of their identity as the children of the Father can be read in this statement (see 5,45). Forgiveness is part of their filial identity. As the Father is forgiving, so too are the children (see 5,38-48)! As he is merciful, so too are they (18,33)!

g) Request for Protection

The sixth petition also has two parts. In the first part the children ask the Father not to bring them into temptation (πειρασμός), and in the second part they ask him to rescue them from the evil one. The first part of the petition raises a serious theological problem. Does the Father bring (εἰσφέρω)[220]the children into temptation? Since many find it difficult to accept such an image of the Father, different translations have been proposed.[221]

God bringing his people into temptation in order to test their faith, is quite a well-known and accepted fact in the OT (Gen 22,1; Exod 15,25; 16,4; 20,20; Deut 4,34; 13,4 – in all these verses the verb πειράζω is used). Similarly, there are texts in Matthew and also in some other NT books where temptation is understood in a permissive sense, as part of the divine programme (see Matt 4,1; Mark 1,12-13; Luke 4,1; John 6,6; 1Cor 10,13; Heb 4,15; 11,17; Rev 2,10). It is true that there is a theological problem in viewing

---

[219] The function of the aorist form, ἀφήκαμεν has been discussed and disputed much in scholarly circles. The main question is whether one should take this aorist form as an accomplished fact ("we have forgiven") or as the translation of an underlying Semitic word indicating durational or consequential action ("we forgive"). See H.D. BETZ, *Sermon on the Mount*, 404, for a summary of various positions. In this study we treat forgiveness as a quality that manifests the authentic identity of the children. Every moment of their life the children share this quality of their Father, and so the question of "when" is not very significant for us.

[220] The verb εἰσφέρω is used only in the present verse in Matthew. Luke uses it on three more occasions besides in the model prayer (Luke 5,18.19; 12,11). In Luke 5,18-19, it is in the narrative text where the evangelist relates the attempt of the men who wanted to *bring* the paralytic to Jesus. In Luke 12,11 it is in the teaching of Jesus as he foretells to the disciples the forthcoming trials where their opponents would *bring* them before the synagogue authorities. The other NT occurrences of this word (Acts 17,20; 1Tim 6,7; Heb 13,11) also communicate the same idea of "bringing" something.

[221] For example: "do not subject us" (NAB); "keep us from" (CEV); "do not cause us" (LOUW–NIDA, I, § 90:93, 810). For a survey of various interpretations of this petition see C.F.D. MOULE, "An Unsolved Problem", 65-75; H.D. BETZ, *Sermon on the Mount*, 408-409.

the Father as the one who brings the children into temptation, especially when temptation is seen exclusively as a negative experience. But such a perspective on temptation expresses a conviction that nothing happens to the children, even the worst of situations, without the knowledge of their Father.[222] The realization that even when they are tempted they are in the presence of the Father would strengthen the children to overcome the temptations. It may be easier to see the presence of God in the so-called consolations in life, but to experience God also in desolations and trials they need an unwavering faith.

In Matthew the substantive πειρασμός appears twice (6,13; 26,41) and the verb πειράζω six times (4,1.3; 16,1; 19,3; 22,18.35). Wherever the verb πειράζω is used in Matthew, it refers to the temptation or test Jesus had to face from his opponents.[223] Through their trickeries they challenged his identity as the Son of God or tried to dissuade him from fulfilling his God-given mission. But Jesus never yielded to their temptations. At the same time, as the author of the letter to the Hebrews says, from his own experience Jesus was aware of the pressure of temptations in human life (Heb 4,15).

Referring to the vulnerability of human nature Jesus asks his disciples at Gethsemane to stay awake and pray not to enter into (εἰσέρχομαι) temptation (26,41). The context of this verse clearly explains the kind of temptation the disciples are to face. When Jesus undergoes the pain of death, the disciples remain unmoved as if they had no relationship with him (26,37-40.43.45). When he is arrested they all flee from him. When he is handed over and crucified in order to fulfil God's will for the redemption of human beings, they deny him and their fellowship with him (26,69-75). For their own safety and security they abandon Jesus and his words, and they forget the will of the Father. Thus, at least for a short time, they break off their relationship with the Father and Jesus. Though not as acute as this, there are several other occasions where the disciples succumb to temptations against their filial identity (e.g. 14,30-31; 16,7-8.22-23; 17,25; 20,20-27). In the model prayer when the children ask their Father not to bring them into temptation, it could be viewed primarily as a sincere confession of their human frailty. Being

---

[222] As CYPRIAN, "The Lord's Prayer", 25, 149, puts it, "In this part it is shown that the adversary has no power against us, unless God has previously permitted it, in order that all our fear and devotion and obedience may be turned to God, since in temptations nothing is permitted evil, unless the power is granted by Him." See also, AUGUSTINE, *Sermon on the Mount*, II, 9:30-34, 138-142.

[223] The devil (4,1.3), Pharisees and Sadducees (16,1), Pharisees (19,3), disciples of the Pharisees and Herodians (22,18), a scribe (22,35).

aware of their "humanness", the children ask their Father to protect them from entering/falling into (εἰσέρχομαι) temptations[224] and being separated from their filial relationship with him.[225]

After confessing their human weaknesses in confronting temptations, in the second part of the petition the children ask the Father to deliver (ῥύομαι) them from the evil one.[226] The adversative ἀλλά links the second part with the first part. It is not enough that they be spared from falling into temptation, but they need the Father's protection from the evil one who is trying to destroy them and separate them from their Father.

The adjective πονηρός appears twenty-six times in Matthew qualifying both the concrete and abstract reality of evil in a variety of ways.[227] Since in 5,37 and 6,13 it is in the genitive (τοῦ πονηροῦ), it can be a genitive of ὁ πονηρός "the evil one", or τό πονηρόν "the evil".[228] The evil one, ὁ πονηρός, as a personified reality, confusing the children of the kingdom, is mentioned in 13,19 and 13,38. So, it is possible to interpret τοῦ πονηροῦ in 5,37 and 6,13 also as referring to the "evil one" as in 13,19.38.[229]

---

[224] As ORIGEN, "Prayer", 29:9, 117, exhorts, "[...] let us pray to be delivered from temptation, not that we should not be tempted – which is impossible, especially for those on earth – but that we may not yield when we are tempted."

[225] "Many and diverse are the temptations which beset the Christian. Satan attacks him on every side, if haply he might cause him to fall. Sometimes the attack takes the form of a false sense of security, and sometimes of ungodly doubt. But the disciple is conscious of his weakness, and does not expose himself unnecessarily to temptation in order to test the strength of his faith. Christians ask God not to put their puny faith to the test, but to preserve them in the hour of temptation." D. BONHOEFFER, *The Cost of Discipleship*, 167. See also P. MARECEK, *La Preghiera di Gesù*, 88-89; M. NGOWI, *Jesus' Teaching on Prayer*, 90.

[226] This part appears also in *Didache* 8,2 but not in Luke.

[227] Fourteen of these occurrences are in the singular. The qualified subject is unambiguous in all the texts except in 5,37.39 and 6,13.

[228] Most of the Fathers of the Church before Augustine interpret it as the "evil one" referring to the "tempter" or "Satan"; see ORIGEN, "Prayer", 30:1-3, 127-129; TERTULLIAN, "Prayer", 8:3.5, 166-167; CYPRIAN, "The Lord's Prayer", 27, 150-151; GREGORY OF NYSSA, "The Lord's Prayer", 5, 83-84; J. CHRYSOSTOM, *Homilies*, 19:10, 136-137. But Augustine interprets it as neuter, and takes this term for evil in general; see *Sermon on the Mount*, II, 9:35, 143-144.

[229] Investigating the meaning of the prepositions ἀπό and ἐκ after ῥύομαι and kindred verbs, and examining the gender of the phrase ἀπὸ τοῦ πονηροῦ from the gospels, epistles and early Christian literature, F.H. CHASE, *The Lord's Prayer*, 70-167, concludes that in Matt 6,13 ἀπὸ τοῦ πονηροῦ refers to the evil one: "The record of our Lord's life and teaching in the gospels gives what I cannot but think is a conclusive confirmation of the view that Christ taught His followers in the closing petition of the Prayer to ask for deliverance from Satan in his manifold enmity against man" (p. 166). So also, W. HENDRIKSEN, *Matthew*, 336; R.A. GUELICH, *The Sermon on the Mount*, 297; J. LAMBRECHT, *The Sermon on the Mount,* 145; S. SABUGAL, *El*

The verb ῥύομαι is used only three times in the gospels (Matt 6,13; 27,43; Luke 1,74), always with God as the deliverer and human person(s) as the object of deliverance.[230] To conquer the evil one who is continuously trying to block their journey towards their Father – by snatching away the word sown in their hearts (13,19) and sowing weeds to destroy their growth (13,38) – the children need the Father's protection. He alone can deliver them from the wiles and lures of the enemy.

It is possible to interpret this petition also from an eschatological perspective. In that case, it can be seen as a continuation of the petitions in the first part of the model prayer. As the children pray for the eschatological coming of the kingdom and the will of the Father upon earth, they also pray for the situation where there will not be any temptation or trials as God will have destroyed the kingdom of the evil one and delivered the children.[231]

The model prayer that Jesus teaches the disciples in Matt 6,9-13 reflects different characteristics of the filial status to which Jesus calls his disciples. By asking them to address God as "our Father", he underscores, at the outset, their already attained filial identity. Similarly it also emphasizes their relationship with the other children. Together as a family they call God "our Father". Thus they implicitly profess their fraternity and equality among themselves. Their Father is the "heavenly Father". As the children of that Father they are heirs of heaven – an inheritance they are waiting to receive in the future.

The model prayer invites the disciples to look forward to and pray for the final consummation when the Father's name will be hallowed by every one, when his kingdom will triumph over all other kingdoms, and when everything on earth will be governed by his will as it is in heaven. The petitions for the

---

padrenuestro, 396-398; W.D. DAVIES – D.C. ALLISON, *Matthew,* I, 614; D.A. HAGNER, *Matthew 1–13*, 151; U. VANNI, "Il Padre Nostro", 354; D.A. CARSON, *Matthew 1–12*, 174. Taking 1Tim 4,18 and *Didache* 10,5 as the oldest probable interpretations of the petition, and pointing out the absence of the use of the term "evil one" as a designation for Satan in Judaism, U. LUZ, *Matthew 1–7*, 385 argues that in 6,13 τοῦ πονηροῦ refers to evil in general. See also D. HILL, *Matthew*, 139; L. MORRIS, *Matthew*, 149; H.D. BETZ, *Sermon on the Mount*, 413; J. NOLLAND, *Matthew*, 293 for a similar view.

[230] In the rest of the NT (fourteen times more), either God or Jesus Christ appears as the subject of this verb.

[231] For an eschatological explanation of the sixth petition see R.E. BROWN, "The Pater Noster", 248-253; J.P. MEIER, *Matthew*, 62.

final consummation also express the disciples' longing to enter into and dwell in the kingdom of the Father as his children. Then, they will be freed from all trials and temptations that hinder them today in their process, and they will be relieved of all their human vulnerabilities.

The model prayer exhorts the disciples to live as the authentic children of the Father. They are not to seek their glory but the glorification of the name of the Father; not to put themselves under anybody's authority but only the Father's; not to do the will of another but of the Father. It also encourages the disciples to ask the Father's grace to continue their journey in this world as his children without submitting themselves to any earthly powers that would block their way to the Father. They can approach their Father for all their needs. Their Father is the supreme authority over earth and heaven. So they can be confident that nothing happens in their life – even temptations and trials – without his knowledge. He will forgive all their sins, if they forgive their brothers and sisters; he will deliver them from all enemies, if they live as his children.

3.3.4 An Addendum on Forgiveness (6,14-15)

Forgiveness, the subject matter of the fifth petition (6,12), is taken up again in 6,14-15. What is prayed for and promised in 6,12 is given here as an additional teaching. Since the petition against temptation and the evil one comes in between (6,13), in the present structure of the text, this teaching on forgiveness stands as an addendum – a rationale for the fifth petition. The explanatory conjunction γάρ at the beginning of v.14 indicates this part's connection with the fifth petition.[232]

The verb ἀφίημι which appears twice in the fifth petition is used four times in this section.[233] The Father's firm and uncompromising stand regarding forgiveness is made clear in this text both positively and negatively. The children will receive forgiveness from the Father, if and only if they forgive others. It is not given as a general moral teaching on forgiveness applicable to anybody but as a specific demand of the Father to his

---

[232] Instead of the aorist imperatives in the model prayer, this part has conditional sentences in both the verses, composed of an aorist subjunctive in the protasis and a future indicative in the apodosis. These two verses are organized as antithetical parallels. Authors who apply a diachronic approach see this text as a Matthean addition to the Lord's Prayer. Strecker regards it as a "typically Matthean interpretation of the Lord's Prayer", while Luz finds a paraenetical application of v.12 here. See G. STRECKER, *The Sermon on the Mount*, 125; U. LUZ, *Matthew 1–7*, 389.

[233] See above for a discussion on the meaning and usage of this word in Matthew.

children.[234] Therefore, forgiveness is not merely one of the several qualities the children should have, but it is an obligatory and essential aspect of the Father-child relationship.[235]

The inflexible stance of the Father and of Jesus regarding the issue of one's forgiving the other is elaborately given in the parable of the Unforgiving Servant (18,23-35). This parable is told in the context of Peter's question concerning the number of times one should forgive one's brother (18,21). Transforming Peter's seemingly very generous "as many as seven?" into "seventy times seven", Jesus affirms the unlimited nature of the forgiveness demanded of them. The parable explains why they should forgive others unconditionally and without limits.[236] The demand for fraternal forgiveness is stressed in the parable based on the king's incomparable mercy towards his wicked servant. Concluding the parable Jesus says, "So also my heavenly Father will do to every one of you, if you do not forgive your brother from your heart" (18,35). Evidently, the response of the Father to an unforgiving person is compared to that of the king to his servant. Conversely, though not mentioned explicitly, the mercy of the king in the parable represents the mercy of the Father. It is that paternal mercy lavished on every child that makes the Father's demand for mutual forgiveness obligatory.

Though the word "hypocrite" is not used in 6,14-15, the teaching on forgiveness in this section is also a call against hypocrisy. Forgiving the other is an expression of one's acceptance of human nature. Only a person who is aware of his/her limitations, who is willing to accept that limitation, and who is aware of the forgiveness received in his/her life, can really forgive other people. There is nobody in the world without any sin. So, when one hesitates to forgive, one behaves like a hypocrite. They never accept their weaknesses; rather they pretend that they are perfect people. That is why they see the speck in a brother's eye overlooking the log in their own (7,3-4; also see Luke 18,9-14).

---

[234] See the use of the phrase πατὴρ ὑμῶν twice here.

[235] A parallel to this teaching is found in Mark 11,25, and that is the only context in the gospel where Jesus refers to God to the disciples as "your Father who is in heaven."

[236] The king in the parable was extremely kind to his servant when he pleaded for some more time to pay back his huge debt. The king, instead of extending the time, remitted all his debt. The same king turned furious and merciless when he heard that the servant maltreated a poor fellow servant who had borrowed a very small amount from him. Summoning the unforgiving servant, the king asked him: "You wicked slave! I forgave you all that debt because you pleaded with me. Should you not have had mercy on your fellow slave, as I had mercy on you?" (18,32-33). Then the king handed him over to the torturers.

In contrast, forgiveness is the hallmark of the children of the Father. Every time they forgive, they manifest their true identity (5.45.48). In fact, by forgiving others they may lead others to glorify the Father (9,1-8). More than all, by forgiving others the children participate in the salvific mission of Jesus who shed his blood for the forgiveness of sins (26,28).

3.4 *On Fasting (6,16-18)*

After instructing the disciples about the false prayer models of the hypocrites and the Gentiles, and after teaching them a model prayer followed by an additional instruction on forgiveness, Jesus speaks about a third act of righteousness, namely fasting (6,16-18). The disciples are warned, as before, not to assimilate to the fasting style of the hypocrites. An evident similarity to 6,2-4 and 6,5-6 can be observed regarding the structure, theme and vocabulary of this section. The subordinating conjunction ὅταν resumes the exhortative style established in 6,2 and repeated in 6,5.[237]

Fasting in general is regarded as a symbolic act by which people confess their unworthiness and ask for God's forgiveness and blessing.[238] The verb νηστεύω (to fast) appears eight times in Matthew, of which four are in 6,16-18.[239] Fasting was esteemed highly in the Judaism of Jesus' time.[240] For the

---

[237] Similar to the previous sections on almsgiving and prayer, this section also begins with an opening prohibition; unlike them a present imperative is used here and it presents the prohibition as a general principle. The disciples should not be sullen faced like the hypocrites when they fast. Here again the action of the hypocrites (ἀφανίζουσιν) is given in the present indicative as in 6,2 and 6,5. As mentioned above, this points to the habitual nature of their pretence. The rationale of the prohibition is also the same as that of the previous sections: they will have no reward from the Father.

[238] The Hebrew root צום (νηστεύω and its cognates in the LXX) is used in the OT to refer to different types of fasting. People fasted on various occasions: as a sign of repentance (1Sam 7,6; Neh 9,1-3; Dan 9,3-5; Joel 1,13-14), to seek God's guidance (Deut 9,9; Judg 20,26-28; Ezra 8,21; Dan 9,1-13), to prepare to receive divine revelations (Exod 34,28; Deut 9,9.18; Dan 9,3), to implore God's intervention (2Chr 20,2-4; Esth 4,16; Ps 35,13-17), to avoid punishment (Joel 2,12-15; Jonah 3,5-9), to express sorrow and distress (2Sam 1,11-12; 3,35; 1Chr 10,11-12) etc. See J. BEHM, "νῆστις", *TDNT*, IV, 924-935; H.A. BRONGERS, "Fasting in Israel", 1-3; K.D. BERGHUIS, "A Biblical Perspective of Fasting", 92-95. According to the study of Berghuis, the Bible mentions fasting from food in about fifty-nine contexts: forty-three in the OT and sixteen in the NT.

[239] Matt 4,2; 6,16[2],17.18; 9,14[2].15; Some late manuscripts (א[2] C D L W *f*[1.13] 𝔐 sy[h]) add ει μη εν προσευχη και νηστεια in Matt 17,21. The first instance of fasting in Matthew is Jesus' forty-day fast in the wilderness (4,2) which resembles the fasting of Moses on Mount Sinai – the first biblical instance of fasting (Exod 34,28). From the context it is clear that Jesus' fasting was a preparation for his mission. The other three are in a context of a controversy about

Gentiles fasting was an identifying mark of the Jew.[241] This would explain why the hypocrites used it as a means to acquire the attention and praise of people.

3.4.1 Fasting of the Hypocrites

Whilst genuine fasting is a religious act by which one submits oneself to God – repenting or seeking his forgiveness and guidance – the hypocrites fast to impress people and draw their attention and praise. The adjective σκυθρωποί used in the predicative position with οἱ ὑποκριταί in 6,16 displays the pretence of the hypocrites. The compound word σκυθρωπός, made up of σκυθρός ("serious", "sad") and οπ-, means "serious or sad looking".[242] This word appears only once again in the NT where it is used to describe the sad countenance of the disciples who went to Emmaus after the death of Jesus (Luke 24,17). Their sad appearance resulted from their genuine feeling of loss, frustration and confusion (Luke 24,18-24).

An additional description of their charade is shown with the phrase, "they disfigure (ἀφανίζω) their faces". The same verb ἀφανίζω appears twice in the pericope that follows this unit referring to the decaying of earthly treasure by moth and rust (6,19-20).[243] In the present context "disfiguring of face" (making it unrecognizable ἀ-φανίζω)[244] may refer to putting ashes on one's face, which is again a genuine gesture of penitence (see Jonah 3,6; Jer 6,26;

---

fasting. When the disciples of John the Baptist asked Jesus why his disciples did not fast while they and the Pharisees fasted, Jesus defended his disciples with the parable of the bridegroom and the wedding guests (Matt 9,14-15). As mentioned above, the bridegroom and the marriage feast are metaphors of the eschatological banquet in the kingdom (Matt 22,2; 25,1; 2Cor 11,2; Eph 5,23-32; Rev 19,7.9; 21,2). In the presence of Jesus, the bridegroom, the disciples are enjoying that banquet, and it is a moment of joy and celebration, not of sorrow and lamentation. But they will fast when the bridegroom will be taken away from them (9,15). See R.T. FRANCE, *Matthew*, 169; D.A. CARSON, *Matthew 1–12*, 226; cf. L.M. FEDRIGOTTI, *An Exegetical Study of the Nuptial Symbolism*, 187-242.

[240] Luke reports of the prophetess Anna (Luke 2,36-38) who spent her widowhood in the temple praying and fasting; the Pharisee in the parable of the Pharisee and the Tax Collector claims that he fasts twice a week (Luke 18,21). The disciples of John the Baptist, the Pharisees (Matt 9,14) and the discples of the Pharisees (Mark 2,18) seem to have fasted regularly.

[241] J. BEHM, "νῆστις", *TDNT*, IV, 929.

[242] W. BIEDER, "σκυθρωπός", *TDNT*, VII, 450.

[243] See also Acts 13,41 and Jas 4,14 for the negative imagery of this verb.

[244] M. ZERWICK – M. GROSVENOR, *Grammatical Analysis*, 16.

Dan 9,3). Thus they deliberately show their fasting to others so that others may praise them as ascetic, penitent and pious people.[245]

3.4.2 Fasting of the Children

In contrast to the practice of the hypocrites, the disciples should anoint (ἀλείφω) their heads and wash (νίπτω) their faces while they fast so that others may not notice their fasting.[246] Anointing the head and washing the face would make one appear fresh before others (see Qoh 9,8; Ruth 3,3; Amos 6,6).[247] If the hypocrites deliberately invite others' attention by disfiguring their face, the disciples should consciously avoid such attention by keeping their face and appearance fresh.

Different from the teachings on almsgiving and prayer where the intention of the disciples' piety is not given explicitly but implied in the suggested mode, here in the teaching on fasting their intention is given explicitly. The disciples' fasting is not to be seen by people but by their Father who is in secret.[248] Fasting is an expression of one's surrender to and humbling before God. The children should certainly practise fasting, but this should not be with an eye to earn reverence and praise from people, but to grow in communion with their Father. The honour they could receive from people is short-lived; it cannot help them in their journey towards the Father's home. The Father alone can forgive their sins and permit them to continue their journey; he alone can give them the reward of childrenship that is eternal and irrevocable. To him alone they should manifest the tears of their heart.

---

[245] In fact, this calculated disfiguring of faces and the exhibition of their fasting show their real attitude towards fasting. Either they do not consider it as a real religious act performed before God but a means for obtaining human praise, or they think that they can trick God with appearances as they trick human beings.

[246] Like 6,6 the pronoun σύ with the conjunction δέ gives emphasis to their identity and consequent behaviour in contrast to that of the hypocrites. Moreover, the redundant use of σου with the genitives of κεφαλή and πρόσωπον makes the imperative intensely direct and personal.

[247] People anointed their heads "for a festive occasion and for a joyous celebration, and for an every day cosmetic" (Ru 3,3; Jdt 16,7). It had a connotation of gladness (Ps 45,7) and was not practised in the time of mourning (2Sam 14,2; Dan 10,3; Jdt 10,3). S. SZIKSZAI, "Anoint", *IDB*, I, 138-139; see also C.C. MITCHELL, "The Practice of Fasting", 459.

[248] As A. KEE, "The Question about Fasting", 168, puts it, "Jesus approves it as a means of expressing to God feelings of penitence and sorrow, but strongly disapproves of it as a [public] exercise which can quickly lead to pride and self-righteousness (Lk. xviii 12)."

4. **Conclusion**

In this chapter we have studied the central section of the SM (6,1-18), giving special attention to the repeated use of the divine appellation Father for God in this unit. In our analysis of the Father passages in Matthew, we have seen that Jesus presents God as the Father only to his disciples and the people who followed him. Only they are worthy of being told of the Father.[249]

From our study we can conclude that discipleship is viewed here as a process of becoming children of the Father. Two stages of this process are indicated in this unit: the present stage and the future stage. The sphere of the present stage is the world, and that of the future is the kingdom; we call these the "earthly stage" and the "kingdom stage".

The disciples are treated also in the earthly stage as the children of God,[250] but their present filial identity is not irrevocable or eternal. We have identified this as an "already" but "not yet" status. By responding positively to Jesus and his message, the disciples have received the grace to become children of God. Jesus, by presenting God repeatedly as their Father and teaching them to call him "our Father", underscores their already given, presently enjoyed filial status. On the other hand, with his constant warnings against acts of false righteousness and his instructions on the right mode of behaviour, he reminds them of the "not yet" aspect of this filial identity. In other words, if they do not continue living as the authentic children of the Father, they will lose this grace and be removed from the process.

The instructions on the right manner of doing righteousness are to help the disciples to go through the present stage of the process successfully as the children of the Father. As in other parts of the SM, righteousness is understood here also as the "divine demand upon human persons". More concretely, it is the "exceeding righteousness" Jesus taught and lived. Doing righteousness would mean fulfilling the will of God as revealed through the life and mission of Jesus. Three concrete expressions of this divine demand are discussed here: almsgiving, prayer, and fasting. The disciples should practise these pious activities, which are expressions of their relationship with the Father, but not like the hypocrites who perform them in order to be seen by others and be glorified by them, but as the children of the Father. Otherwise, like the hypocrites they will have to be content with the transient human rewards they receive for their theatrical performance. In all their

---

[249] We have used the term disciples in this study to refer to all people (actual disciples and would-be disciples) who respond positively and affirmatively to Jesus and his message.

[250] Thus, God is presented to them as "your Father".

actions the children should aim at the glory of the Father; he is the centre and the ultimate goal of their life. They need to believe that he is with them now and sees in secret all their good deeds done in secret. Evidently, the manner of doing righteousness expected of the disciples should not be limited to the three acts discussed here, but it should be applied to every aspect of their life. On the whole it refers to a lifestyle anchored in the Father, trusting in his unceasing presence, and longing for the reward with him.

In his teaching on prayer, Jesus warns the disciples not to babble like the Gentiles who do not even know the Father. As his children they should be confident that their Father knows all their needs even before they ask him. The model prayer Jesus teaches the disciples shows them how they should progress in their journey trusting in the Father and seeking his glory. The children should deeply desire the sanctification of the Father's name, the coming of his kingdom, and the fulfilment of his will on earth. All the same, the model prayer encourages them to ask for help from the Father to overcome all the hurdles that come their way, and for his protection from all the enemies who attempt to undermine their filial relationship with him. The additional instruction on forgiveness given at the conclusion of the prayer section reminds them that forgiveness is an essential aspect of their identity as the children: if they do not forgive others, their Father will also not forgive them. Evidently, without forgiving others they cannot remain as the children of the Father and continue their process.

The repeated references to the reward and the differentiation between the human reward and the Father's reward mentioned in this unit point out to the disciples the future stage of their process.[251] Right living as the children of the Father in the present earthly process will lead them to a future state of bliss, a reward with the Father. Though the reward passages in the present unit do not specify the nature of the reward, it is clear from the use of this concept elsewhere in the gospel that it refers to the disciples' final reception into the kingdom of the Father as his children. When they arrive at that state of bliss, it will be the culmination of the process. Then they will dwell as their Father's children in his kingdom for ever. The eschatological character of the model prayer also points towards this future stage. Looking forward to being in this blissful state, the children pray for the final consummation when their Father's kingdom will rule over every other kingdom, when their Father's programme

---

[251] The reward with the Father is given as the motivating factor for their right mode of practising righteousness.

will be carried out everywhere, and when they will have completed the process of becoming his children for ever.

CHAPTER II

The Father and Children in the Rest of the Sermon on the Mount

Besides its ten occurrences in Matt 6,1-18 the appellation πατήρ for God appears seven more times in the SM, in six of these cases again referring to him as the Father of the disciples (5,16.45.48; 6,26.32; 7,11), and the remaining and the last one presenting him as the Father of Jesus (7,21). In all these sections highlighting the disciples' filial relationship with the Father, Jesus instructs them how to live as the authentic children of the Father. Presenting himself as the judge of the final day in 7,21, he describes to them the criterion by which one will be accepted or rejected into the kingdom. In this chapter we will study these πατήρ passages with their context and show how discipleship has been viewed as a process of becoming children of the Father in these sections.

1. The Mission of the Children in the World (5,16)

The first reference to God as the Father of the disciples in Matthew occurs in 5,16. Having identified the disciples as the salt of the earth and the light of the world in the previous verses (5,13-15), Jesus commands them in 5,16: "Let your light so shine before men, that they may see your good works and give glory to your Father who is in heaven."[1]

---

[1] We take v.16 as belonging to the discourse unit 5,13-16. There are several elements that support its literary unity: the two identity-defining maxims introduced by ὑμεῖς ἐστε in vv.13 and 14 are parallel in form (τὸ ἅλας τῆς γῆς; τὸ φῶς τοῦ κόσμου); different words connected with

In 5,13-16 Jesus gives an orientation to the disciples regarding their identity and mission in the world, its consequence and goal. Using the metaphors of salt and light and the examples of a city built on a hill and a lighted lamp in a house he shows them how their identity as the children of God is a blessing to the world:[2] through them the world can know the Father and worship him as the true God.

1.1 *Good Works of the Children and Glory to the Father*

Three human actions are envisaged in the teaching in 5,16: the disciples' shining their light (the main action), which may cause people to see their good works (the first resultant action), which may lead people to glorify the Father (the second resultant and final action). So the focus of 5,16 is not so much on the disciples' glorifying the Father themselves but more on their mediatory role of leading others to glorify him. Similarly, the disciples are asked to guide others not through their words or teachings but through their "good works" (τὰ καλὰ ἔργα), which people themselves will see in the Father's children.

Jesus does not identify any special group of people whom the disciples should inspire and influence to glorify the Father; rather he uses a generic term "men" (ἄνθρωποι) to refer to them. These "men" may also include the people who stay far away from the Father – the bad, the wicked (5,45), the foolish (7,24-27; 25,1-13), the weeds (13,24-30), the faithless (25,14-30) the goats (25,31-46) etc..[3] As long as the children are in the world they have to

---

light (φῶς, καίω, λύχνος, λυχνία, λάμπω) bind vv.14-16 semantically; the same genitive plural τῶν ἀνθρώπων is used in vv.13 and 16 (an *inclusio*) though its function is different in each context. See R.A. GUELICH, *The Sermon on the Mount*, 120; U. LUZ, *Matthew 1–7*, 247; J. GNILKA, *Matthäusevangelium*, I, 133; W.D. DAVIES – D.C. ALLISON, *Matthew*, I, 470; D.A. HAGNER, *Matthew 1–13*, 98; H.D. BETZ, *The Sermon on the Mount*, 155; M. PÖTTNER, "Metaphern der universalen Liebe", 106-108.

[2] The metaphors of salt and light are found also in Mark and Luke (salt: Mark 9,50; Luke 14,34-35; light: Mark 4,21; Luke 8,16; 11,35). But they do not identify the disciples with these metaphors as Matthew does in 5,13-16. The following elements are unique to the Matthean text: i) the introductory declarations, "You are the salt of the earth" (5,13a) and "You are the light of the world" (5,14a); ii) a picturesque presentation of the contemptuous treatment of the "tasteless salt" by people (5,13c); iii) the example of a city set on a hill (5,14b); iv) the concluding exhortation (5,16), which sets the goal of the mission of the disciples and presents God as their Father. See W.D. DAVIES – D.C. ALLISON, *Matthew*, I, 470-471 and D.A. HAGNER, *Matthew 1–13*, 98, for a detailed comparison of the synoptic parallels.

[3] According to W.D. DAVIES – D.C. ALLISON, *Matthew*, I, 478, "men" in the present text "refers to Jews and Gentiles outside the church".

coexist and interact with all these people. The response they receive from people during their life in this world may be varied. Some may receive them in their houses and accept their message (10,11.40-41). But they may be hated, tempted and persecuted by many others (5,10-12; 10,16-25; 24,9).

The disciples have only one way of dealing with all these situations and with all these people: the way of the children of God (see 5,45). They will not respond to the world according to its standards but will act according to the standard of God's children as shown by Jesus. Their nature as the children of God will be radiated in their every act. This is what most probably is meant by the "good works" (τὰ καλὰ ἔργα) of the disciples – a lifestyle that befits their identity as the children of God (see 1Pet 2,12).[4]

Such a way of life may open the eyes of people. They may realize that it is because of the disciples' relationship with the Father that they are able to live and respond differently from them. In fact, people may recognize in the disciples the nature of their Father and his ways. This may influence them to turn towards the Father, to seek him, and to give glory to him. The conversion that people may undergo, owing to the life of the disciples, will be a sign that people profit from the filial identity of the disciples and from their being a blessing to the world.

Glorifying the Father would mean adoring him and worshipping him as the true God.[5] If people intend to glorify the Father, first of all they should know him and believe in him and in the Son who reveals him. Therefore, people's glorifying the Father would imply that they have gone through this process of faith. This means that even though they were away from the Father before, they come closer to him now thanks to the life of the disciples. Thus

---

[4] There are different suggestions regarding the intended meaning of the expression τὰ καλὰ ἔργα: i) "Good deeds, like righteousness, are the life lived consistent with the new relationship established by Jesus' ministry between God and humankind (5:6; 6:33)": R.A. GUELICH, *The Sermon on the Mount*, 124; ii) they are works of mercy ("Werke der Barmherzigkeit"): J. GNILKA, *Matthäusevangelium*, I, 137; iii) they "are to be identified with the acts commanded in 5,17–7,12": W.D. DAVIES – D.C. ALLISON, *Matthew*, I, 479; iv) "The love commandment provides the foundation for these good works (cf. 22,37-40)": D.A. HAGNER, *Matthew 1–13*, 101; v) they refer primarily to the beatitudes; but they also include all that is described in the SM under the word "righteousness" (5,20–7,12): M. DUMAIS, *Le Sermon sur la Montagne*, 169. All the above interpretations (and many more could be added!) are valid and sound. No doubt the "good works" of the disciples include all of these.

[5] See Ch. I,3.2.1 b) for an explanation of the use of the verb δοξάζω in Matthew. The hypocrites seek their own glory through their deeds (6,1-18), the children the glory of their Father.

they, too, receive the grace to join the family of the children in their journey towards the Father.[6]

1.2 *"Shine your light before men"*

Though the "good works" of the disciples may lead others to the Father, Jesus does not ask them to show their good works directly to people. Rather he asks them to shine their light before them, so that others may see their good works and give glory to the Father. The disciples' shining the light needs to be understood from vv.14-15 where Jesus identifies them as the light of the world.

In v.14 Jesus emphatically tells the disciples, "You are the light of the world."[7] The light is depicted in the Bible as an attribute of God and his salvific presence (see Pss 27,1; 36,9; Isa 60,19; 1John 1,5). By identifying the disciples with the light Jesus acknowledges them as God's children who share the quality of their Father. Being the light of the world thus means being an instrument of God's salvific presence in the world. It is a divine mission, and the OT mentions many of God's appointed servants who engaged in such a mission (see Isa 9,1-2; 42,6-7; 49,6; 60,1-5.19-20; Dan 12,3; Mic 7,8; Job 29,3; also, Acts 13,47). God chose these servants to be the light of the world, so that his salvation might reach to the ends of the earth (Isa 49,6). Like them, the disciples function in the world as the agents of God's salvation.

The identity of the disciples as the light of the world mirrors Jesus' own identity. Introducing the ministry of Jesus in 4,12-17 the evangelist quotes the prophet Isaiah who prophesied the coming of the Messiah as a light to the nations, "[...] the people who sat in darkness have seen a great light, and for those who sat in the region and shadow of death light has dawned" (4,16). The word φῶς which occurs twice in this quotation refers evidently to Jesus and his mission (see Isa 9,1). In the gospel of John Jesus says about himself, "I am the light of the world; he who follows me will not walk in darkness, but will

---

[6] Therefore the purpose clause ὅπως ... καὶ δοξάσωσιν τὸν πατέρα ὑμῶν... can indicate their glorifying the Father in the present earthly life as well as in the future life in the kingdom.

[7] See the subject ὑμεῖς. It sounds exclusive, referring only to the disciples. "You, you alone are the light of the world." See L. MORRIS, *Matthew*, 104; D.A. HAGNER, *Matthew 1–13*, 101-102. Light is a metaphor that is usually reserved in Judaism for Israel, the Torah, the Messiah, the Temple and Jerusalem. The Messiah is designated as the "star" of Jacob (Num 24,17) and the light of the nations (Isa 42,61); Jerusalem is told that the light has come upon her and is asked to shine that light (Isa 60,1). See Str-B, I, 237; O. DA SPINETOLI, *Matteo*, 150; R.A. GUELICH, *The Sermon on the Mount*, 122; G.M. SOARES PRABHU, "The Church as Mission", 277.

have the light of life" (John 8,12; see also, 1,4-5.9; 9,5; 11,10; 12,35.46). Luke, citing Isa 42,6, presents Jesus as the light of the Gentiles (Luke 2,32). By declaring that the disciples are the light of the world, Jesus is regarding them also as his co-workers in the light-giving mission entrusted to him.[8]

When they live in this light, all their activities will reflect the light. In other words, their life will radiate the light, and it will illuminate their surroundings. Their light will be visible to all who come across them. To elucidate the visibility of the disciples' light, Jesus uses the imagery of a city built on a hill (5,14).[9] It is improbable that someone would not notice a city on a hill. More likely, it would serve as a point of reference and orientation for the whole surrounding territory.[10] Similarly, the disciples' being the light of the world will be perceptible to others, and it cannot be hid. Owing to their light the disciples may be "lifted up out of the world"[11] as an orienting indicator for the world.

Evidently, the disciples' being the light of the world is a blessing to the world. It will dispel the darkness of the people and brighten their lives. However, the disciples may be tempted to hide this light and run away from their mission of illuminating the world (see 25,18). They should overcome such temptations; the grace they have received as the children of God should be used for fulfilling its purpose. Jesus reminds the disciples of their mission with the example of a lighted lamp in a house (5,15). Everybody knows that

---

[8] As Frankemölle summarises: "Wie Jahwe in der Schrift als Gott Israels der Gott für alle ist, so ist auch Jesus und so sind auch die Jünger (vgl. 10,5f; 28,19) Licht für Israel und für die Welt." H. FRANKEMÖLLE, *Matthäus,* I, 217. G.G. GAMBA, *Vangelo di San Matteo*, 75, "Essa viene detta dei discepoli per partecipazione, in quanto il loro compito è di mantenere vivo l'insegnamento di Gesù" (see Acts 13,47).

[9] Referring to texts like Isa 2,2-4; 60,1-22; Mic 4,1-3; Rev 21,10-11 some scholars (e.g. von Rad, Schnackenburg, Campbell, Donaldson, Guelich, Gnilka, Derrett, Hagner) suggest that the example of the city built on a hilltop refers to "Jerusalem" or the eschatologically "new Jerusalem". This conjecture seems to be wrong in the context, since the emphasis of the example here lies on its visibility and not on the "city" itself (agreeing with Meier, Luz, Davies–Allison, and Dumais). Moreover, there is no definite article before the word πόλις so that it cannot be considered as referring to any particular city. Cf. G. VON RAD, "Die Stadt auf dem Berge", 439-447; R. SCHNACKENBURG, "Ihr seid das Salz der Erde", 191-192; K.M. CAMPBELL, "The New Jerusalem in Matthew 5.14", 335-363; J.P. MEIER, *Matthew*, 45; W.J. DUMBRELL, "The Logic of the Rule of the Law", 14-16; R.A. GUELICH, *The Sermon on the Mount*, 122; T.L. DONALDSON, *Jesus on the Mountain*, 117; U. LUZ, *Matthew 1–7*, 251; J. GNILKA, *Matthäusevangelium*, I, 135-136; W.D. DAVIES – D.C. ALLISON, *Matthew*, I, 475; J.D.M. DERRETT, "The Light and the City", 174-175; D.A. HAGNER, *Matthew 1–13*, 100; M. DUMAIS, *Le Sermon sur la Montagne*, 169.

[10] See K. STOCK, *Jesus Künder der Seligkeit*, 40.

[11] G. STRECKER, *The Sermon on the Mount*, 50.

the purpose of a lamp is to give light, and nobody will put it under a bushel but on a lamp stand. Permitting an allegorical interpretation, we may identify the lamp(s) as the disciples; Jesus is the one who lights these lamps.[12] He has lit their lamps not to be concealed but to be seen by all and to give light to all in the house. If they conceal their lamps under the bushel, the light will go out, and the world will remain in darkness.[13]

In 5,14 the disciples are identified with the light (ὑμεῖς ἐστε τὸ φῶς); in 5,16 the light is presented as a quality of the disciples (τὸ φῶς ὑμῶν). Since the disciples are the light, they have the light. Their existence emanates from their essence. So the imperative in 5,16 (λαμψάτω) is an invitation to radiate that light which is actually their essence as the children of God.[14] The light of the disciples will illumine "those who sit in darkness"; as a result their eyes will be opened and they will be able to recognize the nature of the Father in the children and glorify him (see 9,8; 15,31). Thus, through their lifestyle the disciples will be able to reveal the nature of the Father and gain others for him.[15]

In 5,16, "your light" (τὸ φῶς ὑμῶν) and "your good works" (ὑμῶν τὰ καλὰ ἔργα) are given in parallel. The light of the disciples and their good works are not two different things but two aspects of the same reality. When they live as the children of the Father by listening to Jesus and following his model, all their works will be good works. It is these good works that shine as their light before people. In other words, their good works are the concrete expression of their being the light, being the disciples of Jesus, being the children of the Father.

They can shine the light so long as they are the light and have the light. Though not mentioned explicitly, there is a possibility that they may extinguish their light. As we have seen before, they can rupture their relationship with the Father at any time during their life in the world and so discontinue their process of being and becoming his children. Then they will

---

[12] See CHROMATIUS, "Tractatus in Matthaeum", 285.

[13] G. Schneider beautifully summarizes the meaning of the examples of the city and the lighted lamp: "Der Spruch von der Stadt auf dem Berge sagt, daß das Licht nicht verborgen bleiben kann. Der Spruch von der Lampe sagt hingegen, daß das Licht nicht verborgen werden darf." G. SCHNEIDER, "Das Bildwort von der Lampe", 134.

[14] Hagner's interpretation of the shining of the light as "living according to the perfection of the kingdom and thus manifesting the righteousness of the Torah according to its correct interpretation" is correct but incomplete. Not only their way of living but also their whole being as the light is reflected in this imagery. Cf. D.A. HAGNER, *Matthew 1–13*, 101.

[15] As K. STOCK, *Jesus Künder der Seligkeit*, 41, puts it: "Durch die, die als seine Kinder leben, will Gott als guter Vater bekannt werden und immer mehr Menschen an sich ziehen."

no longer be a blessing to the world, and their works will not be "good works"; nobody will glorify the Father upon seeing their way of life! The reality of the disciples' being a blessing to the world and the possibility of their failing to live in this grace are shown more clearly in the metaphor of salt given at the beginning of this unit (5,13).

1.3 *"You are the salt of the earth; but..."*

Salt is a simple condiment which could be found in every house, irrespective of one's economic or social status. People use it for adding taste to food and as a preservative. Besides these normal functions, according to the OT salt was used also for sacrifices (Lev 2,13; Ezra 6,9; Ezek 43,24; 47,11), for purification (2Kigs 2,20-21), and for medicinal purposes (Ezek 16,4).[16] By telling the disciples "You are the salt of the earth" Jesus seems to be referring to the functional role of the disciples who, as the "salt", would give taste to the life of people, who would function as the preservative of society, and who would purify and heal others.[17]

Salt can be taken also as a symbol of self-emptying. In the process of serving a particular purpose it dissolves and becomes part of the substance which uses it. Thus it loses its existence, but its essence remains. Like Jesus, who was rejected, persecuted and killed by the very people whom he came to save, the disciples may lose their lives in their mission of salting the earth (see 5,11-12).[18]

---

[16] See J.E. LATHAM, *The Religious Symbolism of Salt*, 29-82.160-192; W.D. DAVIES – D.C. ALLISON, *Matthew*, I, 472-473, for various other uses of salt mentioned in Jewish and Greek religious texts. Since it is almost impossible to decide which quality of salt is intended here, as Hagner suggests, "it may be best simply to take the metaphor broadly and inclusively as meaning something that is vitally important to the world in a religious sense, as salt is vitally necessary for everyday life." D.A. HAGNER, *Matthew 1–13*, 99; see also, W.S. WOOD, "The Salt of the Earth", 170.

[17] As a rule, predicate nouns are *anarthrous* in NT Greek. But here both ἅλας and φῶς (v.14) have the definite article. This may be to underscore the unique role of the disciples as the salt and the light. BDF § 273:1, 143.

[18] Several authors interpret the salt metaphor in 5,13 as a continuation of the theme of persecution given in 5,11-12. J.B. SOUČEK, "Salz der Erde", 289-299, explains the function of salt in 5,13 referring to its function in Lev 2,13 and interprets the teaching principally as a call to be "the salt of the sacrifice" for the world. According to this interpretation, to be the "salt of the earth" implies inevitable persecution. See also, J. DUPONT, *Les Béatitudes,* III, 315-329; W.J. DUMBRELL, "The Logic of the Rule of the Law", 2-3.13-14; R.H. GUNDRY, *Matthew: Mixed Church*, 74; P.S. MINEAR, "The Salt of the Earth", 31-41.

The earth refers to "the realm of human existence"[19] where the divine project of God will be fulfilled. The Father is the Lord of the earth (11,25), and Jesus is given authority over it (28,18).[20] The earth is the abode created and sustained by God for his creatures to live in (Gen 1,1-2; Acts 4,24; 14,15; Rev 10,6). The disciples, the children of the Father, are the salt of that earth. Through their mission the earth will become a better place in which to live, but without them it will remain tasteless![21] Indeed, their being the salt of the earth is a blessing to the earth.

However, after identifying the disciples as the salt of the earth, Jesus asks a hypothetical question: "But if salt has lost its taste, how shall its saltiness be restored?"[22] The verb μωραίνω, which is translated in the present context as "losing taste", "becoming insipid", or "losing saltiness", occurs only here in Matthew. As a derivative of the noun μωρία it could literally mean "to cause the content of certain thoughts to become devoid of meaning" or "to cause to become nonsense".[23] Saltiness is the essence of salt; without saltiness it is just rubbish. Similarly, if the disciples lose their real essence, then they are like saltless salt. Externally they may appear like the "disciples", but internally they are "essence-less" (see 7,21-23). Nothing can save them from their abject condition.[24]

---

[19] R.A. GUELICH, *The Sermon on the Mount*, 121.

[20] See J. BEUTLER, "Ihr seid das Salz des Landes", 85-94; P. ŠOLTÉS, „*Ihr seid das Salz des Landes*, 85-105, for a semantic analysis of the word γῆ in Matthew.

[21] A call to universal mission is implicit in this teaching. The disciples are the salt of the earth – not only of any particular group or sect. See J. CHRYSOSTOM, *Homilies*, 15:10, 97. To be the salt of the earth they need "to get involved with this earth and its life"; they have to transcend all the barriers – be they of religion or of ethnicity – that could limit their mission. They cannot exclude anybody; both the just and the unjust must be served (5,45). See H.D. BETZ, *The Sermon on the Mount*, 158.

[22] While the "eventual condition" (ἐάν + subjunctive) in the protasis implicitly warns the disciples of the possibility of losing the essence of their identity, the instrumental ἐν with the interrogative τίνι and the indicative future passive ἁλισθήσεται in the apodosis express the inability of any external agent to restore it. See M. ZERWICK, *Biblical Greek*, § 320, 109.

[23] LOUW–NIDA, I, § 32:59, 388.

[24] W. Tyndale's translation of 5,13ab is worth mentioning here: "Ye are the salt of the earth: but if the salt have lost her saltiness, what can be salted therewith?" D. DANIELL, ed., *Tyndale's New Testament*, 25. According to this translation, the v.13b is referring not to the impossibility of restoring the lost saltiness by an external agent but to the "uselessness" of the saltless salt, that nothing can be salted again with it. If one interprets ἐν as instrumental, one cannot accept this translation. However, in the context where Jesus speaks about the functional identity of the disciples as the salt of the earth, this translation makes good sense. See also W.R. HUTTON, "The Salt Sections", 166-168.

The destiny of the saltless salt is known to all: "It is no longer good for anything except to be thrown out and trodden under foot by men" (5,13b). The double imageries of "throwing" (βάλλω) and "trampling under feet" (καταπατέω) show how salt, which could have a significant function in the daily lives of people, can become useless and an object of contempt if it loses its essence. It is a warning to the disciples; they who are a blessing to the world can become objects of scorn and contempt if they lose their essence and become rubbish.[25]

The imagery of throwing out also alludes to the fate of these men on the day of judgement. They will not be received into the kingdom as children of God but will be thrown out of the kingdom (3,10; 5,29; 7,19; 13,42.48.50; 18,8-9).

Leading people to give glory to their Father is the most important mission that the children are to carry out in the earthly stage. In 5,13-16 this mission is described as a life of witness rather than a verbal proclamation or teaching (see 28,16-20).[26] From their good works people will recognize them and come closer to their Father and glorify him. What the children have to do is to shine their light – to live out the characteristics of their identity – before men, and this will open people's eyes to see the Father and his children. As the children of the Father, the disciples are a blessing to the world; they are its salt and light. Thanks to them the world will be salted and lighted. However, when they cease to exist as the children of the Father, then they will no more be a blessing to the world but will be useless objects to be thrown out and trampled over.

The metaphors and imagery used in this unit (5,13-16) referring to the identity and mission of the disciples indicate that it is not possible for them to continue their process while ignoring their brethren in the world.[27] They have a responsibility to guide them through their life of witness to the Father. In short, in the earthly stage of their life they have a double mission: to live as

---

[25] According to P.S. MINEAR, "The Salt of the Earth", 36, "whenever the disciples refuse to accept the suffering required by their vocation, the salt loses its power."

[26] See G.M. SOARES PRABHU, "The Church as Mission", 273.

[27] "Il vero discepolo di Cristo deve rimanere allo scoperto e non rifugiarsi nella propria quiete o bearsi per proprio conforto della luce che possiede. Per vocazione egli deve parteciparla agli altri. Non si può essere carenti di luce, e più ancora non si può mancare di ripercussione e di influenza comunitaria." O. DA SPINETOLI, *Matteo*, 151.

the children of the Father, and to lead others to the Father so that they may believe in him, glorify him, and become his children (see 28,19).

2. **Being and Becoming the Children of the Father (5,45.48)**

The persons who leave everything and follow Jesus enter into a filial relationship with God. They are given the grace to be the salt of the earth and the light of the world, and their lifestyle should lead the world to salvation, to the praise of their heavenly Father (5,13-16). The sections that follow 5,16 treat in detail various aspects of their daily life, especially, their approach to the Law and their living it. In 5,17-19 Jesus declares that he has come not to abolish the Law and the prophets but to fulfil them. But his understanding of the Law and its fulfilment is not like that of the scribes and Pharisees. In 5,20 he warns the disciples that if their righteousness does not exceed that of the scribes and Pharisees they will never enter the kingdom. In the antitheses that follow (5,21-48), Jesus reinterprets the Law in the light of this "exceeding righteousness" and instructs the disciples how they should practise it.

In the concluding section of the antitheses (5,43-47) pointing out the inadequacy of the love commandment of the Torah, Jesus gives them a new love commandment: "Love your enemies, and pray for those who persecute you." He gives the rationale of the new commandment in 5,45: "so that you might become sons of your heavenly Father." This verse is particularly important for our study as it explicitly refers to the disciples as the ones becoming the "sons of the Father". As his children the disciples are to follow the paradigm of the Father. The exceeding nature of love demanded of the disciples is further emphasized in 5,46-47, which invites them to contrast their love-expressions with those of two counter models.[28] The teaching in this unit

---

[28] Thematically 5,43-47 could be considered a continuation of the previous section, the teaching on retaliation (5,38-42). But the borderline between them is clearly drawn using distinct literary markers. Following the general pattern of the antitheses, 5,43 begins with the introductory attention-calling formula ἠκούσατε ὅτι ἐρρέθη (see 5,21.27.33.38) followed by a reference to a teaching from the Law (see 5,21.27.31.33.38). Similarly the new teaching is introduced by the formula ἐγὼ δὲ λέγω ὑμῖν (see 5,22.28.32.34.39). Several pairs and parallels bind this section stylistically. Two opening commandments ("Love your enemy", "Pray for those who persecute you" 5,44); two things the Father does (makes the sun rise and makes the rain fall, 5,45); two classes of people (the good and the bad, the just and the unjust); two rhetorical questions ("if you love those who love you…" 5,46a, "if you greet only your brothers…" 5,47a); two examples of counter models (the tax collectors, 5,46b, and the Gentiles 5,47b). Three words ἀγαπάω (5,43.44.46), πατήρ (5,45.48), and ποιέω (5,46.47) function as the basic unifying factors of this antithesis. See W.D. DAVIES – D.C. ALLISON, *Matthew*, I, 548.

insists in different ways on the love for enemies as a must for the disciples in their process of becoming children of God.

Jesus concludes the antitheses by exhorting the disciples to be perfect as their heavenly Father is perfect (5,48). Being the perfect children of the Father, that is the ideal the disciples should strive for in the earthly stage of life; thus they become children of the Father in the eternal kingdom.[29]

2.1 *A New Love Commandment for the Children*

"Love the loving, hate the hating" – this is the common rule of the world. This is the moral principle that the disciples have heard also from the OT.[30] But the children of the Father should surpass such "give-in-return" morality; they should love their enemies and pray for their persecutors.

As in the previous antithetical teachings, Jesus begins (v.43) by calling their attention to the teaching of the OT: "You have heard that it was said,

---

[29] The main theme of the teaching in Matt 5,43-48, "love of enemies" has parallel material in Luke (6,27-28.32-36). Source and redaction critics are engaged with the question of whether both Matthew and Luke depended on the same source or on independent sources for the composition of this teaching (see H.D. BETZ, *The Sermon on the Mount*, 298-300, for a discussion on various possibilities regarding their origin). In any case, there are many notable differences between these two texts: i) Matthew begins this section referring to the OT Law (quoting Lev 19,18 partially and adding an additional saying to it) and presents the whole section as an antithesis to this old teaching. In Luke the quotation from Leviticus is missing and he presents this teaching as a continuation of the section on "blessing and woes" (Luke 6,20-26). ii) In Matthew the disciples are asked to pray for those who persecute (διώκω) them, in Luke for those who abuse (ἐπηρεάζω) them. iii) The Matthean text is more vivid on the rationale of the new commandment: the relationship of the disciples with the Father is emphasized here presenting them as "sons of your Father" (υἱοὶ τοῦ πατρὸς ὑμῶν); in Luke God is not called Father, and there is no personal pronoun that shows the disciples' relationship with God; according to Luke, those who love their enemies will become "sons of the Most High" (υἱοὶ ὑψίστου). iv) In Matthew the benevolence of the Father is illustrated with two concrete examples (sunshine and rain); in Luke no concrete example is given. Similarly Matthew presents two specific examples of counter model (the tax collectors and the Gentiles); Luke uses the same term "sinners" three times to refer to the counter models. v) Both the deserving and the undeserving beneficiaries of the kindness of the Father are mentioned in Matthew; in Luke only the undeserving are referred to. vi) In Matthew the disciples are exhorted to be perfect (τέλειος) as their heavenly Father is perfect; in Luke they are asked to be merciful (οἰκτίρμων) as their Father is merciful. See D.A. HAGNER, *Matthew 1–13*, 133, for some other differences found in these texts.

[30] "The prevailing opinion in both Greek and Jewish thought would have considered hatred of one's enemy as legitimate, and never would have considered prayer for the well-being of that enemy as logical." T.M. TEHAN – D. ABERNATHY, *An Exegetical Summary*, 92; see also C.S. KEENER, *The IVP Bible*, 60-61.

'You shall love your neighbour and hate your enemy'." The first part of the reference, "you shall love your neighbour", corresponds to the teaching in Lev 19,18.[31] The second part, "you shall hate your enemy", does not have a verbatim parallel anywhere in the OT. However, hating the wicked and destroying the enemies have been justified on various occasions in the OT (e.g. Exod 17,14-16; Deut 7,2; 20,16; 23,3-6; 25,17-19; Pss 41,7-12; 139,19-22).[32]

The neighbour (רע) in Lev 19,18 needs to be understood as any fellow Israelite rather than our common understanding of neighbour as a person who lives next door (see Luke 10,29.36).[33] This means that the basis of the commandment to love the neighbour in Leviticus was their religio-ethnic identity as Israelites. The commandment appears to be unconcerned with non-Israelites. Usually they were considered "enemies" by the people of Israel as they did not belong to their community.[34] Therefore the statement "and you shall hate your enemy" in v. 43b can be taken as a corollary added to disclose the inadequacy of the love commandment given in Lev 19,18.[35]

---

[31] Jesus quotes this text two more times in Matthew (19,19; 22,39).

[32] A teaching close to 5,43 is found in the Dead Sea Scrolls where "sons of light" are asked to hate the "sons of darkness"; see 1QS 1,9-11. Similarly, Josephus in his account of the Essenes (*Jewish War* II, 8,13) notes that the newcomers before being allowed to enter into the community were required to promise under oath "always to hate the wicked and help the righteous." See O.J.F. SEITZ, "Love Your Enemies", 49-51. These texts show that, as V.P. FURNISH, *The Love Command*, 47, argues, "there was current in Palestinian Judaism, shortly before Jesus' day, a counsel to 'hate' one's enemies." See also M. SMITH, "Mt. 5.43: 'Hate Thine Enemy'", 71-73.

[33] See the injunction in Lev 19,18a that leads to this commandment: "You shall not take vengeance or bear any grudge against the sons of your people, but..." The phrase בני עמך (sons of your people) parallels the רעך (your neighbour) in the second part. Moreover, רעך is a synonym of אחיך, אמיתך, and בני עמך, which are used interchangeably for neighbour in Lev 19,11-18. All these terms refer to the members of the people of Israel. See O. LINTON, "St. Matthew 5:43", 66-79; O.J.F. SEITZ, "Love Your Enemies", 43; D. HARRINGTON, *Matthew*, 89; G. KEERANKERI, *Love Commandment*, 50-52.

[34] The Israelites normally kept away from the non-Israelites and considered them their enemies. See how the OT presents the enemies of Israel referring to their ethnic identity: the Egyptians (Exod 1,8-11), the Amalekites (Exod 17,8), the Edomites (Num 20,18), the Amorites (Num 21,23), the Canaanites (Josh 11,1-5), the Syrians (Judg 3,8), the Moabites (Judg 3,12), the Midianites (Judg 6,1), the Philistines (Judg 10,7-8), the Assyrians (2Kgs 15,19.29), the Babylonians (2Kgs 24,1) etc.

[35] This view is shared by V.P. FURNISH, *The Love Command*, 51; R.A. GUELICH, *The Sermon on the Mount*, 225-227; G. STRECKER, *The Sermon on the Mount*, 88-89; U. LUZ, *Matthew 1–7*, 343-344; H.D. BETZ, *The Sermon on the Mount*, 304. As O. LINTON, "St. Matthew 5:43", 75, puts it: "[...] the two sentences: 'You shall love your neighbour' and 'You shall hate your enemy' stand as a coherent summing up of the old Law. The latter sentence

Repudiating their old understanding of love based on the religio-ethnic identity, Jesus gives them a corrective, a new commandment of love, which challenges them not only to surpass the borders of their exclusive affections but also to extend their love even to their enemies and persecutors (5,44). There are a few texts in the OT which encourage kindness to one's enemies. One may think of Exod 23,4-5; Lev 19,34; 2Kgs 6,22-23; 2Chr 28,9-15 and Prov 25,21-22 as the best examples for them. The enemies are presented in these texts in an inferior and helpless situation deserving the kindness of God's people. But none of these texts demands that one should love one's enemies and pray for the persecutors. In his new commandment of love Jesus is asking his disciples to show not mere kindness to the enemies who cannot defend themselves but to express genuine love, affection, and compassion (ἀγαπάω)[36] to those who make their life miserable.

The specification of the enemies as "those who persecute you" (τῶν διωκόντων ὑμᾶς) shows the domineering state of the enemy. Physical or mental persecution could be taken as an intense expression of enmity. But Jesus has already told the disciples that they will have to suffer on his account and they should welcome it gladly and willingly (5,10.11.12; see also 10,23; 23,34).

Normally it would be considered a virtuous act if someone is able to forgive his/her persecutors, but Jesus demands much more than this from the disciples. They should even pray (προσεύχομαι) for their persecutors.[37] Obviously forgiveness is intrinsic to prayer. One cannot feel hatred towards a person and at the same time pray for him/her. Through prayer the children intercede for their persecutors (see Luke 23,34; Acts 7,60; Rom 12,14; 1Pet 3,9) asking God to forgive their sins and bless them with his grace.[38]

---

explicates the first one. He, who gives his neighbour the first place, expels *eo ipso* the stranger into the second rank."

[36] See G. QUELL – E. STAUFFER, "ἀγαπάω", *TDNT*, I, 44-48.

[37] See J. CHRYSOSTOM, *Homilies*, 18:4, 126, for a beautiful description of the different steps that one has to ascend before one can pray for one's enemies.

[38] There is at least one reason why the disciples should pray for their persecutors. The disciples are persecuted on account of Jesus and his mission (5,11-12; 10,22; 24,9) and for righteousness' sake (5,10). By persecuting these children of the Father who are the "salt of the earth" and the "light of the world" they are opposing God and his Son and his salvific programme in this world. They need God's grace to come out of their sinfulness and to experience light.

2.2 *"You might become children of your Father in heaven"*

Humanly speaking, loving one's enemies or praying for the persecutors is not effortless. Normally people would pray for the destruction of their persecutors with the hope that it might put an end to their sufferings too. To forgive and love and pray for their enemies who maltreat them, the disciples need to go beyond their normal and "ordinary" human ways. To use the language of the SM, it demands an exceeding righteousness (5,20), or it needs the courage to follow the narrow way (7,13). The disciples can and should surpass the ordinary ways because they are the children of the Father. They have to love and pray for their enemies and persecutors, not because their enemies deserve it but because of their own identity as υἱοὶ τοῦ πατρός.

The verb γίνομαι in the aorist subjunctive (5,45) points to a future state of life into which the disciples are yet to grow (see 13,43).[39] The same verb form (γένησθε) is used in 18,3 where Jesus warns the disciples saying "unless you turn and become like children you will never enter the kingdom."[40] In the present context, loving their enemies is given as an essential requirement for their becoming children of the Father in the kingdom stage.[41]

The futuristic notion of "sonship" is reflected also in the seventh beatitude: "Blessed are the peacemakers, for they will be called sons of God" (5,9).[42] Peacemaking was the mission of Jesus. As the author of the letter to the Ephesians writes, "He is our peace"; he broke the dividing wall of hostility (Eph 2,14). The "peacemakers" are the ones who participate in his mission on

---

[39] See the result clause in v.45 (ὅπως + subjunctive) which functions as the rationale of the new commandment: "so that you may be the sons of your Father who is in heaven."

[40] For an explanation of the dynamic character of the verb γίνομαι in these contexts see W. GRUNDMANN, *Matthäus*, 177-178; M. VELLANICKAL, *The Divine Sonship of Christians*, 61.

[41] As U. LUZ, *Matthew 1–7*, 343, puts it, "those who do love their enemies will be revealed in the last judgement as children of God." See also M.J. LAGRANGE, *Matthieu*, 117; P. BONNARD, *Matthieu*, 75; L. MORRIS, *Matthew*, 131; D.A. CARSON, *Matthew 1–12*, 159. Referring to the use of γίνομαι in Luke 10,36 and John 15,8, several authors suggest that the clause ὅπως γένησθε υἱοὶ τοῦ πατρὸς ὑμῶν... needs to be taken as a command to act according to the disciples' filial identity; by loving their enemies they might show the world that they are God's children. See A. PLUMMER, *Matthew*, 88; M. ZERWICK – M. GROSVENOR, *Grammatical Analysis*, 14; W. HENDRIKSEN, *Matthew*, 314; W.D. DAVIES – D.C. ALLISON, *Matthew*, I, 554; D.A. HAGNER, *Matthew 1–13*, 134; H.D. BETZ, *The Sermon on the Mount*, 315; J. NOLLAND, *Matthew*, 268. Though this interpretation is possible, considering the context where Jesus speaks about "reward" and "merit", it is preferable to interpret this clause as pointing to the future state, to the irrevocable "sonship", into which the disciples are yet to grow.

[42] "Loving one's enemies and praying for one's persecutors is a concrete way of striving for peace." P.J. HARTIN, "Call to be Perfect", 485.

earth; so they will "participate in his dignity also – the divine sonship."[43] The future indicative of καλέω shows that they will be recognized as God's children later on, presumably at the end of the process;[44] the passive of the verb implies that it is God himself who will recognize them as his children at the end.[45]

Jesus gives the example of the Father as the guiding principle for the disciples in their dealings with others. Their Father is omnipotent; he is the creator and the protector of this universe and every reality in it.[46] He makes his sun rise on the evil and on the good (πονηροὺς καὶ ἀγαθούς) and sends rain on the just and on the unjust (δικαίους καὶ ἀδίκους). The present indicative of the verbs ἀνατέλλω and βρέχω draws attention to the ongoing activity of the Father in nature on behalf of all. The disciples are the children of such a great Father![47]

The Father would naturally like everyone to be good and just, but not all respond to him as he would expect of them. Many people rebel against him and choose the way of wickedness. But he is munificent and compassionate towards them. He takes care of their needs, and does not prevent the natural powers from serving them (5,45).[48] His benevolence is not controlled or influenced by human behaviour; he is gracious to all irrespective of their response, because it is his nature. Similarly, since the disciples are children of the Father, – and if they want to become his children – they should treat others, including their enemies and persecutors, as their Father would treat them (see Eph 5,1).[49] To be wicked is the choice of the "non-children". Why should the children be influenced by that choice and behave like them?

---

[43] M. VELLANICKAL, *The Divine Sonship of Christians*, 54.

[44] "It is a thoroughly Hebraic concept that the name reveals and is identical with one's nature and that sons are those who share in their father's nature (Mt 23:31; Jn 8:39,41f; Apoc 21:7 etc.)." M. VELLANICKAL, *The Divine Sonship of Christians*, 56.

[45] See K. STOCK, "I figli sono liberi", 154.

[46] The authority of the Father over the sun and rain is shown by presenting him as the implied subject of the verbs ἀνατέλλω and βρέχω. The use of the possessive, τὸν ἥλιον αὐτοῦ, also highlights this aspect.

[47] How foolish and absurd if the disciples imitate the model of the tax collectors and Gentiles ignoring the model of their Father (see the next page).

[48] As G.L. BORCHERT, "Matthew 5:48", 267, writes, "These words of Jesus represent reality, but they sound strange to human logic. Yet they provide a clue to the operating pattern of a follower of Jesus because they point to the meaning of wholeness."

[49] "The disciples, the sons of this Father, must prove their 'legitimacy' by showing the family likeness, which means loving with the all-embracing love their Father bestows." J.P. MEIER, *Matthew*, 55. Or as Gnilka puts it, "Die Art der Kinder ist die Art des Vaters, sein

2.3 *The Children and the Non-Children*

The disciples' identity as the children of the Father is reiterated indirectly in vv.46-47 inviting them to compare their behaviour and identity with that of the tax collectors and the Gentiles.

Jesus asks the disciples, "For if you love those who love you, what reward have you? Do not even the tax collectors do the same?" (5,46). Reciprocal love is a common characteristic of most creatures. So, if the disciples assume that they are doing something meritorious by loving the people who love them in return, they are mistaken. The love they get back is itself their recompense; they will have no reward with the Father (see 6,1.2.5.16).

As we have seen in the previous chapter, the nature of the reward (μισθός) mentioned in 5,46 can be deciphered in the light of the teaching in 5,45 where the disciples' recompense for loving their enemies is mentioned as their becoming children of the Father.[50] What more can the disciples aspire to than to become the Father's children![51] But their natural affection for their kin and kith or for their neighbours (5,43) alone will not make them worthy of that reward. Rather, when they love those who trouble them and pray for their persecutors, they can be certain of receiving it (5,12.44).

Since mutual love is a possible trait of all creatures and not something unique to the tax collectors, Jesus' reference to them in the rhetorical question, "Do not even the tax collectors do the same?" needs to be understood as representative.[52] Jesus seems to be using society's image of the

---

Wesen ist ihr Wesen, sein Verhalten ist ihr Verhalten. An der Ähnlichkeit erkennt man die Verwandschaft." J. GNILKA, *Matthäusevangelium*, I, 192.

[50] In the Lukan parallel, the great reward that the people receive for loving enemies and doing good to them is clearly specified as their becoming children of the Most High (6,35). See E.M. SIDEBOTTOM, "Reward in Matthew v.46, etc.", 219-220; W. KLASSEN, "The Authenticity of the Command", 399.

[51] See Ch. I,3.1.3, for an explanation of the concept of "reward" in Matthew.

[52] Since Jesus is presented elsewhere in the gospel as a friend of the tax collectors (see 9,10-11; 11,19; 21,31-32), the disparaging reference to them in the present context (also in 18,17) raises questions about consistency. Davies–Allison present three different explanations given by the scholars : i) tradition is wrong in presenting Jesus as a friend of the tax collectors; ii) 5,46 and 18,17 may not be the original sayings of Jesus; iii) Jesus might have disapproved tax collectors' behaviour though he reached out to them. See W.D. DAVIES – D.C. ALLISON, *Matthew*, I, 558. The first position cannot be accepted as a valid solution as we have several instances in the gospels which show Jesus' acquaintance with the tax collectors. The second conjecture may be true, but we are unable to prove it. The third explanation seems to be plausible, as it takes care of both the aspects – Jesus' company with them as well as his disapproval of their character – present in the text. The tax collectors were a despised group, and they held a very low image and identity in the society (Matt 9,10-11; 11,9; 18,7; 21,31;

tax collectors to show the contrast between their identity and the filial identity of the disciples. They symbolize the "non-children", who do not follow the "exceeding way" of the Father. The message is plain: how can the disciples, the children of the Father, debase themselves to the extent of behaving like such people?

Jesus calls the disciples' attention also to their manner of greeting people. He asks them, "And if you salute only your brethren, what more are you doing than others? Do not even the Gentiles do the same?" (5,47). Greeting is an expression of love, respect and recognition. When one greets somebody, one wishes welfare, happiness, peace etc. to that person (see 10,12-14).[53] If one is sincere in what one wishes for others, one may find it difficult to greet some people. It may be easy to greet one's brothers or friends,[54] but not one's enemies. So if the disciples greet only their brothers they are not doing anything exceptional (περισσός);[55] it is quite an ordinary thing, and no special merit can be claimed.

Like the reference to the tax collectors on mutual love, the reference to the Gentiles on brotherly greeting needs to be taken as representative. In 6,7 and 6,32, the Gentiles are portrayed as a counter model to the disciples, as people who do not even know the Father.[56] It is not enough for the disciples to remain on the level of these people and be content with it; they should rise above these ordinary standards of behaviour and live as children of the Father.

One can observe a consistent and continuous call to the disciples in the SM to realize their real identity and conduct themselves in accordance with that identity. The disciples are children of the Father, and they cannot be like the scribes and Pharisees (5,20), the tax collectors (5,46), the Gentiles (5,47; 6,7.32), or the hypocrites (6,2.5.18); their righteousness should exceed the righteousness of all these people, who do not belong to the family of the Father.

Luke 18,11) as they defrauded and extorted their own people for the Romans (Luke 3,13; 19,8). Certainly, theirs was not a lifestyle that was acceptable to Jesus. At the same time, he welcomed them to follow his teachings and experience the love and forgiveness of God through his companionship with them. Several of them repented, gave up their old ways and entered into the family of God as a result of his affirming attitude (Matt 9,9; Luke 19,1-9).

[53] The Jewish greeting *shalom,* "peace", was in fact a prayer. See L. MORRIS, *Matthew*, 133.

[54] See the textual variant: some later manuscripts (L W Θ 𝔐 f h sy^h) add the word φίλους here.

[55] The adjective περισσός reemphasizes the "exceeding" way expected of the disciples in their actions (5,20).

[56] See the explanation of the term Gentiles in Ch. I,3.3.2 a).

2.4 *Perfect Children of the Perfect Father*

Introducing the antitheses Jesus tells the disciples in 5,20 that unless their righteousness exceeds (περισσεύω) that of the scribes and Pharisees, they will never enter the kingdom of heaven. The word "exceeding" (περισσεύω) is rather an open-ended term, and one may ask what the upper limit of this "exceeding righteousness" could be. The concluding command of the antitheses is an answer to such a question.[57] Jesus gives them here an ideal model, an upper limit to strive for in their life: "You therefore, must be perfect, as your heavenly Father is perfect" (5,48).[58] This command of Jesus resonates with the demand of Yahweh in Lev 19,2: "You shall be holy; for I the Lord your God am holy" (see also Lev 11,44-45; 20,7.26; 21,8).

The pronoun "you" (ὑμεῖς) is emphatic here, and it draws attention to the disciples' unique status in contrast to all the other groups previously mentioned.

The adjective τέλειος derives from the noun τέλος which literally means end, goal or limit (10,22; 24,6.13.14.58).[59] So τέλειος could mean, "having reached the end or purpose",[60] and it is normally translated as "perfect" or "whole", conveying the idea of total integrity.[61] This word can be used also to qualify something as "genuine" or "true" or "authentic" (see 1John 4,18).[62]

---

[57] The inferential conjunction οὖν brings together all the previous teachings and binds them to this concluding injunction.

[58] The future indicative of εἰμί (ἔσεσθε) functions here as an imperatival future. The force of the imperatival future "is quite emphatic, in keeping with the combined nature of the indicative mood and future tense. It tends to have a universal, timeless, or solemn force to it." D.B. WALLACE, *Greek Grammar*, 569-570.718.

[59] See M. ZERWICK – M. GROSVENOR, *Grammatical Analysis*, 14. In the LXX τέλειος is used in some places as an equivalent to the Hebrew terms תמים (Gen 6,9; Exod 12,5; Deut 18,13; 2 Sam 22,26), תם (Cant 5,2; 6,9), שלם (1Kgs 8,61; 11,4; 15,3.14; 1Chr 28,9) and תכלית (Ps 139,22, LXX 138,22). All these terms are used in the OT as referring to perfection in an ethical, or a spiritual or even a physical sense, depending on the context. See L. SABOURIN, "Why Is God Called 'Perfect'", 266-267. For a detailed treatment of the meaning of the term τέλειος in Matthew, see R.A. GUELICH, *The Sermon on the Mount*, 234-237.

[60] BAGD, 811-812.

[61] The adjective τέλειος occurs once again in Matthew (nowhere else in the gospels). Jesus tells the rich young man if he wishes to be τέλειος he should sell what he has and give to the poor (19,21). The young man is presented in this episode as one who leads a good life except for one defect. To be τέλειος he has to attend to that defect. So in this context also τέλειος could mean, "without defect" or "perfect" (see Jas 3,2 for a similar meaning).

[62] In 1John 4,18, in his exhortation on God's love, the author describes the real nature of love: φόβος οὐκ ἔστιν ἐν τῇ ἀγάπῃ ἀλλ' ἡ τελεία ἀγάπη ἔξω βάλλει τὸν φόβον. As LOUW–NIDA, I,

Naturally, what is perfect cannot but be genuine or authentic. In the immediate context of 5,48, τέλειος of the Father refers to his gracious dealing with the just and the unjust as it is mentioned in 5,45. His love is perfect and genuine; he extends it to all, to the deserving and the undeserving. In the wider context of 5,21-48, τέλειος may refer to the perfection and authenticity demanded in each of the antitheses.[63] The children may grow perfect as their heavenly Father by orienting themselves completely and exclusively towards the Father, conducting themselves according to his model revealed through Jesus, and living in constant communion with him.[64]

The mandate to be perfect like the heavenly Father points to the disciples' potentiality to attain that perfection. Perhaps this can become true only at the kingdom stage where the children will be free from all trials and temptations.[65] Jesus invites them to unlock that potential and live as the children of the Father in the earthly stage, orienting them towards the perfection of their heavenly Father.[66]

---

§ 73:6, 675, suggest one could easily translate ἡ τελεία ἀγάπη here as "genuine love" or "authentic love".

[63] Interpreting the Father's perfection as "perfection of love" R.H. GUNDRY, *Matthew: Mixed Church*, 100, beautifully summarizes the function of v.48: "This perfection of love brings to a climax the description of surpassing righteousness in the six antitheses. In all of them Matthew has shown that Jesus carried out the tendencies of the OT Law to their true ends: OT prohibitions of murder and adultery escalate to prohibitions of anger and lust; OT limitations on divorce and oaths escalate to demands for marital compassion and simple truthfulness; and the guard against revenge and commands to love neighbours and hate enemies in the OT escalate to the requirements of meekness and love even for enemies."

[64] Scholars have attempted to articulate various aspects of this perfection: a) perfect is the one "who is unreservedly and unconditionally devoted to the will of God": P.J. DU PLESSIS, "Love and Perfection in Matt. 5:43-48", 33; P.J. HARTIN, "Call to be Perfect", 486-487; b) perfection is a "totality of obedience which goes beyond formal adherence to the Law, and which expresses itself in concrete ways toward men": V.P. FURNISH, *The Love Command*, 54; c) "sincere single-hearted devotion to God and man": J.P. MEIER, *Matthew*, 55; d) it refers to "love of enemies": M. VELLANICKAL, *The Divine Sonship of Christians*, 59; U. LUZ, *Matthew 1–7*, 346; e) "a life totally integrated to the will of God, and thus reflecting his character": R.T. FRANCE, *Matthew*, 129; f) it is a call "to love utterly": W.D. DAVIES – D.C. ALLISON, *Matthew*, I, 562; g) "a total giving, a sharing of all that one has": M. BECK, "Be Perfect", 382.

[65] As C. NEERAKKAL, *The Concept of "Perfect"*, 49, notes, one can observe a movement from v.45 to v.48 here: "In v.45 love of enemy is proposed as an obligation of sonship, and its fullness is obtained only by the exercise of sonship, so as to resemble perfectly the heavenly Father and grow towards the eschatological perfection of the sonship."

[66] Applying this call for perfection to Christian life, M. DUMAIS, *Le Sermon sur la Montagne*, 226, writes: "L'éthique de la perfection chrétienne est une éthique du devenir: c'est progressivement que nous imitons la perfection du Père et que nous devenons véritablement ses fils dans notre façon d'être et d'agir." B.B. THURSTON, "Matthew 5:43-48", 173: "Our

Those who follow Jesus and thus receive the grace of being and becoming children of God have to surpass the limits of their familial, ethnic and cultural boundaries in their dealings with others. It is not enough that they love their neighbours following the precepts of the OT Law; they have to extend their affection to all people including their enemies and persecutors. Thus they may be and may become the true children of their Father, who is munificent both to the good and the wicked, the just and the unjust. Living as the perfect children of that perfect Father will lead them to the eternal kingdom where they will be able to share the perfection of their Father himself.

3. **Trust in the Father (6,26.32)**

The disciples of Jesus are the children of the Father. They should not behave like the scribes and Pharisees or the tax collectors or the Gentiles or the hypocrites. In every moment of their life they should grow into the perfection of the Father (5,48). At the same time, they are human persons living in the world. It is possible that human and worldly concerns influence them and tempt them to break up their relationship with the Father. Jesus presents anxiety over sustenance as one of such pressures that has the potential to make them diverge from their identity and function as God's children. Anxiety over needs may compel them to lay up treasures on earth in the belief that this will give them a greater security in their lives. But earthly treasures are corruptible, they can be consumed by moth and rust, and thieves may break in and steal them (6,19-20). Those who go after such worldly treasures (μαμωνᾶς) cannot serve God with an undivided heart; they will become slaves of "mammon" (6,24).

The children of the Father should not store up treasures on earth but in heaven. Then what about their daily life? What shall they eat and drink, or what shall they wear? Are these not serious matters that should be paid attention to during the earthly stage of life? Jesus anticipates such questions and responds to them in his teaching against anxiety in 6,25-34.[67] The phrase

---

perfection is, in modern parlance, 'in process'. It is the process by which we develop our discipleship; it is the 'following after' which the rich young man found so difficult. We 'follow toward' perfection even as Jesus, by his suffering and dying, by his living and rising, was perfected."

[67] The teaching in 6,25-34 is a continuation of the teaching on one's approach to worldly treasures introduced in 6,19. Besides the inferential διὰ τοῦτο clause, which presents the teaching in 6,25 ff. as a conclusion to what preceded, one can also take the words σῶμα (6,22.23.25), δύναμαι (6,24.27), and θεός (6,24.30.33) found in both the sections as indicators that show the connection between these sections. However, the teaching in 6,25-34 is

"your Father" appears twice in this pericope (6,26.32). Referring to the care and protection that the Father provides even for the birds of the sky and the lilies of the field, Jesus challenges the disciples to realize how much more precious they are and how much more their Father will care for them. An invitation to recognize their identity as God's children, an insistence on trusting in the providence of the Father, and a call for conducting themselves in a way that befits their identity are neatly interwoven in this unit.[68]

3.1 *Anxiety, a Threat to the Children in their Process*

In 6,25-34 Jesus sternly warns the disciples that being anxious over material needs is unbecoming of their identity as children of the Father. The verb μεριμνάω, a cognate of μέριμνα which expresses an anxious preoccupation "based on apprehension about possible danger or misfortune",[69] is repeated six times in this unit (6,25.27.28.31.34^2), three times with the negative particle μή (6,25.31.34) forbidding the disciples to worry about the needs of life.[70]

---

demarcated as a distinct unit with its own specific theme. The verb μεριμνάω which occurs six times in 6,25-34 (out of its seven occurrences in Matthew) functions as the axis of the teaching in this unit. The inner unity of this section could be appreciated also from the interrelated use of some other words and phrases: λέγω (25.29.31), ἐσθίω (25.31), πίνω (25.31), ἔνδυμα (25.28), πολύς (25.30), ὁ πατὴρ ὑμῶν ὁ οὐράνιος (26.32), μᾶλλον (26.30), προστίθημι (27.33), ἀγρός (28.30), περιβάλλω (29.31), θεός (30.33), αὔριον (30.34). Similarly, repeated imperatives (vv. 25.26.28.31.33.34), rhetorical questions (vv. 25.26.30), and parallel constructions bind this unit together. See D.A. HAGNER, *Matthew 1–13*, 162, for a thorough treatment of the parallel constructions in this unit.

[68] Except for a few differences in vocabulary and arrangement, the texts on teaching against anxiety in Matthew (6,25-34) and Luke (12,22-31) are similar. The following two differences are significant for our study: i) Matthew uses ὁ πατὴρ ὑμῶν ὁ οὐράνιος as the subject who feeds the birds of the air while Luke ὁ θεός (Matt 6,26; Luke 12,24). ii) In Luke only βασιλεία is mentioned as the "first thing" that the disciples should seek in their life (Luke 12,31), in Matthew βασιλεία and δικαιοσύνη (Matt 6,33).

[69] LOUW–NIDA, I, § 25:225, 313. This word can also have a positive meaning of "care for, be concerned about" (1Cor 7,32-34; 12,25; Phil 2,20); see BAGD, 505. But in the present unit all six times it is treated as a negative quality that the disciples should keep away from in their life. It is used in a negative sense also in 10,19 where the disciples are forewarned of the impending persecution.

[70] Different kinds of anxieties can block the way of the children. The teaching in the present unit deals mainly with anxiety over life (ψυχή) and body (σῶμα). Here ψυχή and σῶμα are not treated in the Greek sense of body and soul as opposite realities, but as integral elements of human life. See M.F. OLSTHOORN, *The Jewish Background*, 23; R.A. GUELICH, *The Sermon on the Mount*, 336; J. GNILKA, *Matthäusevangelium*, I, 247; D. HARRINGTON, *Matthew*, 102; M. CAIROLI, *La Poca Fede*, 25.

The teaching in this unit articulates certain causes of anxiety. First of all, it is a result of one's wrong perspective on life. Jesus asks the disciples, "Is not life more than food and the body more than clothing?" (6,25). In comparison with life and body, which are given freely to humans, how insignificant are food and clothing![71] Being worried about such trivial things the disciples may forget the real goal of their life. Jesus' question describes also an attitude common to anxious people. They tend to identify life (ψυχή) with food and the body with clothing, and they think if they amass wealth their life will be safe.[72]

Another reason why people worry about their lives is their lack of awareness of their own limitations. Jesus asks, "And which of you by being anxious can add (δύναται προσθεῖναι) one cubit to his span (ἡλικία)[73] of life?" (6,27; see 5,36). In Luke (12,25-26) there is a corollary to the question, "If then you are not able to do as small a thing as that, why are you anxious about the rest?" The children should remember the truth that their life is not a "product" of their anxiety but given as a free gift; and it is God who adds (προστίθημι) everything to that life (see v.33).

A more serious problem that causes anxiety in the disciples is their "little faith". Referring to God's clothing of even the short-lived grass of the field,

---

[71] The argument is *a fortiori* here. "If God has given us life and a body, both admittedly more important than food and clothing, will he not also give us the latter?" D.A. CARSON, *Matthew 1–12*, 179; also M. CAIROLI, *La Poca Fede*, 25.

[72] Such an outlook that comes from a materialistic view of life is refuted in 10,39 and 16,25-26: "For what will it profit a man, if he gains the whole world and forfeits his life (ψυχή)? Or what shall a man give in return for his life?" (16,26). The parable of the Rich Fool in Luke (12,15-21) shows the futility of wealth. When he had a plentiful crop the rich man thought that the forthcoming years would be years of ease and merrymaking. Narrating the tragic end of the rich man's foolish calculations and dreams Jesus comments, "So is he who lays up treasure for himself, and is not rich toward God" (Luke 12,21). The rich man might not have thought that life was more important than all that he stored up! It is noteworthy that Luke places the teaching on anxiety between this parable and the teaching on laying up treasures on earth (see Luke 12,13-21.22-31.32-34).

[73] The word ἡλικία could mean either "span of life" or "physical stature". Since the word πῆχυς means "a cubit" or "ell" as a measure of length (Guelich's translation of πῆχυς as "one hour", as he himself admits, is rather liberal; cf. R.A. GUELICH, *The Sermon on the Mount*, 338), some authors prefer to translate ἡλικία as physical stature in the present context. Since addition of a cubit to one's height is not a desirable thing in normal circumstances, the meaning "span of life" is preferable. Whatever the case may be, the sense of the rhetorical question remains the same. It points to the human inability to add even a minute to his life or even an inch to his stature. See BAGD, 345.657, for the meaning of ἡλικία and πῆχυς; M.F. OLSTHOORN, *The Jewish Background*, 41-43, for an analysis of these words in different contexts; M. CAIROLI, *La Poca Fede*, 29, for a list of authors who choose one or another option.

Jesus asks again a rhetorical question to the disciples in 6,30: "But if God so clothes the grass of the field, [...] will he not much more clothe you, O men of little faith?" This question has a double function. On the one hand, it reminds the disciples of their privileged status to be cared for "much more" than the lilies (and other creatures), and, on the other hand, it rebukes them for their failure to remember this privileged status. God who takes care of nature is their Father (v.26), and if he clothes even the grass of the field so beautifully, he will surely clothe his own children with much more care; and if they are authentic children why should they be anxious about anything?

Anxiety is an expression of one's feeling insecure in life and it can undermine the children's relationship with their Father. When people are anxious about something, they normally seek ways and means to tackle the "possible danger or misfortune" they anticipate. So, if they are worried about material needs like food and clothing, they will naturally run after riches with which they can store up these things. Nevertheless, having enough for their needs will not normally satisfy these people; they will crave for more and more to be more and more secure in their lives, and this will eventually make them slaves of μαμωνᾶς (6,24). Thus, mammon will become the centre of their life, and they will certainly forget God, or even hate him in order to assimilate mammon's ways into their life (6,24).

The explanation of the Parable of the Seeds shows how impossible it is for the message of the kingdom to grow and produce fruit in the hearts of anxious people. The cares (ἡ μέριμνα) of the world and the lure of riches choke the word making it unfruitful (13,22). If the word of God is to grow in them, if they are to grow as the Father's children, the disciples have to liberate themselves from the slavery of anxiety, the agent of mammon (see 1Tim 6,10).

Matthew relates the story of a rich young man who had been observing all the commandments of the Law and was willing to do more good deeds so that he may have eternal life (19,16-23). But when he was asked to sell his property and give to the poor, he went out saddened. His attachment to his wealth could be understood as an expression of his worry over the morrows. He might have wondered how he would live if he gave away all that he had accumulated over the years![74] Discipleship is a process that demands an

[74] One may also consider the story of Ananias and Saphira (Acts 5,1-10). As Peter told Ananias, nobody asked them to sell their property and give it to the community. They themselves did it, but they kept a part of it for themselves. Is it not their anxiety over their future that prompted them to lie to God?

absolute trust in the providence of God.[75] Anxiety and trust cannot go together; in fact, anxiety is a symptom of lack of trust in God. Without trusting the Father no one can live as his child.

3.2 *The Father's Devoted Care for His Children*

Though Jesus reproves the disciples for their anxiety and little faith, the purpose of his teaching is not to condemn them for their human weakness but to help them to overcome this temptation and to continue with their process of becoming children of the Father. Pointing out two examples from nature – the birds of the sky and the lilies of the field – Jesus invites the disciples to become aware of their privileged status as the children and of their Father's inestimable care for them. These examples show how God takes care of his creation and how confidently the creatures depend on their creator.[76] In their worry-filled life the disciples might not have seen or realized this truth. What they need to do is to open their eyes and look attentively (ἐμβλέψατε εἰς) and learn from them.

3.2.1 Lesson from the Birds of the Sky

Jesus tells the disciples, "Look at the birds of the sky, they neither sow, nor reap, nor gather into barns, and yet your heavenly Father feeds them" (6,26).[77] The three action verbs attached to the birds are all negative (οὐ σπείρουσιν, οὐδὲ θερίζουσιν, and οὐδὲ συνάγουσιν εἰς ἀποθήκας), and they emphasize the non-action of the birds and their worry-free manner of life. Sowing, reaping, and gathering into barns are activities connected with a farmer's life. By saying that the birds do not perform these activities, Jesus makes a symbolic comparison between human beings who are anxiously involved in production and preservation to make their life safe and secure, and birds that live freely without all these safety precautions (see Luke 12,15-21).[78]

---

[75] See the call narratives: the disciples leave everything they had and follow him (4,20.22; 19,27).

[76] See Gen 1,30; Job 38,41; Pss 104,27; 136,25; 145,15-16; 147,9.

[77] The term birds of the sky is a generic term in the gospels (see Matt 8,20; 13,32; Luke 8,5). Their example can be applied also to other birds and animals. Luke uses κόραξ, a specific group of birds (Luke 12,24; see Lev 11,15; Deut 14,14).

[78] The purpose of this example is not to devalue human labour but to show the irrationality and foolishness of an anxiety-bound life. If the disciples are living such an irrational, anxious life, it is due to their lack of awareness of their own self-worth.

It is to be noted that it is the Father of the disciples (ὁ πατὴρ ὑμῶν) who feeds the birds, and he feeds them continuously (τρέφω in the present indicative).[79] By referring to God, the provider of life, as the Father of the disciples Jesus calls their attention to their privileged status among all creatures. If their Father takes care of the whole universe, how much more he will care for his own children! Jesus lays emphasis on this truth through the rhetorical question, "Are you (ὑμεῖς) not of more value (διαφέρετε) than they?"[80] The present indicative of διαφέρω affirms the existing worth of the disciples.[81] They are his precious children, and he will take care of them.

3.2.2 Lesson from the Lilies of the Field

Having shown the futility of anxiety over food with the example of the birds, Jesus speaks about the silliness of anxiety over clothing with the example of the lilies of the field (6,28-30).[82] The disciples are asked again to look intently at nature: "Consider (καταμανθάνω)[83] the lilies of the field, how they grow, they neither toil nor spin." The call to consider the growth (αὐξάνουσιν) of the lilies without their toiling (οὐ κοπιῶσιν) and spinning (οὐδὲ νήθουσιν) discloses a paradox that takes place everyday in nature.[84]

---

[79] The contrast between the non-action of the birds and the action of the Father underscores the image of God as one who labours for his creation (see Pss 104,14; 136,25; 145,15-16; 147,9).

[80] The pronoun ὑμεῖς is emphasized by presenting it at the beginning of the question. This rhetorical question becomes an assertion in 10,31: "Fear not, therefore; you are of more value (διαφέρετε) than many sparrows." See D.A. HAGNER, *Matthew 1–13*, 164.

[81] In fact, this question mocks the pathetic penury of the anxious disciples. Though they are children of the Father, by being anxious they opt for a miserable life forgetting their true identity and worth.

[82] People's anxiety over clothing can be an expression of their preoccupation with losing human praise and honour. In the world, the worth of a person is measured often on the basis of his/her external appearance. So, "gold rings and fine clothing" might attract people's attention and win their respect (Jas 2,2-4). The teaching in this section implicitly tells the disciples that they should not worry about displaying their worth and acquiring honour (6,1.2.5.16) but should feel secure in their identity as children of the Father.

[83] The verb καταμανθάνω is a *hapax legomenon* in the NT. In the LXX it is found with the connotations "gaze at", "examine", "inspect", "watch", "look intently" etc. (see Gen 24,21; 34,1; Lev 14,36; Job 35,5; Sir 9,5.8; 38,28). R.H. GUNDRY, *Matthew*: *Mixed Church*, 117, suggests that Matthew is substituting καταμάθετε for the Lukan κατανοήσατε in order to carry out his emphasis on discipleship, which is learning.

[84] Toiling and spinning, the two non-actions mentioned of the lilies, like v.26 reflect human labour. The verb κοπιάω conveys the meaning "become weary, be tired, or to work hard, toil, strive, struggle"; it occurs again in Matt 11,28 together with the verb φορτίζω (= to carry a

They do not spin, they do not toil, but who is more beautifully adorned than they are?

Praising the beauty of the lilies of the field, Jesus says that even Solomon in all his glory was not arrayed like one of them. Solomon, the richest of Israel's kings, had the possibility of adorning himself with whatever attire he wanted on earth (see queen Sheba's praise for Solomon's wealth and glory in 1Kgs 10,4-7; 2Chr 9,4-24).[85] But his finest ornamentation, which might have caused a great deal of toil and spinning, is considered inferior to the beauty of these flowers.

The gorgeous appearance of the lilies praised in v.29 is contrasted with their trivial nature and short life in v.30: "[...] today is alive and tomorrow is thrown into the oven". In fact, what are these lilies? For human eyes they are just "grass (χόρτος) of the field";[86] they grow and perish, who cares for them! But for God they are valuable; he clothes (ἀμφιέννυμι) them with great care and attention despite the fact that they have a life that lasts for just a day.[87] If that is the way God treats the grass, how would he treat his own children?[88]

The examples of the birds of the air and the lilies of the field illustrate the irrationality of the disciples' anxiety.[89] Their anxiety is a reflection of their

---

heavy load or burden) where Jesus invites "all who are weary (οἱ κοπιῶντες) and are heavy laden" to come to him, and he promises them rest. The verb νήθω refers more directly to textile process. See M.F. OLSTHOORN, *The Jewish Background*, 47.

[85] The reference to Solomon's glory seems to have ironical overtones. On the one hand, Solomon is a legendary figure in the biblical tradition who has been praised for his political, military, cultural, economic and intellectual superiority over all the other kings of the earth (see 1Kgs 4,29; 10,23; 2Chr 9,22; Ps 89,27); he was perceived by his people as a king endowed with the wisdom of God (1Kgs 3,28) and was revered by the later generations as the one who built the temple of God (Sir 47,13). On the other hand, his weaknesses and moral decline put stains upon his glory (δόξα) and brought wrath upon his children (see Sir 47,20; 1Kgs 11,1-13), and after his death his people realized that his glory was nothing but a folly that put a heavy yoke on their lives (1Kgs 12,4). See also Qoh 2,1-11. How trivial are worldly glories, how shallow are its manifestations! For a detailed presentation of the negative images that Solomon's example suggests in the context, see W. CARTER, "'Solomon in All His Glory'", 3-25.

[86] The term χόρτος denotes "wild grass in contrast to cultivated plants". BAGD, 884. The grass of the field is often used as a metaphor in the OT referring to the transitory nature of human life on earth (see Pss 90,5-6; 103,15; Isa 40,6-8; 51,12).

[87] See J. CHRYSOSTOM, *Homilies*, 22:1, 150.

[88] See the rhetorical question in v.30: "But if God so clothes the grass of the field, which today is alive and tomorrow is thrown into the oven, will he not much more clothe you, O men of little faith?" (6,30).

[89] The birds and the lilies mentioned here are only representative examples. Millions of species of plants and animals – identified and unidentified – are created and being nurtured by the heavenly Father (see Gen 1,1-25; Isa 45,18). He watches over his creation with great care

lack of self-worth as well as their lack of trust in their Father. The teaching does not deny the existence of human needs or devalue human labour, but it instructs the disciples that they should deal with their needs "from the positive perspective of faith rather than from the negative perspective of anxiety."[90]

3.3 *The Distinctive Living Required of the Children*

Those who do not know the Father, and do not believe in him and do not live as his children, are the ones who worry about material things like food, drink and clothing. Once again referring to the wrong model of the Gentiles, Jesus tells the disciples what their priorities in life should be (6,31-33).

3.3.1 Gentiles and the Children

By saying that it is the Gentiles who "run after" (ἐπιζητέω)[91] all these things (food, drink and clothing), Jesus makes it clear anew that he does not expect his disciples to behave like the Gentiles (see 5,47; 6,7-8). Furthermore, in 6,32b by using the phrase, ὁ πατὴρ ὑμῶν, he reminds them once again of their true identity. The reference to the Gentiles' "seeking things" recalls their manner of prayer in 6,7.[92] As they do not know the Father, they cannot put their trust in him; they worry about their life and seek for means to satisfy their physical needs.[93] Their attitude and lifestyle should not be a model for the disciples who are "much more" than these Gentiles.[94]

Being different from the ignorant Gentiles, the disciples should be confident that their Father knows all their needs, as they have already been told in 6,8. In the present context it is developed and explained more logically.

(Ps 33,14) and provides for the needs of everybody (Ps 65,9-13). How sad it is that his children, the crown of his creation (Psalm 8), live a wretched life worrying about the petty things in life!

[90] D. PATTE, *Matthew*, 95.

[91] The verb ἐπιζητέω appears in two more contexts in Matthew (12,39; 16,4). In both the contexts the type of seeking indicated by this verb is negative. See M. CAIROLI, *La Poca Fede*, 35. Normally plural neuter nouns take singular verbs. But here a plural verb (ἐπιζητοῦσιν) is used. It may be because the evangelist wants to stress the individuality of each Gentile, so as to show that seeking material things is basic to their identity. See D.B. WALLACE, *Greek Grammar*, 401.

[92] Arranging Matt 6,7-11 and 6,31-34 synoptically M.F. OLSTHOORN, *The Jewish Background*, 71, has shown the similarity between these texts; see also, R. FABRIS, *Matteo*, 173.

[93] W.D. DAVIES – D.C. ALLISON, *Matthew*, I, 658: "Just as they ignorantly heap up empty phrases when they pray, so too do they fail to trust God's providence."

[94] The Gentiles' seeking for material things can also imply that their vision of life is limited to the material reality around them. They have nothing more to hope for than satisfying their material needs.

If the Father knows even the needs of the birds of the air and lilies of the field and cares for them, how much more he will care for his own children! Such a confidence presupposes, as mentioned above, a deep conviction or faith that the Father knows them personally. In fact, this faith and confidence is intrinsic to a Father-children relationship; when they behave without this faith and confidence, they behave not like the children but like the Gentiles.

3.3.2 The Right Priorities of the Children

It is not enough that the disciples refrain from seeking material things; they have to look actively for "things" that befit their identity. They are to seek (ζητέω) first (πρῶτον) the Father's kingdom[95] and his righteousness (6,33). The adverb πρῶτον emphasizes not only priority but also exclusivity.[96] If the term πρῶτον means "the first in a series", it would imply that after seeking the kingdom and righteousness, one could seek to satisfy one's needs. This is certainly not the point here, especially in a context where an undivided loyalty to God is demanded (see 6,24).[97] The disciples should seek only the kingdom and righteousness of the Father, and everything else will be added to them.

---

[95] In some later manuscripts the phrase τοῦ θεοῦ is added after τὴν βασιλείαν in v.33. *Novum Testamentum Graece* has given them in brackets showing it as a doubtful text; see B.M. METZGER, *A Textual Commentary*, 15-16. Considering the external evidence (missing in two major witnesses ℵ and B) it should be treated as a scribal addition. However, some scholars (W.D. DAVIES – D.C. ALLISON, *Matthew*, I, 660; D.A. HAGNER, *Matthew 1–13*, 161) suggest that it could be an accidental omission, as Matthew rarely uses kingdom without a modifier; they also think "the αὐτοῦ following δικαιοσύνην also is easier with the presence of the expressed antecedent θεοῦ." D.A. HAGNER, *Matthew 1–13*, 161. This argument goes against the principle of *lectio difficilior*. In fact, the absence of the phrase τοῦ θεοῦ links βασιλείαν and δικαιοσύνην to the antecedent πατήρ in 6,32. Thus we may understand this verse as referring to the kingdom of the Father and his righteousness. This fits well in the context as Jesus is talking about the privileged status of the disciples in the previous verses referring to their Father in heaven. This also holds true when we consider the previous occurrence of βασιλεία in 6,11 which is linked with the πατήρ in 6,9. See T. ZAHN, *Matthäus*, 296-297; G. STRECKER, *The Sermon on the Mount,* 139; J. GNILKA, *Matthäusevangelium*, I, 250.

[96] M. CAIROLI, *La Poca Fede*, 38.

[97] So R.A. GUELICH, *The Sermon on the Mount*, 343; also R.H. GUNDRY, *Matthew*: *Mixed Church*, 118: "the adverb is emphatic rather than permissive"; T.E. SCHMIDT, "Burden, Barrier, Blasphemy", 177-178; R.J. DILLON, "Ravens, Lilies, and the Kingdom", 622-623. Against J. SCHMID, *Matthäus*, 143; J. DUPONT, *Les Béatitudes*, III, 275-277 who interpret πρῶτον in terms of a relative priority.

The word ζητέω occurs fourteen times in Matthew.[98] In almost all the contexts "seeking" is presented as a search with an emotional involvement to find somebody or something.[99] In the present context it would mean, "to give oneself unreservedly" to the pursuit of the Father's kingdom and his righteousness.[100]

As seen in the previous chapter, the "kingdom" refers to the dominion and sovereignty of God over his people.[101] So seeking his kingdom would mean seeking God himself as the lord and supreme ruler of their life. At the same time, the kingdom is the end stage of their process. Hence seeking the kingdom would also mean seeking things or living a life that will lead them to the kingdom.[102]

---

[98] Different suggestions regarding the nuance of ζητέω in the present context are given by scholars: a) it is putting forth effort in the service of the imminent kingdom: J. JEREMIAS, *Die Gleichnisse Jesu*, 179; b) it is a call to pray for the kingdom as in the Lord's Prayer: R.V.G. TASKER, *Matthew*, 78; c) it refers to having an attitude, a basic desire for the eschatological kingdom: G. STRECKER, *The Sermon on the Mount*, 139; R.H. GUNDRY, *Matthew*: *Mixed Church*, 119; d) it means to give oneself unreservedly to the pursuit of the kingdom, which is both present and future: R.A. GUELICH, *The Sermon on the Mount*, 342-344; W.D. DAVIES – D.C. ALLISON, *Matthew*, I, 660.

[99] So ζητέω is used in the contexts where the enemies of Jesus, from Herod to the chief priests, seek him (with a determination) to kill him (2,13.20; 21,46; 26,59) or to betray him (26,16). It is used positively in two parables underscoring the great enthusiasm of the merchant who seeks fine pearls (13,45) and the shepherd who seeks his lost sheep (18,2). The emotional involvement is quite explicit in the women seeking the body of Jesus (28,5).

[100] See R.A. GUELICH, *The Sermon on the Mount*, 344; M. CAIROLI, *La Poca Fede*, 38: "Cercare (ζητεῖν) è un verbo che esprime la passione, la tensione, l'iniziativa e la progettazione. Non è un comportamento facoltativo: l'imperativo dice tutta la serietà e l'obbligatorietà di questa ricerca." The dynamic nature of this verb shows, that a disciple is not a "quietist who merely waits upon what God gives through the resources of nature, like an animal", but an active seeker of the Father's kingdom and righteousness. H.D. BETZ, "Cosmogony and Ethics", 114.

[101] See K. STOCK, *Discorso della Montagna*, 32.

[102] There are two predominant views among scholars about the concept of kingdom in the present context. According to one group, it refers to a future eschatological consummation of God's rule in history. So W.G. KÜMMEL, *Promise and Fulfilment*, 125-126; J. SCHMID, *Matthäus*, 143; J. DUPONT, *Les Béatitudes*, III, 293-297; G. STRECKER, *The Sermon on the Mount*, 139. The other group conceives it both as a present and a future reality. See J. SCHNIEWIND, *Matthäus*, 95; D. HILL *Matthew*, 145; E. SCHWEIZER, *Matthäus*, 105; R.A. GUELICH, *The Sermon on the Mount*, 344-345; W.D. DAVIES – D.C. ALLISON, *Matthew*, I, 660-661; G. R. BEASLEY-MURRAY, "Matthew 6:33", 88-89. As Guelich argues, taking the kingdom as God's sovereign rule present and future fits the context of 6,25-34. The following reasons support this view. i) The examples of the birds and the grass and their sustenance point to a God who is actively involved in the creation today. ii) The promise to the disciples that God will take care of their needs so they should not be anxious about them cannot be taken only as a

At this point of their being with Jesus, the disciples have heard much about the kingdom on different occasions.[103] They have been given enough indications to realize that the mission of Jesus is to announce the "good news of the kingdom" and to prepare people to receive it. Later in their life with Jesus they will hear more about it and know that it is to this same mission of preparing the people for the kingdom that they too are called (see especially, 9,35; 10,7; 13,11-52; 16,19; 24,14; 26,29). Therefore, "seeking the kingdom" is in fact nothing but responding positively to the mission of Jesus and being sincere about the mission they are engaged in. Thus they become heirs of the very kingdom they are announcing.

This is the only time in the gospel that the term δικαιοσύνη is given as an attribute relating to the Father.[104] As we have discussed in the preceding chapter, the Father's righteousness is given here as the ideal which the disciples should seek in their lives.[105] They should seek not an ordinary

---

promise for the end times. iii) In Matthew's gospel the concept of kingdom is both present and future.

[103] The kingdom was the central message of the preaching of John the Baptist and Jesus (3,2; 4,17). The evangelist reports that after the call of the first disciples Jesus went about all Galilee and preached the good news of the kingdom (4,23). In the SM, the kingdom is mentioned at the beginning and the end of the beatitudes (5,3.10), in the teaching on the observance of the Law (5,19.20), and in the model prayer (6,10). See Ch. I, 3.3.3 c), for a detailed treatment of the term "kingdom".

[104] The possessive pronoun αὐτοῦ stands for the Father (see v.32).

[105] The understanding of δικαιοσύνη in the present context depends on how one interprets the genitive αὐτοῦ here. Those scholars, who consider it a subjective genitive, interpret God as the subject who offers righteousness. Some of them further argue that it is the future eschatological vindication by God of his people. So, J. SCHNIEWIND, *Matthäus*, 94; F.V. FILSON, *Matthew*, 102; A. SCHLATTER, *Der Evangelist Matthäus*, 234-235; R.H. GUNDRY, *Matthew: Mixed Church*, 118; T.E. SCHMIDT, "Burden, Barrier, Blasphemy", 176-177; S.H. BROOKS, "Apocalyptic Paraenesis", 103. On the other hand, those who take αὐτοῦ as an objective genitive interpret righteousness as human conduct pleasing to God. See W. TRILLING, *Das wahre Israel*, 146-147; J. SCHMID, *Matthäus*, 143; D. HILL, *Matthew*, 145; J. DUPONT, *Les Béatitudes*, III, 303-304; B. PRZYBYLSKI, *Righteousness in Matthew*, 89-91; R.A. GUELICH, *The Sermon on the Mount*, 346-347; G. STRECKER, *The Sermon on the Mount*, 140; G. MANGATT, "The Kingdom of God", 128; W.D. DAVIES – D.C. ALLISON, *Matthew*, I, 661; R.J. DILLON, "Ravens, Lilies, and the Kingdom", 625; D.A. CARSON, *Matthew 1–12*, 182. Considering the Matthean use of this term elsewhere in the SM, we take αὐτοῦ primarily as an objective genitive and the righteousness demanded here as the right conduct the Father requires of the disciples. At the same time, in line with our interpretation of δικαιοσύνη in 5,20 and 6,1 as "exceeding righteousness", it is possible to interpret αὐτοῦ as a subjective genitive since the "righteousness of the Father" could be taken as the ideal of righteousness that the disciples are asked to seek in their life. As W.D. DAVIES – D.C. ALLISON, *Matthew*, I, 661 put it, "God's righteousness is

righteousness but an exceeding righteousness, as exceeding as that of the righteousness of the Father. In fact, seeking the Father's kingdom involves seeking his righteousness, and seeking the Father's righteousness will lead one to his kingdom (5,20).[106] To those who make the Father's kingdom their priority and live according to his righteousness everything else will be added (19,29).[107]

3.3.3 Faith: an Essential Requirement in the Process

Jesus correlates the disciples' anxiety, resulting from their inability to realize their worth and the Father's care for them, with their little faith (6,30). His calling the disciples "men of little faith" (ὀλιγόπιστοι) is a serious charge against them. The adjective ὀλιγόπιστος appears three more times in Matthew (8,26; 14,31; 16,8; see also 17,20).[108] In all three contexts the disciples (in 14,31 Peter) are called ὀλιγόπιστοι for their failure to put trust in Jesus. In the present context it is for their anxiety that Jesus rebukes them using this adjective. Thus their anxiety is rightly interpreted here as a symptom which manifests their "broken faith or insufficient faith".

Faith is an essential requirement for the disciples in their process. In fact, it is intrinsic to their identity as the children of the Father. It is through faith that they can see the Father who is invisible to their physical eyes but present everywhere (6,4.6.18). It is through faith that they can perceive this universe and all the wonders happening here as the handiwork of their Father; only with the eyes of faith can they see their Father feeding the birds and clothing the lilies (6,26.30). Similarly, it is through faith that they can recognize Jesus

---

here the norm for human righteousness, just as in 5,48 God's perfection is the norm for human perfection."

[106] F.X. D'SA, "'Dhvani' as Method of Interpretation", 288, interprets 6,33 as a directive to grow in the Father-children relationship: "The final conclusion is a praxis oriented directive to the implicit suggestion that with God being our heavenly Father we should cultivate a relationship of 'sonship'. How do we come to such a new relationship with Him, how do we develop this relationship? 'Seek first His Kingdom and His righteousness and all these things shall be yours as well'. Make His value your values, His priorities yours!"

[107] The future tense of the verb προστίθημι makes it clear that the disciples' seeking the kingdom and righteousness is a basic condition for them to receive the blessings; the divine passive affirms the truth that it is God who adds everything (ταῦτα πάντα) to their life; and it stands in contrast to the human inability to add even a cubit to one's span of life (see the use of the verb προστίθημι in v.27 and 33).

[108] Matthew uses this word ὀλιγόπιστοι to depict the wavering faith of the disciples. Outside Matthew this word occurs only once in the NT (Luke 12,28). See M. CAIROLI, *La Poca Fede*, for an elaborate study of this term.

as the Son of the Father and trust in his words (14,33); only through faith can they be convinced that by following Jesus, by hearing and doing his words, they too become children of God (19,29). It is only through faith that they can be confident that their Father is with them (10,20), that he knows all their needs (6,8.32), and that they can entrust their ψυχή and σῶμα and all other concerns into his hands and continue their journey towards him.

The teaching in 6,25-34 deals with the issue of the disciples' anxiety over daily needs like food and clothing during the earthly stage of the process. Jesus gives them clear directions about what they should not do and what they should do. As in the other sections we analyzed above, here again the identity of the disciples as the children of the Father is the basic rationale of the behaviour pattern expected of them.

God is the provider of the whole universe, and he attends even to the birds and the grass with great care. But for the disciples he is their Father (6,26.32). For him they are worth much more than anybody and anything else. He knows all their needs, and he will give them all.

The disciples have to recognize their worth and live a life in accordance with the demands of the great privilege they have received. They should not worry about the needs of life and body but trust in the Father and grow as men of faith, and they should not remain as "men of little faith". They should not behave like the Gentiles who seek "things" to make their lives safe. They are the children, and their priorities should be of the children. They should live seeking the kingdom of the Father, which is the real goal of their life, practising an exceeding righteousness as that of the Father.

4. **Reliability of the Father (7,11)**

Living as the children of the Father in the earthly stage is not simple. Narrow is the gate and hard is the road that leads to life (7,14). To enter through this narrow gate, the children have to resist the attractions of the broad-ways (7,13). Sometimes it may demand of them to go through pain, persecution, and even death (5,10-12.44; 10,23; 16,21; 17,22-23; 20,17-19; 23,34; 26,2). Their human nature may tempt them to see such experiences as negative and dreadful (16,22-23; 27,41-44). They may be confronted with the basic needs of life and body (6,25-34). How can the disciples face such situations? To whom can they go seeking help? We have seen in the previous section that Jesus asks the disciples not to worry over their needs but trust in their heavenly Father to whom they are "much more" precious than anybody and anything else (6,25-34). Jesus re-emphasizes the trustworthiness of the Father in 7,7-11; the children can ask and approach him for all their needs.[109] In the concluding verse of this unit God is presented as the Father of the disciples for the last time in the SM. Referring to the example of the human fathers who give good gifts to their children, Jesus urges the disciples here to realize how much more their heavenly Father will give good things to them, his children, when they ask him (7,11).[110]

4.1 *Encouragement to Ask, Seek and Knock*

Jesus encourages the disciples to ask, seek and knock and assures them of getting a proper response (7,7).[111] The present imperative of αἰτέω, ζητέω and κρούω implies that their asking, seeking and knocking need to be continuous.[112] The verbs δίδωμι and ἀνοίγω are in the passive, but the agent of the action is not specified. Who gives to the disciples when they ask? Who

---

[109] The unity of 7,7-11 and its thematic difference from its neighbouring units are easily recognizable. The verse just prior to it appears to be a warning against profanity (7,6). No element of this warning, except the verb δίδωμι, is continued in 7,7-11. Moreover, while 7,6 is a prohibitive exhortation with three negative particles, 7,7-11 is a permissive teaching, encouraging the disciples to ask their Father. The "Golden Rule" (7,12) that follows our unit is a conclusive summary of all the particular norms discussed previously. Referring to the teaching of the Law and the prophets, 7,12 functions as an *inclusio* with 5,17. In form and content 7,12 is distinctly different from 7,7-11.

[110] The teaching in Matthew 7,7-11 has a very close parallel in Luke 11,9-13. One can find even verbatim correspondences between some verses. However, there are some notable differences, and the following ones are particularly significant for our study. i) While Luke uses the word πατήρ to refer to the human fathers who give good things to their children (11,11), Matthew uses the term ἄνθρωπος (7,9). ii) God is presented in Luke without a modifying pronoun, ὁ πατὴρ [ὁ] ἐξ οὐρανοῦ (11,13), but in Matthew as the Father of the disciples, ὁ πατὴρ ὑμῶν ὁ ἐν τοῖς οὐρανοῖς (7,11). iii) According to the Lukan text the Father will give the Holy Spirit to those who ask him, (11,13) but in the Matthean text the gift of the Father is unspecified; he gives "good things" to his children.

[111] Matt 7,7 introduces the thesis using three sets of the *imperative* + *καί* + *future indicative* construction. The imperative in this construction is called a "conditional imperative", as it is used here to state a condition (protasis) on which the fulfilment (apodosis) of another verb depends. This use of the imperative conveys the idea, "[if] you ask (and you should), it will be given to you; if you seek, you will find; if you knock it will be opened to you." D.B. WALLACE, *Greek Grammar*, 489.

[112] The present tense of the imperative shows the *iterative* force of the action commanded. They need to "keep on asking…keep on seeking… keep on knocking". See M. ZERWICK – M. GROSVENOR, *Grammatical Analysis*, 19; D.B. WALLACE, *Greek Grammar*, 722.

opens the door when they knock? We may take them as divine passives;[113] they suggest the hidden presence of the Father who responds to the needs of his children.

No specific direction is given regarding what they should ask and seek for, or where they should knock.[114] The verb αἰτέω appears fourteen times in Matthew of which five are in the present context (7,7.8.9.10.11). In two other contexts also this verb has the same function: to encourage the disciples to ask the Father for what they need (18,19; 21,22). In 18,19 they are promised that their request will be heard on the grounds of their brotherly communion. On the other hand, in 21,22 asking is linked with prayer, and faith is given as the basic condition for their request to be granted. These texts in common emphasize the fact that the disciples, on the strength of their relation with the Father, can ask him confidently, and he will attend to their needs. Similar to 7,7, in these texts too αἰτέω does not have any definite object. The absence of a specific object in these contexts seems to be deliberate. It underscores the absolute reliability of the Father; the children can ask anything of him.[115]

The second and the third imperatives ("seek" and "knock") also do not have a specific object. For the second, the immediate context offers a

---

[113] See W.D. DAVIES – D.C. ALLISON, *Matthew*, I, 679; D.A. HAGNER, *Matthew 1–13*, 174; C.L. BLOMBERG, *Matthew*, 130.

[114] Nevertheless, there are some suggestions: a) considering the proverbial character of this teaching, some authors surmise that it is for "wisdom" that the disciples are encouraged to ask, seek and knock. See E. SCHWEIZER, *Matthäus*, 110-111; C.H. TALBERT, *Reading the Sermon on the Mount*, 134; b) J.P. MEIER, *Matthew*, 70, interprets it as "the power to carry out all that Jesus commands in the Sermon and throughout the gospel, in short, the power to do the Father's will"; c) reading it from the background of the Lord's Prayer and the assurance it gives of the Father's awareness of his children's needs before they are voiced, R.A. GUELICH, *The Sermon on the Mount*, 357 claims that it covers "the spectrum of the disciples' desires and needs in view of the Kingdom present and future"; d) connecting it with 6,22, D. PATTE, *Matthew*, 98, suggests that the disciples should ask for a sound and undivided eye to discern what is good and bad for their children and for themselves.

[115] The teaching of Jesus in 7,7-11 may seem to contradict the teaching in 6,7-8 and 6,32 where he tells the disciples that they should not be like the Gentiles who seek anxiously for material things, but they should trust their heavenly Father who knows their needs before they ask him. But they are not contradictory, because the purpose of the teachings in 6,7-8 and 6,32 is not to discourage the disciples from asking but to tell them that their asking – which reflects their priorities in life – should not be like that of the Gentiles who do not know the Father. Indeed, the prayer that follows 6,8 (6,9-13) contains various requests to the Father including a petition for daily bread. As M.E. BORING, "The Gospel of Matthew", 213, puts it: "The encouragement to bring human needs to God in prayer is not to inform or to persuade, but is an expression of the disciples' relation to God as dependent children who ultimately are in control of their lives." See also, J. KOTTACKAL, "The Righteousness Required", 135-136.

possibility for interpretation. We have seen above in 6,33 that the same imperative ζητεῖτε appears with the objects kingdom and righteousness. These are the only things (πρῶτον) the disciples should seek in their life. Hence, this directive "seek and you will find" can be taken as an extension of the teaching in 6,33. Those who live as the Father's children seeking his kingdom and righteousness will find them. Thus the teaching in 7,7-8 functions as an assurance to the disciples that the Father's kingdom into which they are initiated is not an unreachable ideal but an accessible reality which will be found if they continuously strive for it.[116]

The third maxim, "knock and it will be opened to you", can be interpreted in two ways. Like the first maxim, it encourages the children to knock at their Father's door for all their needs and gives them the assurance that it will be opened to them. At the same time, the verbs κρούω and ἀνοίγω evoke the image of a closed gate or door and somebody waiting outside to enter (see Matt 25,11; Luke 12,36; 13,25; Acts 12,13.16; Rev 3,20). In fact, Jesus has used this imagery of "entry" at different times in his reference to the kingdom (5,20; 7,21; 18,3; 19,23.24). Accordingly, the metaphor of knocking at the door and its opening may be interpreted as the successful completion of the process and the resultant entry into the kingdom.[117]

Jesus reiterates his promise presenting it as a general principle in the next verse: "For everyone who asks receives, and he who seeks finds, and to him who knocks it will be opened" (7,8).[118] Though the substantive πᾶς in 7,8 could mean everyone in general, in the context of Jesus' teaching in the SM it

---

[116] This assurance of Jesus resonates with the promise in Jer 29,13 (LXX 36,13): "You will seek me and find me"; see Deut 4,29; Isa 65,1; Amos 5,4.

[117] So, J. JEREMIAS, "θυρα", *TDNT*, III, 178; G. SCHNEIDER, *Botschaft der Bergpredigt*, 94; E. SCHWEIZER, *Matthäus*, 110; D. PATTE, *Matthew*, 97; S. GRASSO, *Matteo*, 208. But R.A. GUELICH, *The Sermon on the Mount*, 357, disagrees with this interpretation and suggests that it is a metaphor for prayer and has nothing to do with the entrance to the kingdom; also L. MORRIS, *Matthew*, 170. W.D. DAVIES – D.C. ALLISON, *Matthew*, I, 679, sees both seeking and knocking as "activities within prayer or identical with prayer".

[118] The thesis in v.7 and the basis in v.8 have three elements in each, and they are parallel to each other. The adjective πᾶς emphasizes the distributive significance of this general principle. The verbs used in the imperatives in v.7 are repeated here as *substantival* participles in which two of them (ὁ αἰτῶν and ὁ ζητῶν) function as subjects and the other one (τῷ κρούοντι) as an indirect object. But the verbs that express the promise (λαμβάνω, εὑρίσκω, ἀνοίγω) are given in the present indicative, emphasizing the assurance part of the saying. For an explanation of *substantival* participles, see D.B. WALLACE, *Greek Grammar*, 619.

evidently refers to those who follow Jesus and thus enter into a filial relationship with the Father.[119]

4.2 *Lesson from the Goodness of Human Fathers*

To illustrate the benevolence of the heavenly Father Jesus gives two examples which show the caring nature of human fathers for their children. "Or what man of you, if his son asks him for bread, will give him a stone? Or if he asks for a fish, will give him a serpent?" (7,9-10).[120] No father will give his son a stone if he asks for bread, or a serpent if he asks for a fish.[121] These examples highlight some of the basic characteristics of an earthly father-child relationship: the natural affection of fathers towards their children, their natural instinct that prevents them from doing anything harmful to their children, the freedom of the children to ask for their needs, and the confidence of the children in their fathers that they will not do anything harmful to them etc.. This is the lived experience of the disciples, both as children and as fathers.[122] Jesus invites them from this experience to look at their heavenly Father's attitude and affection towards them, his children.

4.3 *Assurance of the Giving of the Heavenly Father*

Having pointed out the goodness of human fathers towards their children, Jesus asks the disciples, "If you then, who are evil, know how to give good gifts to your children, how much more will your Father who is in heaven give good things to those who ask him!" (7,11).

This concluding inference accentuates the reliability of the Father making the disciples aware of the contrast between their nature and the Father's nature, and the consequent benevolence. The adjective πονηροί summarizes

---

[119] Agreeing with R.A. GUELICH, *The Sermon on the Mount*, 358; W.D. DAVIES – D.C. ALLISON, *Matthew*, I, 680; different from U. LUZ, *Matthew 1–7*, 421; H.D. BETZ, *The Sermon on the Mount*, 506. Luz takes vv.7-8 as a general teaching on prayer applying to everybody. Betz on the other hand interprets it as a teaching on giving and receiving, and general goodness of life. Considering it a teaching against scepticism, Betz denies the possibility of interpreting it as a call for prayer.

[120] Matthew uses a generic term ἄνθρωπος to refer to human fathers, while Luke uses πατήρ. Since Matthew uses πατήρ elsewhere in the SM only for God, this change may be viewed as deliberate. Thus the evangelist may be avoiding even the least possibility of any equivocation of this term.

[121] Bread and fish represent the basic components of their daily diet (14,13-21; 15,32-39).

[122] The question is applicable to all human fathers in general (ἄνθρωπος); the inclusion of the disciples is stressed with the partitive genitive ἐξ ὑμῶν.

all human imperfection in comparison with the perfection and absolute goodness intrinsic to God.[123] "How much more" (πόσῳ μᾶλλον) of 7,11 reminds us of the "much more" of 6,26 and 6,30.[124]

Despite being imperfect and sinful, the disciples as human fathers show affection towards their own children and do what is good for them. Then how much more will their heavenly Father, who is a perfect Father (5,48), do for his children! The rhetorical question expects the disciples to be convinced that their Father in heaven will give much more to his children than the fathers on the earth give to their children. Conversely, it implies that the disciples have the freedom of children to ask for things confidently of their Father.

It is significant that the object of the Father's giving is entirely unrestricted in Matthew.[125] While Luke specifies it as the Holy Spirit, Matthew presents it as "good things" (ἀγαθά). As in v.7, here also the non-specification of the object seems to be intentional. We may understand "good things" as all that the disciples need to live as the children of the Father in the earthly stage of their process.[126] However, its non-restrictive use assures the disciples that their Father will give them only "good things", and thus it

---

[123] As R.H. GUNDRY, *Matthew*: *Mixed Church*, 125, observes, "Here πονηροί modifies the disciples *considered as human beings*. After all, giving good gifts to one's children represents a human quality, not a quality distinctive of Jesus' disciples." This phrase πονηροί need not be taken with a moral connotation (cf. H.D. BETZ, *Sermon on the Mount*, 506), as though the disciples are wicked. As A.J. HULTGREN, *The Parables of Jesus*, 237, suggests, "It [πονηροί] can be regarded [...] as a comparative term in which a contrast is made between God, who is absolutely good, and human beings, who are not." See also G.G. GAMBA, *Vangelo di San Matteo*, 211.

[124] W.D. DAVIES – D.C. ALLISON, *Matthew*, I, 626, point out three major similarities between the teaching in 6,25-34 and in 7,7-11: i) "both are based on arguments *a minori ad maius*"; ii) "both have been constructed around key words that are repeated five times (μεριμνάω in 6,25-34 and αἰτέω in 7,7-11)"; iii) "both use two major illustrations to make their respective cases (birds/lilies, the son who asks for bread/the.son who asks for fish)."

[125] See J. GNILKA, *Matthäusevangelium*, I, 263; J. MURPHY-O'CONNOR "The Prayer of Petition", 403.

[126] Scholars suggest various possibilities regarding the connotation of "good things" here: a) gifts prayed for in the Lord's prayer: E. SCHWEIZER, *Matthäus*, 111; b) the eschatological benefits of the kingdom present and future: R.A. GUELICH, *The Sermon on the Mount*, 359; c) things required for meeting physical needs: R.A. PIPER, "Matt 7,7-11", 415; d) things related to entrance into the kingdom: D. PATTE, *Matthew*, 97; e) "all that is required to live the life of faithful discipleship as this is set forth in the great sermon": W.D. DAVIES – D.C. ALLISON, *Matthew*, I, 685.

encourages them to live as authentic children putting their trust in the Father.[127]

In 7,7-11, where Jesus presents God as the Father of the disciples for the last time in the SM, the reliability of the Father is underscored. The children can ask the Father confidently, can knock at his door for their needs, and can be certain that their requests will be granted. Pointing out the incomparable goodness of the heavenly Father, Jesus demands a filial trust from the disciples. The teaching in this unit indirectly assures the children that they will find the Father's kingdom – the true goal of their life – if they earnestly seek it.

5. **The Judgement of the Process (7,21)**

In all the units we have studied so far from the SM, Jesus presents God as the Father of the disciples. But in 7,21 he refers to God as "my Father".[128] The change of pronoun (from ὑμῶν to μου) is significant in the context. By referring to God as "my Father" in this concluding section of the SM, Jesus reveals that the Father about whom he has so far spoken to the disciples is his own Father. This adds a new dimension to the understanding of the disciples' identity: they are not only the children of the Father but also the brothers and sisters of Jesus.

However, one cannot claim this identity and its privileges if one does not live according to its demands. On the last day, Jesus, the Son, will appear as the judge to give the verdict on their status. Anticipating a scene from the day

---

[127] Although not mentioned explicitly, a call for a deep faith echoes through this section (see 6,30). Only with faith can one feel confident in the providing care of the heavenly Father. One may easily recognize the goodness of human fathers by means of one's senses, because one can see it, hear it, and feel it. But to experience the greater goodness of the heavenly Father one needs to go beyond one's sensory knowledge. This means one has to surrender oneself in faith (21,22). Only an authentic child who is confident of the parental care of God can ask him boldly and also accept everything confidently (26,39.42.44). See U. LUZ, *Matthew 1–7*, 422; A.J. HULTGREN, *The Parables of Jesus*, 239.

[128] Though we have limited this study basically to the πατήρ passages which refer to God as the Father of the disciples, we take 7,21-23 as an exception considering the following features of this unit: i) here, for the first time in the gospel and the only time in the SM, Jesus speaks about God as his Father (πατρός μου); ii) the two stages – the present and the future – of the disciples' life are explicitly mentioned here; iii) this unit presents Jesus, the Son, as the judge who utters the verdict on people's entry into the kingdom.

of judgement, Jesus teaches the disciples in 7,21-23 about the criterion by which all will be judged at the end.[129] Those who do the will of the Father during their earthly stage of life will be received into the kingdom, while others will be rejected.[130]

5.1 *The Son as the Judge at the End*

The scene of judgement given in 7,21-23 completes Jesus' repeated teaching in the SM on the process of the disciples' becoming children of God.

---

[129] The teaching in 7,21-23 and 7,24-27 are closely related. As we have seen in the general structure of the SM, 7,21-23 belongs to the section of general conclusions (7,13-27). We noted that formally 7,21-27 is arranged as a single whole, and it corresponds to 5,3-10, as in both units Jesus speaks in the third person (see Ch. I, 1.1). One can also find a thematic unity in 7,21-27 as it deals with the issue of "doing the will of the Father" (7,21-23) and "doing the words of Jesus" (7,24-27). Jesus reveals the will of the Father in the SM; so those who do his words will be doing the will of the Father. Regarding our unit's relationship with the previous pericope (7,15-20) there is no consensus. Some scholars, identifying the people mentioned in 7,21-23 with the false prophets of 7,15, take 7,15-23 as a single unit. Cf. D. MARGUERAT, *Le Jugement*, 172; R.A. GUELICH, *The Sermon on the Mount*, 384; U. LUZ, *Matthew 1–7*, 439; J. GNILKA, *Matthäusevangelium*, I, 272; R.H. GUNDRY, *Matthew*: *Mixed Church*, 128; W.D. DAVIES – D.C. ALLISON, *Matthew*, I, 693-694; M. DUMAIS, *Le Sermon sur la Montagne*, 300. Although one can find a certain symbolic correspondence between the characteristics of the false prophets and of the people at the judgement scene (e.g. coming in "sheep's clothing" [7,15] <=> calling "Lord, Lord" [7,21]; "ravenous wolves" [7,15] <=> "evil doers" [7,23]; "false prophets" [7,15] <=> "did we not prophesy in your name" [7,22]), there is no clear evidence to identify them as the same persons. It may be more reasonable to consider 7,21-23 as a unit dealing with "false followers" rather than with "false prophets". See D.A. CARSON, *Matthew 1–12*, 159. The specific theme of the judgement on the last day treated in this pericope favours taking it as a complete unit in itself (see also the unique features of this unit mentioned in the last footnote). The following authors also treat 7,21-23 as a separate unit: J. SCHNIEWIND, *Matthäus*, 104-105; T.W. MANSON, *The Sayings of Jesus*, 176; D. HILL, "False Prophets and Charismatics", 327-348; H.D. BETZ, "An Episode in the Last Judgement", 125-131; G. STRECKER, *The Sermon on the Mount*, 164; J.E. DAVISON, "Anomia", 629; J. LAMBRECHT, *The Sermon on the Mount*, 184-185; D.A. HAGNER, *Matthew 1–13*, 185.

[130] Luke does not have a unit that parallels Matt 7,21-23. However, a teaching similar to Matt 7,21 is found in Luke 6,46, and one similar to Matt 7,22-23 in Luke 13,26-27. There are many differences between these texts especially in their content. We mention four significant aspects which are found in Matthew but not in Luke: i) a direct reference to the entry into the kingdom; ii) a demand for doing the will of Jesus' Father (in Luke the demand is to do Jesus' words, and so functions as an introduction to the parable of the Two Builders, which Matthew treats separately; see Matt 7,24-27; Luke 6,47-49); iii) the rejected ones' claim of having done mighty works in Jesus' name (in Luke they do not mention any of the things they did in his name; rather they give instances of their being together with Jesus, Luke 13,26); iv) a direct presentation of Jesus as the judge (in Luke it is "the householder" who makes the judgement, Luke 13,25).

We have already seen that it is by being a disciple of Jesus that one enters into a Father-child relationship with God, and it is by hearing and doing Jesus' words that one fulfils the process successfully in the earthly stage of one's life. Now the present scene shows that Jesus is not only their guide and master but also the judge of their process.

Matthew presents Jesus on at least three other occasions in the gospel as the judge of the end times (16,27; 19,28; 25,31). In all these three judgement references Jesus has the title the "Son of Man". The same title is used also in 10,23; 13,41; 24,27.30.37.39.44 alluding to Jesus' role as the eschatological judge. He is the appointed judge of the Father (see John 5,22) and his authority is manifested by the glory (δόξα) associated with him and the heavenly cohort (οἱ ἄγγελοι) that accompanies him.[131] He will sit upon his glorious throne, and all the nations will be gathered before him for the final judgement (25,31-32), and he will repay everyone for what each one has done in life (16,27; 25,31-46).

Jesus' role as the judge of the end times is a further confirmation for the disciples that following the way of life shown by him will certainly make them worthy to be judged as the children of the Father.

5.2 *Doing the Will of the Father: the Condition for Reception*

What is the right faith expression that makes one worthy to enter the kingdom? This is the main issue discussed in 7,21-23. The first part of v.21 begins with negating (οὐ) a probable common assumption that all (πᾶς) who say (ὁ λέγων...) to Jesus "Lord, Lord" will enter the kingdom. As a contrast (ἀλλά), the second part of the verse (21b) describes the type of people who will really enter the kingdom. They are identified as the ones who do (ὁ ποιῶν...) the will of the Father of Jesus.

In Matthew the title "Lord" (κύριος) is used for Jesus mostly by the disciples or the people who faithfully submit to his authority (see 8,2.6.8.21.25; 9,28; 14,28.30; 15,22.25.27; 16,22; 17,4.15; 18,21; 20,30.31.33). None of the opponents of Jesus ever addresses him as Lord. So the people who are denied entry into the kingdom are not the ones who oppose Jesus and his message but the ones who proclaim him as the Lord. They even claim that they prophesied, cast out demons, and performed many mighty works in his name.[132]

[131] In 16,27 it is explicitly mentioned that Jesus is coming in the glory of his Father.

[132] In Matthew both John the Baptist (11,9; 21,26) and Jesus are called "prophets" (14,5; 21,11.46); Jesus "casts out the evil spirits" (4,24; 8,16.31; 9,33-34; 12,24.29; 17,18) and the

Normally, having the power to do these things is considered a spiritual gift received from God. In fact, Jesus gives the disciples authority to "heal the sick, raise the dead, cleanse lepers and cast out demons" before he sends them for the mission (10,8). By addressing Jesus as the Lord and repeatedly saying that they did great things in his name,[133] they seem to claim that they too are his disciples and have the right to enter the kingdom.

A contrast between "saying" and "doing" is pointed out here. To be accepted as a child of the Father in the kingdom it is not enough to call (λέγω) Jesus "Lord, Lord"; one must also do (ποιέω) the will of Jesus' Father. Matthew has dealt with this theme of "doing" in contrast to empty "saying" in different contexts. In the parable of the Two Sons (21,28-30), the first son responds to the father's request with a firm "no" (οὐ θέλω) in the beginning.[134] But later he repents and does what his father wanted him to do. On the contrary, the second son is very polite in his words. He shows respect to the father addressing him as κύριε and promises him that he will do the job. But he does not do it. The parable ends with a clear message that only those who do the will of the Father will enter the kingdom. The need to put one's words into practice is stressed again in 23,3, which condemns the insincere preaching of the scribes and Pharisees. Similarly, on the day of the final judgement, the sheep and the goats will be separated and judged according to their deeds and not according to their words (25,31-46).

As we have seen in the previous chapter, the condition to enter the kingdom given in 7,21 needs to be understood in the light of the condition given in 5,20. The exceeding righteousness demanded in 5,20 (and repeated in 6,1) for the entry into the kingdom is clarified here as doing the will of the Father. Therefore, "doing the will of God" refers here to a life of exceeding righteousness that will make one worthy of the redemption the Father wills for

---

Twelve are given the power to do so (10,1.8); Jesus does many "mighty works" (4,24; 8,3.13; 9,6.22; 11,4-5).

[133] A. Maggi makes an interesting suggestion regarding the use of the phrase τῷ σῷ ὀνόματι in this context comparing it with another phrase ἐπὶ τῷ ὀνόματί μου (18,5; 24,5; Mark 9,37.39; 13,6). According to him, to act ἐπὶ τῷ ὀνόματί τινος would mean assuming the identity of that person and manifesting his presence, while τῷ σῷ ὀνόματι would mean only "using the name" of somebody for one's own gains. A. MAGGI, "Nota sull'uso di 'ΤΩΙ ΣΩΙ ΟΝΟΜΑΤΙ'", 147. Though his distinction makes good sense in the present context, his silence regarding the use of ἐπὶ τῷ ὀνόματί μου in 24,5 makes this suggestion rather less convincing.

[134] The order of the responses of the sons is reversed in several texts. B *Θ* f^{13} 700 al (lat) sa^{mss} present the second son as the one who does the will of the father. As J. NOLLAND, *Matthew*, 860, comments, "The reversal may have taken place under the influence of a salvation-historical reading of the parable in connection with Jews and Gentiles."

human beings.[135] Only by doing the will of the Father can one become a brother and sister of Jesus and a child of the Father (see 12,49-50).

People can come to know about the will of the Father through the life and mission of Jesus.[136] This is mentioned explicitly in the next unit, in the Parable of the Two Builders (7,24-27), which functions as the conclusion to the whole teaching of the SM: "Everyone then who hears these words of mine and does them will be like a wise man who built his house up on the rock; and the rain fell, and the floods came, and the winds blew and beat upon the house, but it did not fall, because it had been founded on the rock" (7,24-25).

5.3 *The Rejection of the Lawless*

It is possible to identify these people who will be denied entry into the kingdom as the ones who accepted the call of Jesus initially, assumed the role of the disciples, and even had the power to prophesy and perform miracles, but who failed to live up to the demands of this call.[137] They may represent the people who begin the process but abandon it later. They still pretend to be the followers of Jesus, but in truth they are not.[138]

Jesus strongly denies any relationship with them declaring that he never knew them (7,23). When Jesus says "I never knew you" (οὐδέποτε ἔγνων ὑμᾶς), it need not mean that he did not know them in the literal sense as the word γινώσκω suggests. Rather it would imply that he had no relation with them at all, neither in the past nor in the present.[139] This means that even if they had been his disciples in the past and thus have received the grace to

---

[135] See Ch. I,3.3.3 d), for an explanation of the phrase "will of the Father".

[136] Some scholars even define the will of the Father as the teachings of Jesus in the SM. See R.A. GUELICH, *The Sermon on the Mount*, 399; W.D. DAVIES – D.C. ALLISON, *Matthew*, I, 712.

[137] See CYRIL OF ALEXANDRIA, "Fragmenta in Matthaeum", § 88, 180.

[138] H.D. BETZ, *The Sermon on the Mount*, 540, identifies this group as the "Christians of Gentile origin" who worship Jesus as the Lord but do not keep the Torah of God. Such an interpretation tends to limit Jesus' teaching in the SM within the walls of the Torah. Some authors, viewing the text from a post-Resurrection context, identify them as "Christian charismatics": D. HILL, "False Prophets and Charismatics", 327-348; G. STRECKER, *The Sermon on the Mount*, 165. Some others, as we have noted above, identify them as false prophets. They certainly remind us of false prophets who come in sheep's clothing, performing great signs and wonders to lead the believers astray (7,15; 24,11.24), but we may not identify them as false prophets. Nowhere is it mentioned that false prophets address Jesus as "Lord" or claim entry into the kingdom.

[139] W.D. DAVIES – D.C. ALLISON, *Matthew*, I, 717, notes that "'I never knew' is a formula of renunciation, and it means 'I never recognized you as one of my own'" (see John 10,14; 1Cor 8,3; 2Tim 2,19). See also R.H. GUNDRY, *Matthew*: *Mixed Church*, 132.

become children of the Father, if they have not lived the requirements of this call throughout the earthly stage, they cannot claim any relationship with Jesus; they will not be granted entry into the kingdom which is reserved for the true brothers and sisters of Jesus (12,50).

Their claim that they did great works in Jesus' name may be true, but their being able to perform these signs does not mean that they belong to him. They might have performed them as the hypocrites perform acts of righteousness, not to give glory to God but to seek their own glory, not to do the will of the Father but to do their own will.

The judge will chase these people out saying, "depart from me you doers of lawlessness!" (7,23). This condemnation expresses the displeasure of the judge at their presence in front of him. A similar rebuke is found in Ps 6,9, where the Psalmist makes a retort to his enemies who put him in a sinful situation.[140] These people who claim to have done great works in Jesus' name are like the enemies of the Psalmist, whose deeds took the Psalmist away from God and pushed him into terror and misery. How many people might have been misled by their lawlessness!

The "iniquity" or "lawlessness" (ἀνομία) that they are accused of commiting may be better understood in the present context as their disregard for the will of the Father revealed by Jesus.[141] The same word "lawlessness" is used in 13,41 referring to the weeds that hinder the growth of the sons of the kingdom. In 23,28 it is given as the characteristic of the scribes and Pharisees together with hypocrisy. In the end times many people will fall victim to this "lawlessness"; as a result their love will grow cold, and they will be led into sin (24,12). No wonder the judge drives out these men of iniquity from his presence: they have been a threat to the children of the Father and because of them many have fallen away (13,26-27.38-39; 24,10).

By revealing God as his Father in 7,21 Jesus implicitly acknowledges his fraternal relationship with the disciples. At the same time, doing the will of his Father is given as the absolute condition for anyone to be accepted as "his own". On the last day when he appears as the judge, he will allow only those who have successfully completed their process in the earthly stage by doing the will of the Father to enter the kingdom. All others, even if they had been

---

[140] In the Psalm the imperative ἀπόστητε is used instead of ἀποχωρεῖτε (see Luke 13,27); ἀπόστητε ἀπ' ἐμοῦ πάντες οἱ ἐργαζόμενοι τὴν ἀνομίαν (Ps 6,9)

[141] See D.J. HARRINGTON, *Matthew*, 108; D.A. HAGNER, *Matthew 1–13*, 189.

his disciples earlier and had been able to do great works in his name, will be disowned and rejected.

6. **Conclusion**

Also in the rest of the Father passages in the SM – other than those in 6,1-18 – discipleship is viewed as a process of becoming children of God. In 5,16, where God is presented as the Father of the disciples for the first time in the gospel, the disciples are asked to shine their light – which is their "good works" – before people and thus help them to know the Father and glorify him. Identifying the disciples as the light of the world (and the salt of the earth), the teaching in this section indicates that they are the children of God, the Supreme Light, and the participants of the light-giving mission of Jesus. Being the disciples of Jesus they are a blessing to the world and are instruments of its salvation; without them the earth will be "tasteless" and the world will be "lightless". They should not allow their light to go out by hiding it, or their salt to become useless by losing its saltiness. The description of the destiny of "saltless salt" mirrors the fate of the disciples who fail to live according to the demands of their call (5,13). They will be thrown out and trodden under foot (see 7,21-23).

The idea of the disciples' becoming children of the Father in a future stage is explicitly given in 5,45. At the same time, this text and its context underscore also the present filial status of the disciples, especially by inviting them to contrast their identity and behaviour with that of the tax collectors and the Gentiles. To reach the final stage where they will be the Father's children for ever, the disciples have to live as his children in the present stage, imitating his character. The benevolence of the Father is unlimited and impartial; to be his children they have to surpass all the boundaries, even the ones set by the Law, which make their love and affection conditional and restricted. The love commandment of Jesus clearly shows the disciples how they can be and become the children of the Father (5,44).

The concluding command of the antitheses, "Be perfect…as your heavenly Father is perfect" (5,48), also envisages a dynamic growth process at the end of which the children will be absorbed into the perfection of their Father. The disciples will grow into the perfection of the Father by orienting themselves absolutely and exclusively towards the Father and imitating his model revealed through Jesus. The fullness of this perfection may be accomplished only in the eternal kingdom.

Jesus rebukes the disciples in 6,25-34 for their anxiety over material needs. Pointing to the examples of the birds of the air and the lilies of the field, Jesus invites the disciples to realize how much more precious they are than all other creatures, and how much more their Father will care for them, his children, than he cares for others (6,26.30). If they are still anxious about their needs, it is because they do not know their worth, or because of their lack of trust – "little faith" – in their heavenly Father. Worrying over worldly needs they depart from their filial status and sink to the level of the Gentiles who do not even know the Father. The disciples are exhorted here to live seeking the true goal of their call – the kingdom of the Father and his righteousness (6,33).

The reliability of the Father is reaffirmed in the teaching in 7,7-11. Referring to the goodness of human fathers towards their children, Jesus asks the disciples to consider how much more their heavenly Father will be good to them, his children (7,11). Jesus encourages the disciples to approach their Father for all their needs, and he promises them that the Father will give them "good things". The maxims, "seek and you will find" and "knock and it will be opened to you", assure them implicitly that they will find the kingdom and will be received into it if they live seeking for it (see 6,33).

In 7,21, referring to God as his Father (πατήρ μου), Jesus indirectly discloses his fraternal relationship with the disciples. The life of the disciples is clearly depicted in this section (7,21-23) as a two-stage process. At the end of the first stage Jesus will appear as the judge. He will acknowledge as his own and receive into his Father's kingdom only those who have done the will of his Father, revealed by him, in their earthly stage of life (see 7,24-27).

CHAPTER III

The Father and Children in the Other Great Discourses in Matthew

From the study of the "Father" passages in the SM, we have come to the conclusion that in the SM discipleship is viewed as a process of becoming children of the Father. Matthew takes up his presentation of the disciples as the children of the Father and the brothers and sisters of Jesus in other places in the gospel. There are at least three more occasions where God is referred to as the Father of the disciples using the term "your Father" as in the SM (10,20.29; 18,14). In addition, in 23,9 Jesus explicitly tells the disciples that they should call no man their father on earth as they have one Father who is in heaven. There is one more instance in the gospel, in 13,43, where God is portrayed as the Father of human beings. He is presented in this verse as the Father of the "righteous". Our study of this passage and its context will show that these righteous represent the ideal disciples who have successfully completed their process in the earthly stage and have proved worthy of being received into the kingdom.

Remarkably, all the above references appear in the Great Discourses of Jesus. In the present chapter we will take each discourse separately and analyse the above verses and their context with a view to understanding the process of discipleship depicted in these texts.

1. The Father and Children in the Mission (10,20.29)

Jesus called his first disciples to become fishers of men in 4,18-22. In the SM he told them and others who followed him about their new identity as the children of the Father and taught them how they should live this identity in the world. Coming down from the mountain, they accompany Jesus as he engages in his triple ministry of teaching, preaching the gospel of the kingdom, and healing the sick (8,1–9,35). In 9,36, when Jesus sees gathered around him multitudes of people who are harassed and helpless, like sheep without shepherds, he expresses the need of human collaboration for the care of this people. He asks his followers to pray to the Lord of the harvest to send more labourers into his harvest (9,37-38). Immediately afterwards, Jesus calls his twelve disciples to him and gives them authority over unclean spirits to cast them out and to heal every disease and every infirmity (10,1-4). Then he sends them out for the mission with a series of instructions concerning their life in the mission field (10,5-42).

The word πατήρ occurs seven times in the Missionary Discourse (MD) in which four of them (10,20.29.32.33) refer to God. In verses 10,20.29 Jesus mentions God as the Father of the disciples (your Father) while in 10,32.33 he is referred to as his Father (my Father).

1.1 *The Father's Children under Trial*

The first "your Father" text in the MD appears in the literary unit 10,16-25.[1] The teaching in this unit begins with a warning: "Behold, I send you out as sheep in the midst of wolves; so be wise as serpents and innocent as doves" (10,16). People will deliver the disciples up to the councils and flog them in their synagogues; they will be dragged before kings and governors (17-18). Now, how are they going to face all these trials? Where can they look for help? Jesus consoles the disciples, promising them that they will be given what they are to say in that hour (19). He further assures them that it will not be they who speak before their persecutors but the Spirit of their Father through them (20).[2]

---

[1] Several scholars consider 10,16-25 as a single unit (e.g. J. GNILKA, *Matthäusevangelium*, I, 372; A. STOCK, *The Method and Message of Matthew*, 168; S. GRASSO, *Matteo*, 276; W. WIEFEL, *Matthäus*, 194); others (e.g. F.W. BEARE, *Matthew*, 244; W.D. DAVIES – D.C. ALLISON, *Matthew*, II, 184; D.A. HAGNER, *Matthew 1–13*, 275-276; D. SENIOR, *The Gospel of Matthew*, 116) take 10,16-23 as a unit.

[2] We may divide 10,16-25 into the following subunits: a general cautioning against the forthcoming dangers (16); a prediction on persecution from the authorities (17-18); encouragement and assurance of help at the time of trial (19-20); a prediction on persecution from family circles (21-22a); encouragement to endure (22b); the command to flee from persecution, and the promise of the coming of the Son of Man (23); the rationale for the sufferings of the disciples (24-25).

1.1.1 On Children's Worry at the Time of Trial

Jesus has already told the disciples in the SM that they will have to suffer persecution and opposition as they follow him (5,10-12.44). Nonetheless, the imagery referring to persecution given in 10,16-18, such as "sheep in the midst of wolves", "floggings", "dragging before governors and kings", could be terrifying to them. It would be entirely reasonable for them to worry about how they might defend themselves against their mighty tormentors. Foreseeing their possible anxieties, Jesus prepares them to face such persecutions with great confidence.

Though the teaching is addressed to the twelve disciples whom Jesus is sending for the mission, the pronoun "you" (ὑμεῖς) can be taken as referring to all the disciples who will undergo persecution for the mission.[3] From the "sending" to the "witness" (μαρτύριον) there is a long journey. We may presume that those envisioned here as facing persecutions are the ones who have been faithful and loyal to their master and to his call. Up until this point they have lived as the authentic children of the Father committing themselves to proclaim the good news of his kingdom. But the ears of some people are reluctant to hear that good news. The mission of the Father's children annoys and angers them; it disturbs their "evil and adulterous" ways (14,4; see Wis 2,12-16). They want to get rid of them, and so they bring the children before the worldly authorities for judgement (v.18).

The disciples' relationship with Jesus is reflected clearly in the description of their persecution. The verb παραδίδωμι, which has been used three times (10,17.19.21) in the present context referring to the "delivery"[4] of the disciples into the hands of their persecutors, appears repeatedly in the context of the passion and death of Jesus (see 17,22; 20,18.19; 26,2.15.16.21.23.24.26.45; 27,2.4.18.26).[5] Thus the trial of these disciples is identified with the passion and death of Jesus himself.[6] Moreover, verses 24-25 make it explicit that it is because the disciples belong to the household (οἰκιακός) of Jesus that they have to undergo all these sufferings.

---

[3] See O. DA SPINETOLI, *Matteo*, 314.

[4] Technically παραδίδωμι means "handing over a person for a judicial process". In a normal judicial process the jury questions the defendant to verify the charges against him. But the process the missionaries are going to face is an unjust one. There will be no verification of the truth. In any case, it will end with the execution of the accused (see 4,12 and 14,10).

[5] In addition, ὁ παραδούς / ὁ παραδιδούς are used for the "betrayer" (10,4; 26,25.46.48; 27,3).

[6] This word is used once again to refer to the suffering of the disciples in 24,9.

Jesus consoles the disciples telling them not to worry (μὴ μεριμνήσητε) about how they are to speak and what they are to say during their trial. Since the verb is given here in the aorist subjunctive, the worry it implies can be understood in two ways. It may be the actual feeling of the twelve as they hear about the coming persecutions.[7] Or, more probably, it refers to the worry of the disciples standing before the persecutors in the future. In either case, this consolatory command parallels the teaching in 6,25-34 where the disciples' worry over material needs is explained as a symptom of their lack of trust in their heavenly Father. Certainly, in the present context, the situation is much more severe as their life itself is in peril. If the disciples do not trust in the Father and in his Son and in their own identity as the children, they will not be able to take up this mission. Similarly, the imperative "do not worry" can make sense only to those who are confident in the protection of their heavenly Father.

The anxiety of the disciples is specified as their preoccupation about what they are to say when they are brought to trial before their enemies. In a fair and judicial process the accused has the right to defend himself. But Jesus certainly knows that the trial his disciples are going to face will be nothing but a mockery. Whatever they say, their words will be like the bleating of a sheep before the howling ravenous wolves. By hook or by crook their adversaries will prove them guilty (see 26,57-66). Naturally, this would be a terrifying moment for anyone who has some attachment to his/her life (see 10,39). However, the anxiety of the disciples mentioned here should not be interpreted as their worry over protecting their lives. If that had been their preoccupation they would not have taken up this mission. Rather, their worry should be understood in the light of v.18, where persecution is viewed as an occasion for testimony. For the authentic disciples persecution is not a tragedy but an opportunity to proclaim their faith in Jesus and their commitment to his mission (Acts 4,1-22; 5,27-32. 40-42; 7,1-53; 16,19-34; 20,24; 23,11). All the same, they are human beings. Confronted by the might and malice of their adversaries, they may fumble out of fear and be tempted to give up their conviction and faith. Thus they may fail to defend the cause for which they have lived up to now. Seen from this perspective, the worry mentioned here could be considered as the genuine feeling of a disciple, who is fully aware of his fragile human nature (see 26,41.69-75; Rom 7,18-25).

---

[7] In that case, we may translate 19a as the following: "But do not worry (*now*) about how you are to speak and what you are to say when they deliver you up."

1.1.2 Promise of Help

Jesus gives the reason why they should not be anxious about their defence during their trial: "for what you are to say will be given to you at that hour" (19b). Thus they are assured of God's help (see the divine passive δοθήσεται) to stand up to their enemies at that time (ἐν ἐκείνῃ τῇ ὥρᾳ). In verse 20 Jesus further makes explicit (γάρ) the type of help they are going to receive. In a contrastive statement that makes use of an οὐ …ἀλλά construction, they are told emphatically that it will not be they who speak but the Spirit of their Father (τὸ πνεῦμα τοῦ πατρὸς ὑμῶν).

a) "You will be given"

The verb δίδωμι is used on various occasions in the gospel to refer to God's giving to his children (eg. 7,7.11; 9,8; 13,11; 28,18).[8] On the other hand, it is also used to show his "not giving" to the people who do not belong to him (12,39; 13,11; 16,4). The disciples who suffer persecution are God's children. They are brought before their enemies because of their involvement in his mission. He, who knows all their needs and attends to them, will not abandon them and will not allow them to stumble as they defend his cause.[9] With the help of God, they will be able to face their persecutors boldly. Therefore they do not have to worry about their human weaknesses in front of the ghastly power of their enemies. The assurance that God will give them what they are to say makes them confident that God knows their sufferings and acts on their behalf. Such a confidence would be quite enough for the disciples to face the persecutions courageously. Yet, Jesus emboldens them further, telling them, "For it is not you who speak, but the Spirit of your Father speaking through you" (10,20).

b) "The Spirit of your Father"

Matt 10,20 is the only text in the whole Bible where the phrase "the Spirit of your Father" referring to the divine Spirit occurs. In the parallel texts in both Mark and Luke, the term "Holy Spirit" is used (Mark 13,11; Luke 12,12). Various other forms referring to the Spirit of God are found in Matthew: the Holy Spirit (1,18.20; 3,11; 12,32; 28,19), the Spirit of God

---

[8] The passive forms of δίδωμι with God as the implicit subject occur eleven times in Matthew (δοθήσεται 7x; δέδοται 3x; ἐδόθη 1x).

[9] See Exod 4,12; Jer 1,9; Eph 6,19.

(3,16; 12,28), the Spirit (4,1; 12,31; 22,43) and my Spirit (12,18). All these appellations refer to the same reality.

The Spirit is presented in the gospel as the power of the Father active in Jesus, the Son. He was born of this Spirit (1,18.20); the Spirit alighted upon him during the baptism (3,16; cf 12,18), guided him (4,1), and was active in his mission (12,18.28.31.32, see 3,11).[10] The interrelatedness of the Father, the Son and the Spirit is explicitly shown at the conclusion of the gospel by mentioning them in connection with the one name (28,19).[11]

In 10,20 the same Spirit is promised to the disciples as their advocate (see John 15,26). He will defend their case against their enemies. The Spirit will be functioning not as an external agent but from within and through (ἐν ὑμῖν) them. That means, the disciples will be filled with the Spirit, and they will function as the "trumpets of the Spirit".[12]

The presence of the Spirit in the disciples recalls the coming of the Spirit upon Jesus after his baptism. What followed was the divine proclamation of the Sonship of Jesus (3,16-17; see 12,18). Afterwards the same Spirit led Jesus to the wilderness where he triumphed over the temptations of the devil and proved himself the Son of God (4,1-11). Similarly, the presence of the Spirit of the Father in the disciples at the time of persecution can be seen as a sign of the Father's acceptance of them as his authentic children. With the Spirit they will be able to endure the threats and temptations of their persecutors and testify that they are the true children of God (see Wis 2,13.16; Acts 7,55).

Furthermore, Jesus' reference to the Spirit in 10,20 as the "Spirit of your Father" gives clear emphasis to the filial identity of the disciples. The Spirit that comes to their aid is that of their Father. Naturally, what belongs to the Father belongs to the children, and they have the right of inheritance.[13] At the same time, the Spirit of the Father is not separable from the Father; it is the power of the Father.[14] In fact, it is the Father himself who will be acting on

---

[10] See K. STOCK, *I racconti pasquali*, 106.

[11] In Matt 28,19 the word ὄνομα occurs only once, but three genitives (τοῦ πατρὸς καὶ τοῦ υἱοῦ καὶ τοῦ ἁγίου πνεύματος) are linked to it. This shows that there is only one God (so one name), but the one God is revealed and understood as the Father and the Son and the Holy Spirit. See K. STOCK, *I racconti pasquali*, 105.

[12] W.D. DAVIES – D.C. ALLISON, *Matthew*, II, 185.

[13] This explains why the earthly households of the disciples turn against them. They no longer belong to them (see 10,21-22. 35-37).

[14] See D.J. WEAVER, *Matthew's Missionary Discourse*, 96.

behalf of his beloved children as he has been acting through his beloved Son, Jesus.[15]

As mentioned above, the situation described here is futuristic. The disciples envisioned here are the ones who have lived their identity as the children. It is due to their commitment to the mission of Jesus, the Son of the Father, that they are suffering now, and it is for his sake that they are delivered up to their adversaries. Certainly, their Father will be with them to defend them from their enemies.

1.2 *The Father's Precious Children*

Matt 10,29, the second "your Father" verse in the MD, belongs to the literary unit of 10,26-31. The thrice repeated imperative of φοβέω with the negative particle μή binds this unit together.[16] However, v.26 is presented as an inferential conclusion (οὖν) of the teaching in vv.24-25, where Jesus explains to the disciples why they will be persecuted. The reason is simple: as his disciples they belong to his household. If he himself was called Beelzebul, how much more will they malign those of his household (10,25)? As we have seen above, from a human point of view, the threat of persecution can cause real fear in anyone. In the face of mockeries, tortures, and execution one might feel abandoned and forsaken even by God (see 27,46). Unless one has a very strong faith one may fail to endure these pains. Reminding the disciples of their true identity in vv.29-31, Jesus empowers them to face the persecutions fearlessly. They are the Father's precious children; nothing happens to them without the knowledge and will of their Father.

---

[15] As M. GRILLI, *Communità e Missione*, 132.271, observes, the testimony of the disciples is presented here as a Trinitarian act: "[...] al momento della persecuzione, è la Trinità stessa ad essere coinvolta (cf. anche 28,19). Chi di loro, infatti, è 'consegnato', è, al pari di Gesù (10,19; cf. 26,2) sotto la protezione del 'Padre' (10,20) presente mediante lo 'Spirito' (10,20)." See also G. MANGATT, "Reflections on the Apostolic Discourse", 201; E. MANICARDI, "Dio Padre", 86.

[16] 10,26-31 can be divided into three interconnected subunits each one carrying an injunction "do not fear". Referring to the definite eschatological revelation of God's truth in 26-27, Jesus exhorts the disciples to proclaim his message without fear. Different pairs of contrasts (covered/revealed, hidden/known, in the dark/in the light, hear in the ear/proclaim upon the housetops) distinguish this subunit from the other two. The second subunit (v.28) consists of two parallel injunctions, one negative and the other positive: "do not fear..., rather fear". The disciples should not fear those who kill the body but cannot kill the soul; rather they should fear the one who can destroy both soul and body in hell. The substantive, "sparrows" (στρουθίον), functions as an *inclusio* for the third subunit (29-31). The imperative "do not fear" appears again in the last verse (31) forming an *inclusio* with v.26 and concluding the teaching of 26-31.

1.2.1 The Omniscient Father

The children may believe that after their struggles and trials in this world they will be received into the Father's kingdom. Is that all? Has God no control over the things that happen to his children in the earthly stage of their life? To make the disciples confident of their Father's intimate knowledge of and care for them, Jesus tells them how their Father is involved even in the insignificant happenings of the world and how he has control over them.

a) The Sparrows

Jesus asks the disciples an open-ended question: "Are not two sparrows sold for a small coin?" (29a). The question highlights the triviality of the birds in various ways. First of all, there are two diminutives, one to show the smallness of the bird (στρουθίον) and the other its minimal value (ἀσσάριον).[17] Again, for such a low price not one but two sparrows are sold. As the sparrows are insignificant, so too is the transaction (see the passive πωλεῖται); nothing is mentioned about the seller or buyer;[18] the text is also silent on the purpose for which they are being bought and sold.[19]

But before the eyes of the Father, these birds are not so insignificant. Not even one of them falls (πίπτω) to the ground[20] without (ἄνευ) his will and consent (29b).[21] The affirmation "one of them" contrasts with the "two" in the previous sentence. The negative οὐ with the future indicative of πίπτω asserts that the Father's knowledge of the sparrow's fall is not casual but definite.

---

[17] στρουθίον is the diminutive of στρουθός, and ἀσσάριον is the diminutive of the Latin *as*, worth about one-sixteenth of a denarius. See M. ZERWICK – M. GROSVENOR, *Grammatical Analysis*, 31.

[18] J.D.M. DERRETT, "Light on Sparrows and Hairs", 344, identifies the sellers as the fowlers who trap the sparrows (see Amos 3,5), but this conjecture has no textual support.

[19] As some scholars suggest, (e.g. A. DEISSMANN, *Licht vom Osten*, 204-206; R.T. FRANCE, *Matthew*, 187; J. NOLLAND, *Matthew*, 437), they might be sold and bought for meat. However, the silence of the text regarding the purpose of the transaction seems to be deliberate. Thus it indicates again the insignificance of the birds.

[20] Some interpret the falling of the sparrow to the ground as a metaphor for its death. Cf. J. GNILKA, *Matthäusevangelium*, I, 388; E.C. PARK, *The Mission Discourse*, 148.

[21] Luke uses the word ἐπιλανθάνομαι in place of ἄνευ in Matthew. ἄνευ is a rare word in the NT. It appears only twice more in the NT, in the first letter of Peter (1Pet 3,1; 4,9). According to BAGD, 65, when used of persons this preposition would mean "without the knowledge and consent" of the person. In that case, while the Lukan text indicates God's "non-forgetting" of these birds, the Matthean text lays stress on his personal involvement in their destiny. See J.G. COOK, "The Sparrow's Fall in Mt 10,29b", 138-144, for a discussion on the various possible meanings of the word ἄνευ in the present context.

They are not just objects which are sold and bought by anonymous persons; they have an owner who knows them and controls their movements. Evidently, the sparrow is a representative of all the creatures in this universe whose movements are controlled by the Father.

Now, this sovereign Lord of all the creatures is the Father of the disciples (πατρὸς ὑμῶν). The argument is *a fortiori* here: if the fall of such an insignificant, sold-for-nothing sparrow happens only with the will and consent of him, how much more will he have control over the things that befall his own children? Jesus does not put such a question directly to the disciples, but he hints at their great identity and privilege by referring to God as "your Father".[22] By addressing the same Father as his Father in verses 32-33 (πατρός μου), Jesus hints also at their fraternal relationship with him, the Son. The Father's care for the children is further highlighted with the affirmation, "Even all the hairs of your head are numbered" (10,30).

b) "The hairs of your head"

Their Father (the implicit subject of the divine passive ἠριθμημέναι) knows even the number of the hairs of their head! Normally, nobody bothers to count one's hairs; they are "too small and too numerous",[23] and their number is not a serious matter that affects one's life. Compared to other parts of the body, hair has a less important function. Therefore, when it is said "even the hairs of your head are numbered", it has a metaphorical effect. It points to the Father's total care of and attention to his children.[24] Growth and loss of hairs and their number may be immaterial to them, but for their Father they are not without value. He knows his children through and through; nothing happens to them, even so-called insignificant things, without his consent.

This metaphor of the "numbered hairs" is noteworthy in the context of the disciples' undergoing persecution. If their Father is so attentive even to such an unimportant thing, how much more will he be involved in a situation where his children are ill-treated for a just cause? The metaphor strengthens and encourages the disciples. When they are persecuted, they are not abandoned or forsaken. Their Father is with them; even their persecution is part of his divine will (26,39.42).

---

[22] Luke uses "God" in place of Matthew's "your Father" (Luke 12,6).
[23] D.C. ALLISON, Jr, "The hairs of your head", 334.
[24] See W. WIEFEL, *Matthäus*, 200.

1.2.2 The Invaluable Children

The inference (οὖν) of the "sparrow story" is given in v.31 with the concluding consolatory imperative: "fear not" (μὴ ...φοβεῖσθε), and with the assertion: "you (ὑμεῖς emphatic) are of more value than many sparrows".

The command "fear not" in v.31 comes as the climax of a set of three "fear not" imperatives in the unit 10,26-31. In the first two "fear not" commands, the disciples are given two other reasons for why they should not fear their persecutors. In 10,26 Jesus tells the disciples, "So have no fear of them; for nothing is covered that will not be revealed, or hidden that will not be known." The revelation of the truth is definite. Today their enemies may oppose their mission and persecute them, but "God will see to it that truth will be victorious."[25] They can boldly proclaim the message of Jesus. It is the truth, and it will not deceive them (10,27). The second "fear not" command shows the inability of the persecutors to do anything against the soul. They can kill only the body; they are not the ones who should be feared. The disciples should fear rather the one who can destroy both body and soul in hell (10,28).[26]

The teaching in vv.29-30 focuses on the involvement of the Father's knowledge and will in all the things that happen in the life of the disciples and of all the creatures. In that context, we may interpret the "fear" mentioned in v.31 as the mental agony and crisis the disciples may experience during persecution.[27] When they undergo the tortures of the enemies, they may even doubt whether God really knows their suffering or not! Is he with them or has he abandoned them?[28] If God has not forsaken them why does he allow their enemies to crush them? If the disciples are confident of their identity and worth and of their Father's care for them, such a fear will not strike them; even if it shakes them for a while, they can readily overcome it. The sparrow

---

[25] W.D. DAVIES – D.C. ALLISON, *Matthew*, II, 203.

[26] See I.H. MARSHALL, "Fear Him who Can Destroy", 276-280.

[27] In fact, by presenting God as the Father of the disciples, Jesus has already shown their great worth in contrast to the sparrows in 10,29. He affirms it again in v.31. If the fall of a sparrow (ἓν ἐξ αὐτῶν) to the ground happens only with the knowledge and consent of their Father, what about the sufferings and persecutions of the disciples who are of more value than many (πολλῶν) sparrows?

[28] Consider the way the enemies of Jesus interpreted his suffering and death. They derided him saying, "If you are the Son of God, come down from the cross"; "He saved others; he cannot save himself"; "He trusts in God; let God deliver him now" (27,39-43). Even Jesus himself cried out, "My God, my God, why have you forsaken me" (27,47).

story encourages the disciples to believe that they are the Father's precious children;[29] he cannot and will not abandon them in their sufferings.[30]

One may still ask: if the disciples are God's precious children how can he permit them to be persecuted and killed? Does not Jesus' soothing promise sound rather absurd considering the reality of persecution? In fact, only an authentic child of God can comprehend and live this seemingly paradoxical reality. For many, life is only an episode that begins with birth and ends with death. They may see sufferings and death as a terrible tragedy, as they believe that with death everything comes to an end. Probably, the persecutors share this vision of life. That may be the reason why they use threats, torments and death as a means to silence the children of God. They do not realize that they can only kill them but nothing more than that (v.28). But the disciples' vision of life is different. They are called to be the children of God. For them, life in this world is not the end but a transitory stage. After death they will continue their life in their Father's home. That does not mean that they can just ignore their life in this world. Quite the opposite, this interim period is an opportunity given to them to live as the children of the Father. By following the Son and doing his words they will become worthy of entering their eternal home. If that is the case, when they are persecuted and killed for the sake of the Son and his mission, why should they fear? In fact, they should rejoice and be glad for having received this grace (5,10-12).

1.3 *Assimilation into the Sonship of Jesus through the Mission*

In the foregoing analysis we have seen how Jesus emboldens the disciples to face the persecutions that result from their involvement in the mission, as the authentic children of the Father. In actual fact, their participation in the mission itself can be viewed as a process through which they are assimilated into the Sonship of Jesus.

1.3.1 Participation in the Mission of the Son

The mission the disciples are entrusted with is the same mission that Jesus himself is involved in. In fact, it is the mission of the Father. He is the Lord of

---

[29] See J. CHRYSOSTOM, *Homilies*, 34:2-3, 228-229. As F.W. BEARE, *Matthew*, 248, remarks, "'Of more value than many sparrows' seems like a weak assurance, when the value of the sparrows has been set so low! The thought is, of course, that they are of incomparable value in God's sight."

[30] "Surely, the love which the Father has for his children will manifest itself, and is something the persecuted can turn to in trust and hope." J.J. KILGALLEN, *Matthew*, 88.

the harvest, and it is he who sends labourers into his harvest (9,37-38). The Son, the authorized emissary of the Father, delegates this authority to his disciples (10,1). Thus, they are given power to partake in his ministry of preaching, teaching and healing (see 4,23; 9,35; 10,1.7-8; 28,20). As the Father sent him, Jesus sends them (ἀπέστειλεν) to proclaim the good news of the kingdom (see 4,17.23; 10,5.7). They need to go without precautionary measures for their sustenance, trusting in the providence of God, as he did (see 8,20; 10,9-10).[31] So close is the identity between Jesus and the missionaries that those who receive them receive the Son himself and the Father who sent the Son (10,40).[32] Doubtless, their participation in the Son's mission will cause them to have a share also in his destiny (10,38; 16,24).

1.3.2 Sharing the Fate of the Son

The Son came to the world as a light to those who sat in darkness (4,16); his compassionate mission brought solace to the helpless and the harassed (9,36); he invited the weary and the tired to come to him offering them rest (11,29); and he was gentle and meek, his yoke was easy and burden light (11,30). But, paradoxically, he was received with calumnies, floggings and finally a degrading death on the cross. The disciples who engage in his mission will be treated the same way.[33] Not only an abundant harvest awaits them but also slavering wolves (10,16). They too will be delivered up to the councils, flogged and dragged before kings and governors (10,17-18). Even the members of their family will turn against them as they belong no more to their household (10,21-22.35-36). At the same time, it gives them a confirmation that they are like their master and belong to his household (10,24-25). Thus through their mission, the disciples partake in the sufferings of the Son and identify with him in his carrying the cross (10,38; 16,24; see 1Cor 4,10-13).[34]

Persecution and death are not the last words in the disciples' life. Jesus promises, "he who loses his life for my sake will find it" (10,39). By losing their physical life they give witness to the mission of the Son. Thus they acknowledge before the world their solidarity with the Son and with the

---

[31] For a detailed comparison between the mission of Jesus and the mission of the disciples, see D.R. BAUER, *The Structure*, 57-60.

[32] See G.M. SOARES PRABHU, "Following Jesus in Mission", 35.

[33] See the thrice repeated expression, "for my (name's) sake" (10,18.22.39). G. MANGATT, "Reflections on the Apostolic Discourse", 198.

[34] See, S. BROWN, "The Mission to Israel", 78, for a list of the parallel passages which refer to the mission and suffering of Jesus and that of the disciples.

Father who sent him. In return, the Son will acknowledge them as his own before the Father (10,32; 7,21) and receive them into eternal life.[35]

The mission Jesus entrusts to his disciples is a challenging mission. Though they are sent with the good news of the kingdom, they will not be received by all with great enthusiasm. On the contrary, they will be rejected and persecuted by the enemies of the kingdom and even by their own flesh and blood. Jesus does not promise the disciples that God will fight on their behalf and destroy their enemies. Rather, he strengthens them to face the challenge boldly as God's children. Their involvement in the mission and enduring persecution are part of their belonging to the household (οἰκιακούς) of Jesus (10,25). Through the mission and the resulting sufferings they are assimilated into the Sonship of Jesus, and they bear testimony to their heavenly Father, to Jesus and to their own identity as the children of the Father. Their Father is not unaware of, or indifferent to, their sufferings. They are his precious children; he will be with them in their trials and tribulations; and his Spirit will speak on behalf of them before their enemies.

2. **The Father, Children and the Kingdom (13,43)**

Jesus begins his ministry proclaiming the kingdom and inviting the people to prepare to receive it (4,17). In the SM he presents entry into the kingdom as the goal of the disciples' life in the world (5,20; 7,21). We have seen that only in the kingdom will the disciples have an irrevocable filial relationship with the Father, and only those who live as the authentic children of the Father in the earthly stage will have that privilege (5,20; 7,21-23). Jesus speaks more elaborately on the kingdom in the Parable Discourse (PD). A series of eight parables in this discourse describe the priceless nature of the kingdom and point out the process one has to go through to attain it (13,1-58).

The appellation πατήρ for God appears only once in the PD, in the explanation of the Parable of the Weeds (13,43).[36] God is presented here as the Father of the righteous who have done their part well in the world and are received into the kingdom.

---

[35] See T. KAYALAPARAMBIL, "The Missionary Discourse", 254.

[36] The Parable of the Weeds (13,24-30) and its explanation (13,36-43) are unique to Matthew within the NT; an abbreviated version of the parable is found in the gospel of Thomas, 57. See J. LIEBENBERG, *The Language of the Kingdom*, 177-224, for a comparative study of these texts.

2.1 *The Children in the Kingdom*

We have seen that in Matthew Jesus speaks about the Father only to his followers, and whenever he refers to God as the Father of human beings, he uses a second person pronoun (ὑμῶν/σου), implicitly presenting his followers as the children of the Father. Matt 13,43 is an exception. Here, concluding the explanation of the Parable of the Weeds (13,36-43), Jesus tells his disciples: "Then the righteous will shine like the sun in the kingdom of their Father" (πατρὸς αὐτῶν). It is the only passage where God is referred to as the Father of human beings with the pronoun "their", which stands for its antecedent "the righteous" in the context. Who are these righteous who shine in their Father's kingdom? In the Parable of the Weeds (13,24-30) and in its explanation (13,36-43) they are symbolically presented as the wheat gathered at the time of the harvest (13,30.43). Like a seed which goes through a long process from its sowing to yielding a crop, these righteous have gone through a lengthy process in the world before they shine in their Father's kingdom. We may identify them as the true disciples of Jesus who have lived as the authentic children of the Father in the world and are received into the kingdom.[37] Let us briefly look at the process they have gone through from their origin to the reception into their Father's kingdom.

2.1.1 Sown by the Son of Man

The parable (13,24-30) and its explanation (13,36-43) describe the origin and growth of the righteous. First of all, they are sown by the Son of Man (37). This title "Son of Man", which Jesus uses frequently in the gospel to speak about himself, appears immediately in v.41 referring to him as the owner of the kingdom (τῆς βασιλείας αὐτοῦ).[38] Sowing is an activity that

---

[37] The narrative transition in 13,36, where it is reported that Jesus dismissed the crowd and went into the house, is significant. This transition divides the PD into two sections: 13,1-35 and 13,36-52. In that division the Parable of the Weeds is separated into two parts. The first part appears in the first section where the parable is told to an open crowd (24-30), but its interpretation is in the second section where the recipients are only the disciples (36-43). See S. GRASSO, *Matteo*, 356; D.A. HAGNER, "Matthew's Parables of the Kingdom", 103.

[38] The Son of Man sayings appear in Matthew with a variety of implied meanings. Hagner makes a special note of the following three: i) the glorious coming of the apocalyptic Son of Man (10,23; 13,41; 24,30; 26,64 etc.); ii) the suffering and death of Jesus (Matt 17,12.22; 20,18 etc.); iii) the earthly ministry of Jesus (8,20; 9,6; 11,19; 12,8 etc.). See D.A. HAGNER, *Matthew 1–13*, 214.

causes a seed to sprout out the life within it.[39] This suggests that the righteous are initiated (sown) into the eternal life they are enjoying now in the kingdom by the one who has the authority to do so.

In the parable, the seeds are qualified as good seeds (καλὸν σπέρμα) as opposed to the weeds of the enemy. The quality of the seed depends on its prior source (see 7,17; 12,33). Since at the end God is presented as the Father of the righteous, we may attribute the goodness of the seeds to their origin from the Father. So, when they are sown, they have the potential to be the children of the Father, and it is that potential which germinates and grows. This interpretation is validated by the explanation of the good seeds as the "sons of the kingdom" and the weeds as the "sons of the evil one" in v.38. From the beginning they had the capacity to be subjects of the kingdom.[40]

In 8,12, the same phrase "sons of the kingdom" is used for the people who will be thrown out into the outer darkness. There, "sons of the kingdom" stand in contrast to the pagan centurion who confesses his faith in Jesus. In that context "sons of the kingdom" refers clearly to the people who have a right to the kingdom but lose it due to their unbelief in Jesus.[41] This underscores the fact that being sown as the sons of the kingdom alone does not guarantee a good yield. If a seed does not grow properly, it will not be able to bear fruit. In that case, it will have the same fate as the weeds on the day of harvest (3,10; 7,19). From what we have seen in the previous chapters of our study, the same can be said about the discipleship of Jesus. Everyone who decides to follow Jesus is a potential child of the kingdom. But following is an ongoing process, and only when they produce fruit according to their identity will they be worthy of the kingdom (see 7,21-23).

Their identity as the "sons of the kingdom" as opposed to the "sons of the evil one"[42] in seminal form, and their privilege of being sown by the Son of Man as opposed to the devil, suggest an involvement of grace even at their origin. They were initiated to this world as the sons of the kingdom

---

[39] As M.L. BAILEY, "The Parable of the Tares", 271, suggests, the use of the present participle (σπείρων) may reflect the fact that the sowing by the Son of Man is continuing throughout the present age.

[40] For the interpretation of sons of the kingdom as "the subjects of the kingdom" see M. ZERWICK – M. GROSVENOR, *Grammatical Analysis*, 44.

[41] The "sons of the kingdom" is a useful designation for the good seeds sown by the Son of Man because it "provides a bridge between the historic people of God (as the natural heirs of the kingdom – 8,12) and the actualisation of kingdom membership that is taking place with the coming of Jesus." J. NOLLAND, *Matthew*, 559.

[42] See John 8,44.

gratuitously.[43] To the question, why the others were left as the sons of the devil, we have no answer.

2.1.2 Grown with the Weeds

The wheat had to face many troubles during its growth. The enemy did all that he could to thwart its growth and its bearing fruit.[44] The weeds that grew with it might have taken away the water and manure given to it or might have prevented it from absorbing the sunlight.[45] When the householder (οἰκοδεσπότης)[46] was alerted to the danger, he did not allow his servants to remove the weeds so that the wheat might not be destroyed together with them. Thus he let the weeds grow with his wheat until the harvest. The wheat that resisted the weeds during its growth produced good yield.

The growth of the wheat together with the weeds alludes to the actual situation of the world where the sons of the kingdom are called to bear fruit. They need to withstand the destructive oppositions of the enemy, "all causes of sin and all evildoers" (13,41). This reminds us of the various challenges the disciples are warned of in the gospel, from the lures and temptations of the world (6,24; 19,22; 20,20-28) to the persecution and death they might undergo (5,10-12; 10,16-18.22-25; 24,9), during their journey before being received into the kingdom of their Father.

From the description of their origin and growth, it is clear that the sons of the kingdom, in spite of all the opposition from the enemy, had protection from the Son of Man, the one who sowed them, and that they grew as his beloved ones. He spared even the weeds, sprouted out of the seeds the enemy

---

[43] Therefore, as M. GREEN, *The Message of Matthew*, 157 observes, these righteous owe their position in the kingdom entirely to the initiative of the Son of Man.

[44] In the interpretation of the parable the enemy is identified as the devil (διάβολος) in v.39, who is also portrayed as the evil one (πονηρός) in v.38. The devil is the tempter (4,3). He tries even to tempt (πειράζω) Jesus and deter him from the way of the Father (4,1-11). He will also not leave the disciples; see the way he works in Peter (16,23 ["Satan" is the Hebrew word for the devil]). He has also human agents to do his work of tempting (see, 16,1; 19,3; 22,18.35). The disciples are warned against temptation and are asked to pray to the Father to be spared from falling into temptations (6,13; 26,41). Doubtless, to grow together with the sons of the devil is a great challenge for the sons of the kingdom.

[45] The Greek word ζιζάνιον apparently refers to a noxious tare that closely resembles wheat especially in its early stages. See BAGD, 339; D. HARRINGTON, *Matthew*, 204; C.S. KEENER, *Matthew*, 242. The metaphor of the seeds the devil sowed and cultivated as weeds might represent the people "who appear to be somewhat like Jesus' followers but whose basic allegiance will be made plain at the final harvest" (see 7,21-23). R.H. MOUNCE, *Matthew*, 131.

[46] See 10,25; 13,52; 20,1.11; 21,33; 24,43.

sowed, from destruction in order to save them. In the gospel the disciples are presented as the most beloved ones of Jesus. Just before the PD, he publicly acknowledges that his disciples who do the will of his Father are his brothers, sisters and mother (12,50). In the PD they are treated as a privileged group which has been given to know the secrets of the kingdom of heaven (13,11). It is only to them that he reveals the Father (11,27), to them that he entrusts his mission (10,5-15; 28,16-20).

The image of wheat maturing along with the weeds until the harvest addresses an existential situation the disciples encounter in their lives in the world.[47] As one looks around, one sees many people who do not listen to the word of Jesus or believe in him. Many prefer to enter through the broad gate (7,13) and lead a life counter to the values of the kingdom. Moreover, some of them plot against the sons of the kingdom, persecute them and annihilate them (10,16-39).[48] In spite of their wicked ways, they often flourish and triumph over the sons of the kingdom. They might even mock the sons for their faith in God saying, "He trusts in God; let God deliver him now" (27,43). The natural question could be: why does God their Father permit all these evils? Why doesn't he come down from the heavens and intervene directly for their cause, burn the wicked alive and rescue his children (see Luke 9,54)?[49] The response of the owner of the field to his servants, who offer their service to pull up the weeds immediately, shows the approach of the Father. There is no other way; the children have to coexist with the wicked and wait until the harvest to be separated from them. In fact, here lies the challenge of discipleship. They cannot escape from this world and from its temptations and threats, but they must face them as the authentic children of their Father. They need to continue their journey until the day of the harvest, when they will be judged "righteous".[50]

---

[47] We may identify the servants of the householder (see, 10,24-25) as the disciples of Jesus (they address him as κύριος). Their question to the master betrays their confusion regarding the present situation: "from where do the weeds come?" (13,27). See J.D. KINGSBURY, *The Parables*, 68; R. FABRIS, *Matteo*, 306; R.H. SMITH, *Matthew*, 175; D.A. HAGNER, *Matthew 1–13*, 383.

[48] As Kingsbury suggests, the enemy (ἐχθρός) in the parable (13,25) can be understood in the same sense as it is in 10,36, "the person with whom the disciple comes into conflict because of his allegiance to Jesus." J.D. KINGSBURY, *The Parables*, 70.

[49] Many authors have identified the problem of evil and delay of judgement as the main concern addressed in the parable. See O. DA SPINETOLI, *Matteo*, 392-394; R. FABRIS, *Matteo*, 306-307; C.L. BLOMBERG, *Interpreting the Parables*, 200; S. GRASSO, *Matteo*, 349; D.A. HAGNER, "Matthew's Parables of the Kingdom", 109.

[50] See H. WEDER, *Die Gleichnisse Jesu*, 128.

2.1.3 Judged as the Righteous

The imagery used in connection with the harvest in the parable is allegorically explained as referring to the events at the time of the eschatological judgement (see συντέλεια αἰῶνός in vv.39-40) when the separation of the wheat and weeds takes place.[51] The prediction of the separation of the righteous (δίκαιος) from the wicked appears again in 13,49; 25,37 and 25,46. Though the adjective δίκαιος appears seventeen times in Matthew with different connotations, in the above eschatological contexts it refers specifically to the people who have really lived according to the will of God and hence are chosen for the eternal reward.

The sons of the kingdom who grew together with the weeds and yet produced a yield would be judged as the righteous. From their qualification as the "righteous" it is evident that these people who were sown as "the sons of the kingdom" have done their part. Once they are judged as the righteous, they will be received into the kingdom (13,43; 25,46). This adjective also recalls Jesus' demand for an exceeding righteousness (δικαιοσύνη) from the disciples in order for them to enter the kingdom (5,20; see 6,1.33).[52]

2.1.4 Received as the Children

As the wheat is gathered into the barn, the righteous are received into the kingdom of "their Father". They are the true heirs of it, because it is their Father's. It has been prepared for them from the foundation of the world (25,34). It is this kingdom that they passionately sought after in their life (6,33); for the realization of it they prayed every day to the Father (6,11). Now, their journey has come to its destination; here they have no more trials,

---

[51] The metaphor of the harvest is used also in the OT for the final judgement (see Jer 51,33 [ἄμητος]; Hos 6,11 [τρυγάω]; Joel 3,13 [τρύγητος]; also Rev 14,15-16). For more references see A.J. HULTGREN, *The Parables of Jesus*, 297; J. LIEBENBERG, *The Language of the Kingdom*, 193-194.

[52] This qualification, "the righteous", is a good reason for us to find here a reference to the authentic disciples who have lived out their identity in the world. They are the ones who have withstood "all causes of sin" (τὰ σκάνδαλα, 16,23; 18,7) and "all evil doers" (ποιοῦντας τὴν ἀνομίαν, 7,23; 23,28; 24,12). See Ch. I,3.1.1; see also R. FABRIS, *Matteo*, 313-314; D.A. HAGNER, "Matthew's Parables of the Kingdom", 112. As R.H. SMITH, *Matthew*, 178, mentions, "All the many judgement scenes in Matthew reveal God's own hunger and thirst for human deeds of righteousness and mercy and love, and God's sharp criticism of lawlessness or indifference to the needs of the neighbour (3:10; 7:23,24-27; 13:47-50; 21:28-32; 22:11-14; and especially 25:31-46)."

no persecution, and no temptations. Here they dwell as the perfect children of their perfect Father (5,48).

Their present status as the children of the Father is elucidated also in the description of their blissful appearance in the kingdom: "They will shine like the sun in the kingdom." Since God himself is the source of all light (see Ps 84,12; Isa 9,2; Hab 3,4), their shining like the sun can be taken as a proof of their being in God's presence.[53] The same simile of "shining like the sun"[54] is used for Jesus in the Transfiguration (17,2) where the Father acknowledges the Son saying, "This is my beloved Son, with whom I am well pleased" (17,5). As the Son is manifested with the glory of the Father, these children, who followed the Son in words and deeds (7,24), are manifested here with the same glory.[55]

The sun is the greatest source of light known to human beings. So shining like the sun may be understood as their radiating the light par excellence. This recalls Jesus' command to the disciples to shine their light before men so that they may glorify their Father (5,16). During their journey in the world they already had the light, and they were the light (5,14). They shone this light before others and led them to glorify their Father, and now they radiate this light in its fullness in the kingdom.

2.2 *The Journey towards the Paternal Home*

In the above analysis, we have seen how the Parable of the Weeds and its explanation depict the origin, growth process, and "fruit-bearing" of the disciples. They are sown as good seeds and are expected to yield good crops. However, the process in between is not that easy; they have to grow despite the opposition of the enemy who attempts to destroy them. It is implied in the parable that only those who withstand the enemy and his seeds will be able to produce a yield, be judged righteous, and be received into their Father's kingdom.

---

[53] See J.D. KINGSBURY, *The Parables*, 108.

[54] While in 17,2 the verb λάμπω is used for "shining", in 13,43 ἐκλάμπω – "shining out". Both are from the same family.

[55] The shining of the righteous like the sun seems to allude to Dan 12,3 where it is mentioned that the wise shall shine like the brightness of the firmament. See F.W. BEARE, *Matthew*, 313; W. WIEFEL, *Matthäus*, 260. If that is true,the wise (οἱ συνιέντες) in Daniel can be compared to the wise (ἀνήρ φρόνιμος) in Matt 7,24ff. See D. HARRINGTON, *Matthew*, 206.

The parable treats the life of the disciples in two stages: their life in this world and their life in the Father's kingdom.[56] No doubt, the life in this world is viewed as a preparatory phase for life in their paternal home, the kingdom.[57] Some other parables in the PD also highlight these two stages of life and the process one must go through to reach the kingdom.

2.2.1 Hurdles on the Way

The Parable of the Sower and its explanation show the various hurdles they may experience in their journey towards their home (13,1-9.18-24). First of all, they have to understand (συνίημι) the message of the kingdom, which requires an openness to hear, a desire to know and a willingness to believe. It is not enough to receive the message of the kingdom joyfully; they must allow it to take root in their lives, lest they fade when they meet with persecution and rejection on account of the word (see 5,10-12; 10,16-39). They also must not forget that in the world they are growing along with the weeds, and therefore they must be cautious about the cares and delights of the world as they may obstruct their way to their paternal home (see 6,25-34; 19,16-24). Only those who overcome these oppositions and go forward can bear fruit and be received into their Father's kingdom (see 3,8.10; 7,17.18.19; 12,33).

2.2.2 The Unfolding Kingdom

The parables of the Mustard Seed and the Leaven (13,31-33) suggest that the kingdom reveals itself gradually in this world. In fact, the kingdom towards which the disciples are growing is already present in them (they are the "sons of the kingdom", the "good seeds" sown by the Son of Man).[58] Therefore, their growth towards the kingdom will necessarily cause the

---

[56] Presenting these two stages of human life, the parable exhorts the disciples of the present to grow as the sons of the kingdom. They are encouraged to pursue the reward of the children and are warned about the fate of the non-children.

[57] Referring to the aorist tenses in 13,24-28, Bailey identifies three phases of the kingdom in the Parable of the Weeds. According to him the first phase would pertain to the revelation and development of the purpose of God's kingdom in the OT. M.L. BAILEY, "The Doctrine of the Kingdom in Matthew 13", 445. This association with the OT seems to be imposed; the aorist in the parables may be taken as a narrative device rather than a theological guideline.

[58] The main purpose of these two parables is to show the dynamic power of the kingdom. Though the kingdom appears hidden in the present, it will grow and eventually permeate everything. These parables can be interpreted also as referring to the manifestation of the kingdom in and through the lives of the people who grow towards it. Cf. D.A. HAGNER, "Matthew's Parables of the Kingdom", 116, who considers this possibility as unlikely.

manifestation of the kingdom. As a mustard seed unfolds itself and becomes a tree (13,31-32), and as yeast mixed in with flour slowly but surely leavens the whole flour (13,33), so the kingdom grows and spreads out in them and through them as they grow as God's children (see 5,16).

All the same, as we have seen above, not all the seeds sown will produce fruit, but only the ones who withstand every opposition, be it internal or external. Sometimes the cost of this can be very high (see 19,21), but it is nothing compared to the priceless kingdom of their Father. The parables of the Hidden Treasure and the Pearl Merchant (13,44-46) demonstrate the preciousness of the kingdom. The ones who recognize its worth will have the desire to obtain it (compare 6,19-24), but those who want to obtain it will have to give up everything else.[59]

2.2.3 The Privileged

Explaining the purpose of his speaking in parables Jesus tells the disciples that it is given to them to know the secrets of the kingdom of heaven, but not to others (13,10-11). This saying not only emphasizes the privileged status of the disciples but also presents discipleship as a necessary condition to understand the secrets of the kingdom. The kingdom is of the Father (6,10;13,23), and the disciples, as his potential children, are given the knowledge of it as a gift.[60] As they grow more and more as the children of the Father they will come closer and closer to the kingdom, their paternal home, and finally they will be received into it. Though others are growing with them, they will not be given the same grace either to know the secret of the kingdom or to enter it. Rather they will be separated from the children at the end as good and bad fish are sorted by fishermen (13,47-49).[61]

The structural frame of the PD also invites us to understand the kingdom as the real home of the children of the Father. In the pericope that precedes the PD, when Jesus is told that his mother and brothers are waiting for him, he replies that his mother and brothers are the disciples who do the will of his Father in heaven (12,46-50). One's mother and brothers are indicators of one's family identity. Here Jesus defines his family relationships as not based

---

[59] See C.S. KEENER, *Matthew*, 245; C.L. BLOMBERG, *Interpreting the Parables*, 279.

[60] Consider the divine passive δέδοται in 13,11. It is God who gives the disciples the knowledge about the mysteries of the kingdom.

[61] The message of the Parable of the Net is the same as that of the Parable of the Weeds. The righteous and the wicked will grow together in the present world, but at the end they will be separated and judged. The righteous ones will be accepted and the wicked will be rejected (see 25,31-46). See H. WEDER, *Die Gleichnisse Jesu*, 123-124.

on his biological (earthly) identity but on his heavenly identity (see Luke 2,49).[62] In the pericope that follows the PD we find a similar situation. The people at the synagogue who are astonished at his wisdom speak about his family. They identify him as the son of the carpenter and Mary and the brother of James, Joseph, Simon and Judah (13,53-58). The evangelist comments in 13,57 that they took offence at him. What was their offence? We may interpret it as their failure to recognize his heavenly identity and their attempt to confine him to his biological family. Jesus reacts to this very strongly. The evangelist interprets the people's attitude as unbelief (ἀπιστία), because of which Jesus did not do many mighty works there (13,58). Now the PD, where Jesus speaks about the kingdom using different parables, can be seen as his presentation of the heavenly home which transcends the earthly home and family ties. No wonder others will not fathom it, given that they do not belong to this heavenly family (13,10-15).

The righteous who shine in the kingdom of their Father (13,43) are the ideal disciples of Jesus who have lived in this world as the authentic children of the Father, fulfilling his will and following the exceeding righteousness taught by Jesus. Sown by the Son of Man as the sons of the kingdom, they grew together with the weeds sown by the devil. During their life in the world they resisted every attempt of the enemy to lead them astray, and they proved themselves true children of the Father, bearing fruit worthy of their identity.

3. **The Father, Children and the Community (18,14)**

In the opening verse of the Community Discourse (CD),[63] the disciples come to Jesus with a question "Who then is the greatest in the kingdom?"[64] This question does not seem to be a genuine question that emerges from their fervour to know more about the secrets of the kingdom (see 13,11); rather it is calculated to determine who among them is the greatest.[65] In effect, their

---

[62] It is significant to note that Jesus gives the PD on the "same day" (13,1) on which he speaks about his true family (12,46-50). See W. CARTER, "Challenging by Confirming", 416.

[63] This is the fourth of Jesus' Great Discourses in Matthew, and the audience of the discourse is his disciples. See W.G. THOMPSON, *Matthew's Advice*, 71-72, for a detailed discussion of the audience of the CD.

[64] See Mark 9,33-37; Luke 9,46-48.

[65] This interpretation is supported by the fact that when the disciples came to Jesus with this question, he was talking privately to Peter (see the phrase ἐν ἐκείνῃ τῇ ὥρᾳ). It might have bred

question betrays their human desire to be counted greater than the others. We are not sure whether they conceived the kingdom as a present reality or a future reality.[66] In any case, their question indicates that they had thought of themselves as worthy of inheriting it.

Presenting a child in their midst, Jesus tells them, "Truly, I say to you, unless you turn and become like children, you will never enter the kingdom of heaven" (18,3). Through this declaration Jesus seemingly corrects the assumption implied in their question that they all will inherit the kingdom. Afterwards he answers their question, "Whoever humbles himself like this child, he is the greatest in the kingdom of heaven" (18,4). In the subsequent verses of the CD Jesus instructs the disciples concerning their mutual relationship: their living and working together, their accepting, forgiving and supporting one another (18,6-22).[67]

God is referred to as the Father four times in this discourse, three times as the Father of Jesus (18,10.19.35) and once as the Father of the disciples (τοῦ πατρὸς ὑμῶν, 18,14).[68] As we have seen before, Jesus' use of the term "your Father" for God is a reminder to the disciples of their identity as the children. We shall examine how this reminder functions in its immediate context and in the whole context of the CD.

---

some jealousy in others. In addition, two of them come with their mother at a later point to request an honoured position for themselves in the kingdom (20,20-29). See ORIGEN, "Commentary on Matthew", 13:14, 482-483; D.A. CARSON, *Matthew 13–28*, 396. Some scholars consider the disciples' question in 18,1 as a general question. See R.H. GUNDRY, *Matthew: Mixed Church*, 359; U. LUZ, *Matthew 8–20*, 426.

[66] From the question of the disciples, it is not easy to decide whether they understood the kingdom as a present reality or a future reality. The Greek ἐστίν can refer both to the present and to the future. The interest of the disciples seems to be the present position. However the response of Jesus presents the kingdom as a future reality here (see the apodosis οὐ μὴ εἰσέλθητε εἰς τὴν βασιλείαν τῶν οὐρανῶν, in 18,3).

[67] See F. FOULKES, *A Guide to St Matthew's Gospel*, 159.

[68] The textual tradition is divided. Some manuscripts (B N Γ Θ 078. 0281 f^{13} 33. 579. 700. 892. 1241. 1424. *pm* $sy^{s.h}$) read μου instead of ὑμῶν (ℵ D K L W Δ f^{1} 565 *pm* latt $sy^{c.p.hmg}$). Most scholars favour ὑμῶν considering μου as an attempt to conform to the μου of 18,10. So, B.M. METZGER, *A Textual Commentary*, 45; J. GNILKA, *Matthäusevangelium*, II, 129; D.J. HARRINGTON, *Matthew*, 265; D.A. HAGNER, *Matthew 14–28*, 525; J. NOLLAND, *Matthew*, 740. For an opposing view cf. R.H. GUNDRY, *Matthew: Mixed Church*, 367. He admits that μου arises out of the parallel influence from v.10 but argues that Matthew loves parallelisms.

3.1 *The Father's Will for the Little Ones*

Matt 18,14 appears in the literary unit 18,6-14.[69] Describing how highly God regards the "little ones" (οἱ μικροί), Jesus tells the disciples here how they should treat them. This unit can be divided into two parts. In the first part, verses 6-9, a general exhortation against causing scandal to these little ones is given. The second part begins with an injunction to the disciples that they should not despise these little ones (v.10a); the reason for the injunction is specified in 10b.[70] It is followed by a parable (vv.12-13) in which the disciples are invited to consider the model of a shepherd who goes in search of his lost sheep and finds it. The shepherd will certainly rejoice more over the one which was lost and now is found than over the others which never went astray. Applying this parable to God's dealing with the little ones, Jesus says to the disciples that it is not the will of their Father (πατρὸς ὑμῶν) that any of them should perish (18,14).

3.1.1 The Little Ones

The expression "little ones" (οἱ μικροί) appears three times in the pericope (18,6.10.14). The same expression ἕνα τῶν μικρῶν τούτων appears in 10,42, where it refers explicitly to the disciples of Jesus. In 18,6 the little ones are qualified as the ones who believe in Jesus. They are presented here as vulnerable people who could be led astray. Their "faith and vulnerability" mirror the actual condition of the disciples. Though they believe in Jesus, as long as they are in the world they are susceptible to scandals.[71] Some of them may resist the scandals but the others may trip and fall.[72] These little ones are precious to God; so he does not want any of them be lost, though he respects

---

[69] We follow the division suggested by W. TRILLING, *Matthäus*, II, 130; J.P. MEIER, *Matthew*, 202. Several authors take verses 5-9 and 10-14 as separate units: W.G. THOMPSON, *Matthew's Advice*, 153; J. GNILKA, *Matthäusevangelium*, II, 124; D.A. HAGNER, *Matthew 14–28*, 515. But W.D. DAVIES – D.C. ALLISON, *Matthew*, II, 750, considers 6-9 (not 5-9) and 10-14 as two units.

[70] Verse 11 is omitted as it is not attested in the ancient versions. There is a fair consensus among the scholars that it is a gloss, an assimilation to Luke 19,10. See W.G. THOMPSON, *Matthew's Advice*, 156; F.W. BEARE, *Matthew*, 374; J. LAMBRECHT, *Out of the Treasure*, 38.

[71] The verb σκανδαλίζω and its noun σκάνδαλον appear six times in the present context (see 5,29-30; 11,6; 13,21.41.57; 15,12; 16,23; 17,27; 24,10; 26,31.33). As Harrington defines, "a scandal is a trap or stumbling block upon the way. In a religious or moral context it refers to temptation to sin or enticement to apostasy." D.J. HARRINGTON, *Matthew*, 264.

[72] Jesus has warned them often about this danger. In fact, as we have seen in the explanation of the Parable of the Weeds, it is their challenge to grow together with the weeds without being affected by them.

their freedom to go astray (v.12). Therefore, whoever causes them to stumble is an enemy of God, and he will not go unpunished (vv.6-9).[73]

In verse 18,10 the disciples are told that they should not despise (καταφρονέω) any of the little ones. The verb καταφρονέω is used in 6,24 conveying a strong contempt for as opposed to an affective faithfulness (ἀντέχω) to somebody. The despising of the other signals that one does not consider the other as worthy of respect. Jesus' warning in 18,10, saying that the angels of these little ones always behold the face of his Father, functions as a response to such an attitude.[74] Measured by worldly standards, all who follow Jesus may not be of equal calibre and competence.[75] That does not mean that they are insignificant and worthless. They are represented in heaven by their angels, who are continually in the presence of the Father.[76]

In the context of the CD, these admonitions of Jesus seem to be aimed at every individual disciple, asking them to take care of their fellow-disciples. Therefore, as in 10,42, the "little ones" in the CD also refers most likely to the disciples; evidently, each one of them is a "little one", who is to be cared for and supported by others.[77]

---

[73] Scandals can come from outsiders who do not belong to the family of the Father or from insiders who walk together as the children of the Father. In the present context, while the impersonal third person usages in vv.6-7 seem to refer to scandals in general (from the outsiders?), the direct second person usages in vv.8-9 point to the sins caused by insiders.

[74] It reflects the common belief that God has appointed a "guardian angel" for each person – an idea which is well attested in Jewish sources: Pss 34,7; 91,11; 1QH 5,20; Jub 35,17. See W.D. DAVIES – D.C. ALLISON, *Matthew*, II, 770, for more Jewish and Hellenistic references on guardian angels. According to Matt 24,36, the angels belong to the celestial hierarchy (angels…Son…Father). See ORIGEN, "Commentary on Matthew", 13:26-28, 490-491; W.G. THOMPSON, *Matthew's Advice*, 154.

[75] Some scholars qualify the "little ones" as "the insignificant disciples"; cf. J.P. MEIER, *Matthew*, 202-203.

[76] We may assume that these angels are the intercessors or mediators between the Father and the little ones (Job 33,23; Tob 12,15); see W.D. DAVIES – D.C. ALLISON, *Matthew*, II, 770. Or as Thompson writes, "Whatever the precise nuance, this doctrinal statement teaches that through their angels in heaven 'these little ones' constantly enjoy a special relationship to the Father." W.G. THOMPSON, *Matthew's Advice*, 154.

[77] So also W.G. THOMPSON, *Matthew's Advice*, 119; U. LUZ, *Matthew 8–20*, 434; R.T. FRANCE, *Matthew*, 271-272; D.A. CARSON, *Matthew 13–28*, 398-399; J. NOLLAND, *Matthew*, 735.

3.1.2 The Father's Will as the Model for the Children

We have already seen the "will of the Father" as his divine programme revealed through the life and mission of Jesus.[78] According to this divine programme the Father has sent his Son to the world to save everyone, and he does not want any one to perish (9,13; 20,28; 26,28; see John 3,16-17; 1Tim 2,4; 2Pet 3,9).[79] Since the disciples are living in the world, they might be influenced by the attractions of the world to go away from their Father.[80] If that happens, is it possible for them to come back and continue their journey? The answer we get from 18,12-14 is affirmative.[81] The little ones are the Father's beloved children, who believe in the Son and participate in his mission; he certainly will not want any of them be lost. Like a good shepherd who loves his sheep, he takes the initiative and goes in search of the lost ones to find them (see Ezek 34,10-11.13.16).[82] Jesus emphatically says (ἀμὴν λέγω ὑμῖν) that the shepherd will rejoice over the lost-and-now-found more than over the rest which never went astray.[83]

In this context Jesus' using the term "your Father" for God functions as a reminder to the disciples of their identity and their journey as the Father's

---

[78] Ch. I,3.3.3 d).

[79] A sentence added by some later manuscripts (D L^{mg} W Θ^{c} 078^{vid} 𝔐 lat sy$^{c.p.h}$ bo^{pt}) after v.10: ηλθεν γαρ ο υιος του ανθρωπου σωσαι το απολωλος, explains this aspect clearly.

[80] As C.J. CADOUX, *The Historic Mission of Jesus*, 216-217, points out, the idea of loss (ἀπόλλυμι) forms in the present context "the exact antithesis of 'salvation'. It stands for the fate of those who stray from God's purpose for them." See also Matt 10,6; 15,24.

[81] In 18,12-13 Matthew gives the Parable of the Lost Sheep. A similar parable is found also in Luke 15,3-7, in the gospel of Thomas, 107, and in the gospel of Truth 31-32. For a comparative study of their forms, origin, setting and theology see W.L. PETERSEN, "The Parable of the Lost Sheep", 128-147; J. LAMBRECHT, *Out of the Treasure*, 37-52; A.J. HULTGREN, *The Parables of Jesus*, 46-63.

[82] The shepherd's leaving the ninety-nine on the mountains (Luke 15,4 in the wilderness) and going in search of the lost is significant. As A.J. HULTGREN, *The Parables of Jesus*, 54, puts it, "If the shepherd leaves the ninety-nine sheep in a protected enclosure in order to go fetch the one that is lost, he is simply being portrayed as frugal. But if he (quickly) abandons them to search for the one that is lost, he is being portrayed as one who is willing to risk all he has for the sake of the one that is lost." However, there is no assurance that the shepherd will always find the lost ones. See the conditional clause, "if he finds" in 18,13. See W.G. THOMPSON, *Matthew's Advice*, 164.

[83] This attitude of God towards his children presented here throws light on another theological issue which we have discussed in our study of the model prayer (6,13). Does the Father lead his children into temptation? Verse 18,14 tells us that he will not do anything that leads to the destruction of his children. If the children fall into temptation, it is their choice. The Father respects their choice, though he does not wish them to be lost.

children.[84] Elsewhere in the gospel, seeking and doing the Father's will (θέλημα) are presented as the hallmark of the children (6,10; 7,21; 12,50; 21,31; 26,42). In fact, it is the doing of the will of the Father that makes them members of the Father's family (12,50); and it will be the sole criterion by which they will be judged as the children or non-children on the last day (7,21).

As in everything else, in their dealings with their brothers and sisters, their identity as the children of the Father should be the guiding principle of the disciples' behaviour. In fact, each one of them is a "little one"; each may have his own strengths and weaknesses. Some of them even go away from their family. But they should treat each other as their Father would treat them (5,48). He does not want any one of them to be scandalized, to be looked down upon, or to be lost.[85]

3.2 *The Community as God's Family*

We can observe that family imagery permeates the CD. God is the Father of that family, and Jesus and disciples are his children (see 18,10.14.19.35). This family provides a great opportunity for them to grow as the children. Those who become true children will inherit their heavenly home, the kingdom (18,3).

As the children of the Father, they are brothers and sisters[86] (see 18,15.21.35). In the discourse Jesus prepares his brothers and sisters to live as true members of this family. He presents the Father as the model for their life. They need to follow his will in their dealing with others. When one of their brothers sins against them, they should take all measures to win him back. When all attempts fail (so that he refuses to listen even to the church), then they should treat him like a Gentile and a tax-collector, which means they should not imitate his manner of life (18,15-17; see 5,46-47; 6,7).[87] The

---

[84] As J. LIEBENBERG, *The Language of the Kingdom*, 421-422, observes, "The use of τοῦ πατρὸς ὑμῶν here is bound to catch attention since the phrase used in v.10 was τοῦ πατρός μου. This has the clear implication that Jesus' actions were validated by the Father himself. [...] since Jesus' Father is also their Father, they ought to behave the same way he does towards the 'little ones'."

[85] Jesus fulfils the will of the Father, carrying out the role of the good shepherd in his mission (see 15,24; 26,31; also John 10).

[86] In the Greek text only brothers (ἀδελφός) are mentioned; but cf. 12,50.

[87] Thompson gives an insightful interpretation for the rather obscure saying of 18,16 on "binding and loosing": "Each time the brother refuses to accept the fact of his sinfulness, he and the disciple (along with the witnesses and 'the church') bind his guilt more closely to his

Father does not want any of his children be lost; all the same, he will not be indifferent to them if they scandalize or despise their own brethren (18,7-10).

The Father wants all his children to live joyfully and peacefully in this family. They should forgive their brothers and sisters without limit (18,21-22). Though they are children, each one of them is free to break his/her relationship and go away from the family of the Father (18,12-13; see also the "if clauses" in verses 15-17). But he forgives his children in an unlimited way; he releases all their debts when they beseech him (18,23-27). He wants his children to treat others in the same way. But if they do not forgive their brethren, he too will not forgive them (18,35; see 6,14-15).[88] Left without any excuse, they will be rejected by the Father and will be punished for all their debts (18,34).

In the context of the CD, Jesus' reference to God as "your Father" re-emphasizes the filial identity of the disciples. Every disciple is a child of the Father; thus all of them are brothers and sisters. This identity as the children of the Father should be the criterion for their relationship in the community. They should treat each other as their Father treats them. The disciples are addressed here as the "little ones". No one is perfect; all of them have their strengths and weaknesses. As long as they are in the world they are susceptible to temptations and scandals. But they should not cause their brethren to stumble; they should not despise them or consider them insignificant, but they should love and forgive them even if they go astray. That is the will of their Father, and that is what the children should seek.

4. **The True and the Only Father of the Children (23,9)**

The last of the "Father" appellations for God in relation to the disciples in Matthew occurs in 23,9, within the Final Discourse (FD) of Jesus.[89] This

---

person. But when the brother listens to the correction and accepts his objective guilt, they release his sin. Both actions are immediately ratified in heaven." W.G. THOMPSON, *Matthew's Advice*, 202.

[88] See the nature of forgiveness Jesus demands from the disciples. They should forgive their brethren from their heart (ἀπὸ τῶν καρδιῶν ὑμῶν); such forgiveness must be total and personal; it "excludes all casuistry and legalism". R.T. FRANCE, *Matthew*, 278.

[89] As regards the delimitation of the FD, we follow the scholars who consider chapters 23–25 as a unified whole with two parts 23,1-39 and 24,1–26,1. See W. GRUNDMANN, *Matthäus*, 480-481; J. DUPONT, *Les Béatitudes*, III, 467-468; F.W. BEARE, *Matthew*, 445-447; R.H.

verse belongs to the literary unit 23,1-12 where Jesus, referring to the lifestyle of the scribes and Pharisees, admonishes his followers to live without being influenced by the bad example of these religious leaders. Besides this, in the FD the term πατήρ for God appears two more times: once in an absolute form (24,36) and another referring to him as the Father of Jesus (25,34).

In 23,9 Jesus tells the disciples, "Call no man your father on earth, for one is your Father, the heavenly one." This injunction of Jesus has a triple function in the context: i) it once again reminds the disciples of their real identity as the children of the Father; ii) it gives the rationale for the mode of conduct demanded from them in the pericope (see 23,1-12); iii) it functions as a key for understanding the eschatological sayings that follow in chapters 24 and 25.

4.1 *The Identity of the Disciples as the Children of the Father*

People use the title "father" normally to address their biological father. Sometimes, it is used also as a title of respect. In either case, it reveals the kind of relationship – biological or sociological – existing between two persons.

When Jesus says that the disciples should call no man father on earth, he does not seem to deny their existential relationship with their biological fathers. His charge rather calls attention to their heavenly identity in contrast with their earthly identity. It is true that they were born of human parents and are living in the world, but in reality their existence here on earth is temporary. After a short while, all will have to leave this world and all this-worldly relationships. Therefore, though they are in the world, they are not of the world (see John 15,19; 17,14-16). Similarly, their real father is not the one whom they see on earth but the one who is in heaven (see Mal 2,10).[90] They are God's children. However, this realization of one's true identity as a child of the Father is given as a gift of faith. Those who consider their earthly existence as their ultimate existence cannot experience God as their Father.

The injunction in 23,9 can be taken also as a prohibition against using "father" as a title of honour.[91] Unlike in verses 8 and 10, the verb in v.9 is

---

GUNDRY, *Matthew: Mixed Church*, 453; E. KRENTZ, "Community and Character", 566-568; K. STOCK, *Discorso della Montagna*, 2; J. NOLLAND, *Matthew*, 920.

[90] See Jesus' definition of his kinship relationship in 12,50.

[91] Zerwick notes that πατήρ was an honorary title, especially in addressing the members of the High Council. M. ZERWICK – M. GROSVENOR, *Grammatical Analysis*, 74; see G. DALMAN, *The Words of Jesus*, 339 for the use of *abba*, the Hebrew equivalent of πατήρ before the names

given in the active form (μὴ καλέσητε), which means it is not a command against their seeking the title for themselves but against using it to address others. Now, who are the people whom the disciples may address using the title "father"? As scholars point out, the first pronoun ὑμῶν in v.9 can be interpreted either as a partitive genitive or as an adjective that qualifies πατέρα. Accordingly, two translations are possible: i) "do not call anyone of you father on earth"; ii) "do not call anyone on earth your father".[92] If we take the first option, we may interpret it as a command against using the title among the disciples themselves. Since the second option is universal and includes also the first, it seems to be preferable.[93] In any case, it is a title of authority and honour.

Usually a title of honour indicates the high status a person enjoys in a society. Such titles often create at least a feeling of inferiority or superiority among people. As God's children the disciples are all brothers and sisters, and

---

of people. Most scholars interpret the command of Jesus in 23,9 as a command against the titular use of the term πατήρ. See also K.G.C. NEWPORT, *The Sources*, 95-96; W.D. DAVIES – D.C. ALLISON, *Matthew*, III, 276; U. LUZ, *Matthew 21–28*, 105-106; J. NOLLAND, *Matthew*, 928.

[92] See J.T. TOWNSEND, "Matthew XXIII. 9", 57; D.E. GARLAND, *The Intention of Matthew 23*, 58; W.D. DAVIES – D.C. ALLISON, *Matthew*, III, 276. All of them favour the second option.

[93] Referring to the probable use of this title in first century Palestine, scholars propose two plausible interpretations for our passage. According to D.T. Zahn, πατήρ was not a common title used for addressing the contemporary Jewish leaders, but for the great rabbis of the past. The Jewish teachers of that time referred to the authority of these "fathers" to establish their own authority which was traditionally handed down to them (see Gal 1,14). In view of this background, the injunction in 23,9 could be understood as a warning against depending on the authority of the teachers of the past; as his children the disciples should rely only on the authority of their heavenly Father. Cf. D.T. ZAHN, *Matthäus*, 651-653; J.T. TOWNSEND, "Matthew XXIII. 9", 58; J.R. MICHAELS, "Christian Prophecy and Matthew 23,8-12", 305; see Str-B, I, 918-919, for a discussion on the use of the title πατήρ for the great men of an earlier generation. Digging further into the religious roots of Judaism, J.T. TOWNSEND, "Matthew XXIII. 9", 56-59, points out that πατήρ was a title used more commonly for the patriarchs Abraham, Isaac and Jacob than for the great rabbis of the past. Therefore, he suggests, Jesus' injunction in 23,9 "would mean that his followers were not to call the patriarchs father, i.e. not to boast of their Hebrew ancestry." Townsend's suggestion could be backed by Matt 3,9 where the Baptist warns his hearers not to boast about their identity as the children of Abraham (see also John 8,33; Gal 3,6-9). Connecting the teaching in 23,9 with 3,9, Townsend paraphrases the injunction of Jesus in 23,9 as the following: "Do not make a boast that you are descended from Abraham, for such ancestry is insignificant compared to the fact that you are children of your Father in Heaven." J.T. TOWNSEND, "Matthew XXIII. 9", 59; see also T. ROH, *Die familia dei*, 208.

they are all equal (23,8).[94] So, treating one as inferior or superior goes against their identity as God's children. Similarly, as his children, the disciples are under the authority of God's fatherhood and not under anybody else's authority. Their addressing God as "Father" is an expression of their relationship with him; and they should not replace him with human persons even symbolically.

4.2 *Identity and Lifestyle*

Every aspect of the disciples' life should reflect their identity as the children of the Father. In other words, their identity demands certain behavioural patterns from them. This logical demand, which has already been told to the disciples a number of times, is given very emphatically once again in the present context (23,1-12), pointing to the non-exemplary character of the scribes and Pharisees.[95] From the imperatives given in this unit, one can infer some of the characteristics expected of the disciples in their process of becoming the children of the Father.

4.2.1 Practise and Observe, but Do not Imitate

Jesus commands the disciples to practise and observe whatever the scribes and Pharisees tell them, but not to imitate them. This command includes both permission and prohibition. Jesus gives reasons for both.

The disciples have to put into practice the teachings of the scribes and Pharisees because they "sit on the seat of Moses".[96] Without much doubt we can interpret Jesus' words as a command to revere God's Law.[97] It recalls the

---

[94] See the careful wording in 23,8. Jesus does not tell the disciples that they are all "students" or "learners", which would be corresponding to his being their teacher or master, but he tells them that they are brothers (ἀδελφοί), a designation that reminds them of their mutual relationship.

[95] Concerning the unity of 23,1-12, there is a general consensus among scholars. All the scholars mentioned below consider it as a single unit though each one looks at the content of this unit quite differently (their subtitles, given in brackets, show their focus): J.P. MEIER, *Matthew*, 261 (The Disciples are to Avoid the Rabbinic Style); W.D. DAVIES – D.C. ALLISON, *Matthew*, III, 264 (Warnings against the Scribes and Pharisees); U. LUZ, *Matthew 21–28*, 96 (Against Hypocrisy and the Love of Titles); J. NOLLAND, *Matthew*, 918 (Scribes and Pharisees: Custodians of the Law, but Bad Examples).

[96] The verb καθίζω (sit) denotes authority and power (see 5,1; 24,2).

[97] This imagery, "the seat of Moses", has been interpreted both literally and metaphorically. While, M.J. LAGRANGE, *Saint Matthieu,* 437; W. GRUNDMANN, *Matthäus*, 483; F.W. BEARE, *Matthew*, 448; R.T. FRANCE, *Matthew,* 324, understand it as metaphorical, A. SCHLATTER, *Der Evangelist Matthäus*, 663; J.C. FENTON, *Matthew,* 366; W.F. ALBRIGHT – C.S. MANN,

declaration of Jesus in the SM about his approach towards the Law (5,17-19). There he says that he has come not to abolish the Law but to fulfil it. However, in the following verse he tells the disciples that unless their righteousness exceeds that of the scribes and Pharisees they will not enter the kingdom of heaven (5,20). Thus he makes a distinction between the Law of God and the Law practised by the scribes and Pharisees. He makes a similar distinction in the present context. God's Law should be revered and kept irrespective of the unworthiness of the channel through which the Law is given, because the real lawgiver is God and not the ones who preach the Law.[98] This distinction is important as often the people who teach the Law assume the role of the lawgiver and behave as if they were above the Law. Jesus' prohibition on imitating the lifestyle of the scribes and Pharisees attacks such an attitude.

Jesus criticizes the scribes and Pharisees very severely in the whole of chapter 23. His accusations against them are primarily against their hypocrisy (see 23,13.15.23.25.27.29) and the lack of integrity between their words and deeds.[99] Naturally, their authority to teach and preach the Law may earn them a great deal of social respect.[100] People may even consider them as the ideal

---

Matthew, 278; D. HILL, *Matthew,* 310; R.H. GUNDRY, *Matthew: Mixed Church*, 453-454; K.G.C. NEWPORT, *The Sources*, 85, U. LUZ, *Matthew 21–28*, 99, try to establish that it refers to actual seats whereupon the interpreters of the Torah sat in the synagogues. M.A. POWELL in his article, "Do and Keep What Moses Says (Matthew 23,2-7)", 419-435, has discussed in detail the strengths and weakness of both the above positions. Similarly, W.D. DAVIES – D.C. ALLISON, *Matthew*, III, 268, give four options, including both the possibilities of literal as well as metaphorical interpretations. The question whether such a seat existed or not is immaterial for our study. In any case, it stands as a symbol of authority since it is connected with the name of Moses, the interpreter of God's Law.

[98] Therefore, as Powell concludes, "Jesus' statement that the scribes and the Pharisees 'sit on Moses' seat' is not intended as an endorsement of their authority to teach or interpret the Law [...]. Rather, his statement merely acknowledges the reality of the situation in which his disciples must live and conduct their ministry. If they are to 'do' (ποιέω) and 'teach' (διδάσκω) the commandments (5,19), they must obviously know what Moses says. Since the scribes and Pharisees are currently the keepers of the Torah in the social and religious environment where these disciples live, Jesus' followers must be careful to do (ποιέω) and keep (τηρέω) all the words of Moses that they hear these leaders speak (λέγω)." M.A. POWELL, "Do and Keep What Moses Says", 435.

[99] They preach but do not practise (23,3); they put heavy burdens on people's shoulders, but they themselves will not move them with their fingers (23,4); they strain out a gnat but swallow a camel (23,24).

[100] But if they do not practise what they teach, it shows that they themselves are not convinced of what they say. Then the motive of their teaching is nothing but the glory of their profession.

model to be imitated. Doubtless, for the disciples they are not a model to copy; their lifestyle clearly shows that they do not belong to the family of the heavenly Father. The description of their ostentatious practices (23,5-6) recalls the repeated warnings against hypocrisy in 6,1-18. Their desire for human glory is made explicit in their love for honour at feasts and the best seats in the synagogues, salutations in the market places, and the desire to be called rabbi (23,5-7).[101] The disciples are called to be the perfect children of the Father (5,48); they are to grow in their relationship with the Father by doing his will in words and deeds (7,21-23; 21,28-31; 25,31-40). In their actions they are to seek not their own glory but the glory of their Father (5,16).

4.2.2 Not to be Called Rabbi

Jesus criticizes the scribes and Pharisees for their desire to be addressed as rabbi, and he tells the disciples that they should not be called rabbi. The title "rabbi" literally means "my great one", "my lord" or "my master".[102] It was an honorary title given to the great teachers of the Law;[103] and so he who was addressed as rabbi is naturally acknowledged to be superior to the speaker;[104] hence, the motive of the scribes and Pharisees to be addressed by that title is evident.

Jesus gives the disciples two reasons for why they should not be called rabbi. First of all, they have only one teacher (διδάσκαλος).[105] Though it is not mentioned who this teacher is, it is obvious from the context that it refers to Jesus himself (see 23,10; also, 4,23; 5,2; 7,29; 9,35; 11,1; 13,54; 21,23; 26,55).[106] In their journey as the children of the Father, the disciples have to acknowledge Jesus as their only teacher and follow him (7,24). He is the one who reveals the Father to them (11,27), and it is through him that they learn

---

[101] See E. KRENTZ, "Community and Character", 568.

[102] BAGD, 733; R.E. BROWN, *The Gospel according to John*, I, 74.

[103] BAGD, 733.

[104] See G. DALMAN, *The Words of Jesus*, 334.

[105] It is noteworthy that Jesus does not use the term rabbi here for himself. In Matthew only Judas addresses Jesus as rabbi (see, 26,25.49).

[106] As R. Hoet puts it, "διδάσκαλος signifie dans Mt 23,8 comme dans tout l'Evangile de Mt : celui qui enseigne en vérité la volonté de Dieu. C'est un terme qui indique une autorité religieuse selon sa fonction principale, qui est d'initier à cette volonté divine." R. HOET, *Omnes Autem Vos Fratres Estis*, 128.

(μανθάνω) to live as the children (11,29).[107] The second reason is that they are all brothers (ἀδελφοί). They are brothers because they are the children of the same Father (see 12,49-50). Therefore, they are all equal and should not desire to be treated with greater reverence than others.

4.2.3 Neither be Called Masters

Similar to the injunction in verse 8, in verse 10 Jesus tells the disciples that they should not be called "masters" (καθηγητής). This word καθηγητής occurs only here in the whole Bible. The precise meaning is uncertain, though it is normally translated as "master", "tutor", "guide" etc..[108] The suggestion to take it as a term for a personal teacher or a private tutor seems to be justifiable.[109] To their tutors, the students normally show great respect and reverence and often they take them as the role models for their life. Reciprocally, the tutors may take pride in the achievements and success of their students. To be known or called the καθηγητής of a few bright students would be a great honour for them. Jesus has given the disciples authority to continue his mission. As they go preaching the good news of the kingdom, many people may follow them. Then they may be tempted to feel important and may have a desire to be called καθηγητής. Jesus' command could be understood as a warning against such human temptations and desires of the disciples.

The why of this directive is given in the subsequent clause: "for you have one master, the Christ". The use of the term Christ (Χριστός) gives a theological explanation for the command. Χριστός is a title of Jesus which is connected with his mission (11,2). The Son of God came to this world as the

---

[107] "There is only one from whom the church receives all teaching – namely, Jesus; compared to him all of the church's members, including the scribes and even the evangelist who transmits to the church the teaching of Jesus, are 'disciples' (μαθηταί)." U. LUZ, *Matthew 21–28*, 107.

[108] Several scholars interpret v.10 as a clarification of v.8 and consider καθηγητής as a variant of διδάσκαλος. See G. DALMAN, *The Words of Jesus*, 340; D.E. GARLAND, *The Intention of Matthew 23*, 60; W.D. DAVIES – D.C. ALLISON, *Matthew*, III, 278. C. SPICQ, "Une allusion", 393, suggests that this term is an allusion to the Teacher of Righteousness in the Qumran community as his followers called him "Master" (מורה); see CD 20,28. In modern Greek καθηγητής is the common title for a professor, see U. LUZ, *Matthew 21–28*, 106.

[109] Winter, analysing the use of this term in a first-century papyrus (P. Oxy. 2190 [c. AD 70-90]), concludes: "καθηγητής is thus used in this papyrus to refer to a private tutor in rhetoric who would assist a student on an *ad hoc* basis even though the latter owned a school in which the former had not enrolled." B.W. WINTER, "The Messiah as the Tutor", 155. See J. NOLLAND, *Matthew*, 928.

Christ (16,16; 26,63).[110] Through his salvific mission he leads people to become the children of God. To the disciples of every generation he is the only καθηγητής who accompanies them to the Father (see 28,20).[111]

4.2.4 The Greatest – the Servant

"The greatest among you shall be your servant" (23,11). This concluding injunction summarises the paranetic teachings of the pericope. Their mode of behaviour should not be that of the haughty scribes and Pharisees, but of a humble servant (διάκονος). Jesus has already told them of this model in 20,26, when two of them came with their mother requesting a higher position for themselves in the kingdom. Greatness is defined here in terms not of power and prestige, nor of titles, but of service. The disciples are told explicitly in that context that they should not follow the model of the rulers of the Gentiles who exercise power and authority over others, but the model of the Son of Man who came to serve (διακονέω) and give his life for others (20,25-28). That is what the disciples should learn from their καθηγητής, and in the end they will be judged righteous or wicked based on the service they rendered to the least of his brethren (25,31-46, see the word διακονέω in v.44).

4.3 *Identity and Eschatology*

Jesus' call to the disciples to realize their heavenly identity as the children of the Father in contrast to the earthly identity in 23,9 functions as a key for interpreting the teachings that follow in chapters 24 and 25, which symbolically and dramatically present the events connected with the end times.

---

[110] In this context, it is worth noting the discussion of the "sonship" of Christ in 22,42-45. Jesus questions there the common Jewish understanding of the Christ as the son of David, and he establishes that he is not the son but the Lord (κύριος) of David. Though the question "whose son is he?" is not answered explicitly here, the implication, as Michaels suggests, is "as David's Lord, he is God's son". J.R. MICHAELS, "Christian Prophecy and Matthew 23,8-12", 309.

[111] According to S. BYRSKOG, *Jesus the Only Teacher*, 289-290, this honorary title καθηγητής qualifies Jesus in two ways in the context: "First, it suggests that Jesus the teacher provides his disciples with more than mere information. He is also their guide and leader, which even goes beyond his function as a moral example [...]. Second, the personal and private aspects of καθηγητής are present in Matthew. The group of disciples is according to 23,8f a brotherhood with one heavenly Father. Within this intimate setting, Jesus is not a teacher validated by means of official and institutional titles. While his didactic exousia is universal, he functions as the personal teacher of his disciples."

People's confusion at the end times and their "unpreparedness" for the coming of the Son of Man reflect their blind identification with this worldly life and their negligence of the heavenly life. Thus they continue eating and drinking, marrying and giving in marriage, without knowing what is going to happen to them (24,38-39). Like the unfaithful servants, they may immerse themselves in their own pleasures, ignoring the duty entrusted to them (24,45-50); like the foolish virgins they may take no oil for their lamps (25,1-13); they may hide their talents like the slothful servant (25,14-30) or overlook their needy brethren (25,41-46). But in the end, they will have to leave this world and its lures which were so dear to them, and on that day the doors of the kingdom will be shut against them, and they will be thrown into the eternal punishment (24,51; 25,30.46).

In contrast, those of them who live out their heavenly identity here, will be found doing their works when their master returns (24,45-47); they will be ready to receive the bridegroom with lamps filled with oil (25,1-13); they will come forward to settle their accounts with their master with the fruits of their labour (25,14-30); they will be judged righteous for caring for their needy brethren (25,31-46). They will be set over all the possessions of their master (24,47); they will go in with the bridegroom for the marriage feast (25,10); they will be invited to enter the joy of their master (25,21.23); and they will be welcomed to inherit the kingdom of their Father (25,34).

Jesus' injunction to the disciples in 23,9 points to their eternal heavenly identity as the children of the Father in contrast to their transitory earthly identity. As in other places in the gospel, here also the disciples are asked to live a life befitting that identity. They should not follow the wrong model of the non-children – in the present context scribes and Pharisees – who are immersed in seeking earthly glory and honour. In the end-time sayings that follow, the disciples are exhorted to look at the reality of life from the point of view of their heavenly identity and thus be prepared to inherit their eternal home.

5. **Conclusion**

Our study of the "Father" passages which refer to God as the Father of the disciples in the other Great Discourses in Matthew also confirms our thesis that in the gospel of Matthew discipleship is conceived as a process by which one becomes a child of God.

In the Missionary Discourse this appellation is used in the context of Jesus promising divine help to the disciples who will be undergoing trials and tribulations. The very fact that these disciples are persecuted for the sake of the mission shows that they have been following Jesus in words and deeds. They need not be afraid of their adversaries, because they are the precious children of the Father, and he will not abandon them in their sufferings. He will be with them, and his Spirit will defend their case against their persecutors.

In the Parable of the Weeds the disciples who have borne fruit in their life in the world are judged as the righteous and received as the children in the kingdom of the Father. This parable and its context explain the process the disciples go through from their origin to their reception into the paternal home. They were sown by the Son of Man as the sons of the kingdom, they grew with the weeds without being affected by their destructive presence, and they bore fruit worthy of their identity. They are the Father's true children, and they will shine forth like the sun in his kingdom forever.

Jesus qualifies the disciples as the "little ones" in the Community Discourse. Recalling their relationship with their Father using the term "your Father", Jesus instructs the disciples on how they should treat each of their brothers and sisters in the community who are journeying together with them to the Father's home. They should not cause scandals to their brethren or despise them. Following the model of the Father they should take every measure to get back their brethren if they go astray. If they do not forgive their brothers from their hearts, the Father also will not forgive them, and they will be denied his mercy and compassion.

In the Final Discourse, the disciples are told not to call anyone on earth their father, because their only Father is God. This injunction directly impinges on their true identity as the children of God, which should be manifested in their conduct and lifestyle. When they live in the world they may be tempted by the lifestyle of the non-children. But they should not imitate their ways but live as the children of the Father, preparing themselves for their eternal home. In the end the Father will receive his authentic children into his kingdom.

CHAPTER IV

Becoming the Children through the Son

In the previous chapters of this study we have seen that in Matthew discipleship is viewed as a process of becoming children of God. Now we may ask a practical question: how can one go through this process successfully in this world and grow as a child of God? The evangelist presents Jesus as the answer to such a question. He is the Son of God sent to the world, and it is through his Sonship that one becomes a child of the Father. Conversely, one cannot become a child of God nor even conceive of the "childship" if one ignores the Sonship of Jesus and his unique role as the mediator in this process. In the present chapter we will first highlight some of the texts that demonstrate the identity of Jesus as the Son of God and then mention a few other texts that present the Son as the mediator and model for the disciples in their process of becoming children of the Father.

1. The Identity of the Son

Matthew has presented Jesus with different titles in the gospel.[1] But more than any other designation he is the Son of God. Various instances are given in the gospel where the Father, the disciples, and even his adversaries proclaim the Sonship of Jesus.[2] Directly or indirectly, Jesus also often refers to his identity as the Son of the Father.

---

[1] See J.D. KINGSBURY, *Matthew: Structure*, 40-127 for a detailed discussion of the different titles of Jesus in Matthew.

[2] Jesus is called "Son of God" seventeen times in Matthew (Mark 8x; Luke 9x; John 28x).

1.1 *Authentication by the Father*

The Father is the one who can give the most authoritative and credible testimony to the Sonship of Jesus. Matthew (also Mark and Luke) records two direct testimonies by the Father acknowledging Jesus as his Son: the first one at Jesus' baptism (3,17) and the second at the transfiguration (17,5).

According to Matthew's account three supernatural events followed the baptism of Jesus: the heavens were opened to him, he saw the Spirit of God descending like a dove and alighting on him, and at the climax a voice came from heaven, saying, "This is my beloved Son with whom I am well pleased" (3,16-17).[3]

The testimony of the Father reveals not only the identity of the Son but also the Father's intimacy with the Son. He is his beloved (ὁ ἀγαπητός) Son. In the gospels this adjective is used only to refer to (or allude to) Jesus (Matt 12,18; 17,15; Mark 1,11; 9,7; 12,6; Luke 3,22; 20,13).[4] The Father's affection for the Son is further emphasized by means of the qualification "with whom I am well pleased" (εὐδοκέω). In Matthew, ἀγαπητός and εὐδοκέω appear always together (3,17; 12,18; 17,5). The Father's proclamation of his personal

---

[3] Matthew's description of the divine testimony at the baptism of Jesus is slightly different from that of Mark and Luke. While both of them present the Father's proclamation about the identity of the Son with a second person form ("You are [σὺ εἶ] my beloved Son, with you [ἐν σοί] I am well pleased"), Matthew presents it with a third person form ("This is [οὗτός ἐστιν]...with whom [ἐν ᾧ] ..."). Based on this difference many authors interpret the divine revelation in Matthew as a public testimony addressed to the crowd. E.P. BLAIR, *Jesus in the Gospel of Matthew*, 98; W.F. ALBRIGHT – C.S. MANN, *Matthew*, 31; D. HILL, *Matthew* 97; J.P. MEIER, *Matthew*, 27-28; R.H. GUNDRY, *Matthew: Mixed Church*, 53; U. LUZ, *Matthew 1–7*, 180; W.D. DAVIES – D.C. ALLISON, *Matthew*, I, 339; D.A. CARSON, *Matthew 1–12*, 109. See also J.D. KINGSBURY, *Matthew: Structure*, 14.49 (to John and Jesus). Following the grammatical form, one can interpret it as a public revelation. But considering the fact that the divine revelation at the transfiguration was given to only three of the disciples (17,1-8), a public revelation at the baptism seems to be improbable. See also the prohibition in 17,9: "Tell no one the vision, until the Son of Man is raised from the dead." As R.T. FRANCE, *Matthew*, 95, suggests, in the baptism scene Matthew probably intends the divine revelation "to be understood as addressed to Jesus only".

[4] Since the adjective ἀγαπητός carries a strong nuance of election, some authors suggest that the phrase ὁ υἱός ὁ ἀγαπητός conveys the meaning "only Son" as μονογενής in John (cf. John 1,14.18; 3,16.18). Cf. J.D. KINGSBURY, *Matthew: Structure*, 50; J.P. MEIER, *Matthew*, 28; J. NOLLAND, *Matthew*, 158. But as W.D. DAVIES – D.C. ALLISON, *Matthew*, I, 340, observe, it may not be the sense here. Together with εὐδοκέω it rather brings out an emotional meaning which underscores the affection of the Father for his Son.

affection for the Son augments the credibility of the Son.[5] It also implies that the ways of the Son are "pleasing" to the Father. This has been made more explicit in the proclamation of the Father at the transfiguration.

The divine proclamation of the Sonship of Jesus at the transfiguration is witnessed by a small group of three disciples.[6] In Matthew's account of the transfiguration, the wording of the divine proclamation is identical with that of the baptism except for the additional imperative ἀκούετε αὐτοῦ at the end (17,5).[7] This command, which appears in all the three gospels, points to the authority and reliability of the words of Jesus (see Deut 18,15.18). The Father gives the disciples the assurance that Jesus is his beloved Son and his words should be listened to.[8] Obviously, listening to him is not a passive activity of just hearing but also of doing what he says (7,24; see John 2,5).

Different from the baptism scene, here the voice that proclaims the status of the Son comes out of the clouds. It recalls the OT imagery of a cloud as the symbol of God's presence and glory, especially when the people of Israel journeyed towards the Promised Land (Exod 13,21-22; 24,15-18; 40,34-38; Num 9,15-22; 11,25; 14,14; Deut 31,15 etc.). This imagery of the cloud invites us to link the experience of the disciples with that of their ancestors. The same God who guided their ancestors in their journey is guiding them now through his Son, authenticating him and asking them to listen to him.[9]

---

[5] Similarly, the coming of the Spirit of God also attests to the credibility of the Son. Together with Mark and Luke, Matthew presents it as a personal experience of Jesus.

[6] These three, Peter, James and John, are his first disciples (Andrew is left out), and Jesus takes the same three with him when he goes to Gethsemane (26,37). They function as a representative group of all the disciples.

[7] In Mark (9,7) ἐν ᾧ εὐδόκησα is not included; in Luke (9,35) both ὁ ἀγαπητός and ἐν ᾧ εὐδόκησα are missing, whereas another qualification ὁ ἐκλελεγμένος is given.

[8] The command of the Father to listen to the Son needs to be understood from the background of the previous episode that took place six days before at Caesarea Philippi (16,21-23). After Peter's solemn confession of his identity, Jesus began to tell his disciples about his forthcoming passion, death and resurrection. Then Peter took him and began to rebuke him, which means, he did not want to listen to what Jesus said about his passion. Peter was reproved immediately for not being on the side of God (i.e. not listening to what comes from God) but of men. Now, at the transfiguration, Peter and his two companions are told by the Father to listen to the Son. Thus, the Father authenticates the Son and his words, so that the disciples can follow him wholeheartedly. As U. LUZ, *Matthew 8–20*, 399, puts it, "In the narrative the 'listen to him' (ἀκούετε αὐτοῦ) of the divine voice is, as it were, on the level of everyday life, the Son of God will proclaim to his disciples the will of the Father and the gospel of the kingdom."

[9] The response of the disciples to the voice shows that they recognize the divine presence. Matthew writes, "When the disciples heard this they fell on their face, and were very much afraid" (17,6). Falling on one's face is a gesture expressing reverence and fear before God (Lev

1.2 *Testimony of the Son*

There are many instances in Matthew where Jesus speaks about his Sonship directly and indirectly. We will examine two texts, 11,25-27 and 28,18-19, where Jesus refers overtly to his Sonship and its authority.

The unique relationship between the Father and the Son is explicitly given in 11,25-27. In these three verses the word πατήρ for God appears five times and υἱός for Jesus three times. Verse 27 is particularly significant concerning the authority of the Son. Jesus claims in v.27a, "All things (πάντα) have been delivered to me by my Father." Since in v.25 the Father is qualified as the "Lord of heaven and earth", we may understand the pronoun πάντα in v.27 as referring to all things in heaven and earth.[10] The Father's handing on all authority in heaven and on earth to the Son is restated at the end of the gospel (28,18; see below).[11]

As we have seen elsewhere in this study, the phrase "my Father", which is repeated sixteen times in the gospel, accentuates Jesus' unique filial relationship with God.[12] It should be noted that Jesus, although he refers to God as the Father of the disciples (using the terms "your Father", "our Father" and "their Father") as many as twenty times, never equates his filial relationship to God with their filial relationship.[13]

The mutual and exclusive communion between the Father and the Son is also spelled out plainly in v.27b: "no one knows the Son except the Father and no one knows the Father except the Son."[14] The Father is the Lord of heaven and earth and no one except the Son can comprehend him. The Son knows the

---

9,24; Num 20,6; 1Kgs 18,39; Matt 26,39). The disciples' fear (φοβέω) can be compared to the fear of the crowds in 9,8 and that of the centurion and his companions in 27,54.

[10] For a critical summary of various interpretations of this term see A. MULLOOR, *Jesus' Prayer of Praise*, 103-107.

[11] One can observe here an element of continuity between the earthly ministry of Jesus and his exalted post-resurrection status. At both stages Jesus is given authority over all things on heaven and earth. See D.R. BAUER, *The Structure*, 114.

[12] See 7,21; 10,32.33; 11,27; 12,50; 15,13; 16,17; 18,10.19.35; 20,23; 25,34; 26,29.39.42.53; among these only 11,27 has a parallel (Luke 10,22).

[13] See Ch. I,2.2.

[14] Different philosophical and theological proposals are made by scholars regarding the meaning of "knowing" (ἐπιγινώσκω) in the present context. For a detailed discussion, see R.H. GUNDRY, *Matthew: Mixed Church*, 216-217; U. LUZ, *Matthew 8–20*, 166-169; A. MULLOOR, *Jesus' Prayer of Praise*, 107-110; J. NOLLAND, *Matthew*, 472-473; J.R. KIM, *"...perché io sono mite*, 80-82. We may take it, as Gundry suggests, as a personal and intimate knowledge of identity.

Father because he is his Son. Similarly no one can comprehend the Son because he is the Son of the Father.[15]

Does it mean that the Father and the Son will remain always in a transcendent realm and that no human being will be able to know them? No, all have the possibility to know the Father, but only through the Son. The Son has the authority to reveal the Father, and he does it for whom he wills (βούλομαι). Since the Son's knowledge of the Father is founded on his filial relationship with him, we may infer that such a relationship is a necessary and essential condition for knowing the Father.[16] If that is the case, the people to whom the Son reveals the Father will come to know him by responding positively to the revelation of the Son and becoming the Father's children.[17] The process of revelation given here may be summarized as the following: Jesus is the beloved Son of the Father, the Lord of heaven and earth; the Father knows him and he knows the Father; the Son alone has the authority and power to reveal the Father to others; he reveals the Father to those whom he chooses by guiding them to become children of the Father.[18]

Jesus reiterates his authority and status as the Son in the Great Commissioning with which the gospel of Matthew ends (Matt 28,18-20). The risen Jesus meets his disciples at Galilee on the mountain and tells them, "All authority in heaven and earth are given to me. Go therefore and make disciples of all nations, baptizing them into the name of the Father and of the Son and of the Holy Spirit" (28,18-19). As we have seen above it is the Father, the Lord of heaven and earth (11,25), who gives (see the divine passive of δίδωμι) the authority (ἐξουσία) to Jesus; and his authority is universal.[19] It is with this authority that the Son during his earthly life teaches

---

[15] "Wer so erkennt, ist von dem Erkannten gepackt und erfüllt. Das ist die Erkenntnis, die in einer exklusiven Weise zwischen Jesus und Gott vor sich geht, in vollkommener Gegenseitigkeit." K. STOCK, "Gott, der Vater", 17.

[16] This would explain why the Father has hidden "these things" (things that revealed through Jesus) from the so called intellectuals (σοφοί and συνετοί) but has revealed them to babes (νήπιοι); see 21,15-16.

[17] J.D. KINGSBURY, *Matthew: Structure*, 65, has beautifully articulated how the Father is being revealed through the Son: "In Jesus, the Son, God the Father draws near with his Rule (4:17) to forgive men their sins (1:21; 9:5-8; 26:28) and make them his sons (5:9,45; 13:38), whose distinguishing mark is the greater righteousness (5:20), that is, they do the will of God (6:10; 7:21; 12:50)."

[18] "The Son reveals the Father *as Father*, drawing those to whom he reveals him into the warm circle of the Sonship that he himself enjoys." G.M. SOARES PRABHU, "Jesus in the Gospel of Matthew", 167.

[19] The word ἐξουσία occurs ten times in Matthew, in eight of them referring to the ἐξουσία of Jesus: 7,29; 9,6.8; 21,23².24.27; 28,18.

the people (7,29; 21,23), forgives their sins (9,6.8), chases out the people who profane the temple (21,12-13), and heals the blind and the lame (21,14).[20]

The divine nature and authority of the Son is convincingly underscored by presenting him alongside the Father and the Holy Spirit under a single name (τὸ ὄνομα τοῦ πατρὸς καὶ τοῦ υἱοῦ καὶ τοῦ ἁγίου πνεύματος).[21] This means, the Father, the Son and the Holy Spirit are not three different names, but the relational manifestation of the same name. The Son is presented here "in the fullness of his complete communion with the Father".[22]

1.3 *The Testimonies in the Birth Narrative*

Matthew does not mention in the opening verse of the gospel that Jesus is the Son of God (see Mark 1,1), but he discloses it soon after, in the infancy narrative itself, through different allusions. First of all, Jesus is the child of God (1,18.20),[23] though his legal ancestry is linked to the lineage of Abraham and David through the genealogy (1,1-17).[24] The first person who accepts this truth is his legal father, Joseph himself. He believes the testimony of the angel and takes Mary as his wife. The obedient response of Joseph to the messenger of God stands out here as a credible witness for all to believe that this child is really the Son of God.

---

[20] Some scholars, based on the adjective πᾶσα in 28,18, suggest that, though Jesus had authority during his earthly life, it is only after the resurrection that he was given "all authority". Cf. J.P. MEIER, *Matthew*, 370; R.T. FRANCE, *Matthew*, 413; W.D. DAVIES – D.C. ALLISON, *Matthew,* III, 683. Such a conclusion, which would imply that Jesus had only a limited authority during his pre-Easter existence, seems to be gratuitous. It is true that only in 28,18 is the authority of Jesus qualified as "all authority", but does this necessarily mean that he had been given only partial authority during his earthly life? Does not "all things" (πάντα) of 11,27 include also his authority? Most likely, as Nolland suggests, "a reaffirmation of authority" rather than an augmentation of authority is intended in 28,18. Though the adversaries of Jesus completely rejected his authority by crucifying him, through the resurrection God vindicated it. Jesus is freshly affirming it as he sends his disciples for the mission. J. NOLLAND, *Matthew*, 1265. See also J.D. KINGSBURY, *Matthew: Structure*, 78.

[21] As J.P. MEIER, *Matthew*, 371, writes, "Certainly, one could hardly imagine a more forceful proclamation of Christ's divinity – and, incidentally, of the Spirit's distinct personality – than this listing together, on a level of equality, of Father, Son and Spirit."

[22] M.H. FRANZMANN, *Follow Me*, 221.

[23] The intervention of the Holy Spirit (πνεύματος ἁγίου) recalls "the Spirit of God that appears as the agent of God's activity" in the OT (Gen 1,2; Ezek 37,1-14; Luke 1,35 etc.). See R.T. FRANCE, *Matthew*, 77; W.D. DAVIES – D.C. ALLISON, *Matthew*, I, 200.

[24] Even in the genealogy, as Kingsbury observes, the passive ἐγεννήθη (divine passive) which refers to the birth of Jesus in 1,16 may give an indication to the readers that the child of Mary was born by a special act of God (see 1,20). J.D. KINGSBURY, *Matthew: Structure*, 43.

Matthew quotes several OT texts giving evidence for the involvement of the divine will in the advent of this child.[25] Particularly significant for our study is the citation from the prophet Hosea in 2,15, which attests to Jesus' status as the Son of God. Anticipating the child Jesus' return from Egypt to Israel, the evangelist comments: "This was to fulfil what the Lord had spoken by the prophet, 'Out of Egypt have I called my son'" (2,15).[26] By using the Masoretic Text of Hos 11,1 (לִבְנִי = τὸν υἱόν μου) instead of the LXX reading τὰ τέκνα αὐτοῦ the evangelist emphasizes the personal intimacy between the Father and the Son.[27] In the Hosean text, "my son" refers to the people of Israel who were liberated by the Lord from the slavery of Egypt (Hos 11,1). Some scholars argue that by applying this text to Jesus, Matthew is equating Jesus with the people of Israel, God's chosen race. This interpretation is plausible as a number of "analogical correspondences" between the history of the people of Israel and the history of the Son are found in the gospel.[28] However, Jesus' Sonship is different from the collective "adoptive sonship" of Israel.[29] He is God's unique Son. As we have seen above, Matthew has already mentioned the nature of Jesus' Sonship in the birth prediction (1,18.20), and it has been reaffirmed in the baptism scene and in the temptation episode (see 3,13-4,11).[30]

1.4 *The Confession of the Disciples*

It is evident from the portrayal of the disciples in the gospel that the evangelist does not expect his readers to believe that the disciples understood

---

[25] See 1,23; 2,6.15.18. For a detailed study of these quotations see G.M. SOARES PRABHU, *The Formula Quotations*, 192-293; J. MILER, *Les citations*, 12-78.

[26] As Meier remarks, "This citation is the theological highpoint of the infancy narrative, because here Jesus receives his most exalted definition." J.P. MEIER, *Matthew*, 14.

[27] See T.L. HOWARD, "The Use of Hosea 11,1 in Matthew 2,15", 322.

[28] For example, like Israel he was called out of Egypt, he passed through the Jordan and was tempted in the desert. See J.P. MEIER, *Matthew*, 14; R.T. FRANCE, *Matthew*, 86; T.L. HOWARD, "The Use of Hosea 11,1 in Matthew 2,15", 321.

[29] See J.P. MEIER, *Matthew*, 14.

[30] Jesus' oneness with God in essence and existence is depicted with another OT quotation. After presenting the angel's message to Joseph that Mary will bear a son and he is to call him Jesus for he will save his people from their sins (1,21), the evangelist interprets this event as the fulfilment of Isa 7,14: "Behold, a virgin shall conceive and bear a son, and they shall name him Emmanuel." Matthew then explains the meaning of the Hebrew word "Emmanuel" for his readers: "which means God with us" (1,23). This fulfilment formula gives an orientation to the whole gospel: "in the person of Jesus, his Son, God has drawn near to dwell with his people." The Son through his salvific mission removes the sins of the people and draws them near to God. See J.D. KINGSBURY, *Matthew: Structure*, 53.96.123.

Jesus' identity fully and perfectly during their life with him. In fact, on various occasions Matthew characterizes them bluntly as men of "little faith". On the other hand, there are moments where they manifest a great trust in Jesus, believe in his authority, and follow his way. Particularly, on two occasions they proclaim Jesus' identity as the Son of God (14,33; 16,16).

In 14,33, the disciples, having witnessed Jesus' walking on the sea and his rescuing Peter from sinking (14,22-32), worship him proclaiming: "Truly you are the Son of God."[31] Evidently, their worship and their proclamation emanated from their concrete experience of the power of Jesus. The supernatural elements[32] in this episode function as instruments of revelation of the true identity of Jesus. The disciples respond positively to that revelation this time, and they express it with an act of worship (προσκυνέω).[33] The disciples' recognition of the divine character of Jesus and their worship resemble the people's recognition of Yahweh in the "sea-rescue" narratives in the OT (see Exod 14,31; Ps 107,31-32; Jonah 1,16).[34] The affirmative adverb ἀληθῶς ("truly")[35] in their proclamation suggests that they were fully convinced (at least for the moment) of what they proclaimed.[36]

---

[31] In the Markan parallel (6,45-52) the disciples do not make such a proclamation nor do they worship him. Mark reports that they were utterly astounded. Luke has not included this event in the gospel.

[32] Consider the turbulence in the sea when Jesus was away (v.24) and the ceasing of the wind when he got into the boat (v.32); his walking on the sea (v.25); Peter's walking on the water; his fear and Jesus' saving him from sinking (v.31).

[33] The disciples worship Jesus again when he appears to them after the resurrection (28,17). The verb προσκυνέω recalls the temptation scene where Jesus tells the devil that one should worship only the Lord God (4,10). The same verb, προσκυνέω, occurs eleven times in the gospel with Jesus as the object (altogether it occurs thirteen times in Matthew; Mark 2x; Luke 3x). Thus, besides the disciples, several others – the Magi (2,2.11), the leper (8,2), the ruler (9,18), the Canaanite woman (15,25), the mother of the sons of Zebedee (20,20) and the women who heard the Easter message (28,9) – worship Jesus (or do obeisance before him). Ironically, King Herod too accepts that Jesus should be worshipped (2,8).

[34] See J.P. HEIL, *Jesus Walking on the Sea*, 66; W.D. DAVIES – D.C. ALLISON, *Matthew*, II, 510.

[35] The adverb ἀληθῶς intensifies the credibility of the proclamation. It occurs twice more in Matthew (26,73; 27,54). In all the contexts, the speakers use ἀληθῶς to emphasize the truth that they have inferred from their personal experience.

[36] Connecting the present episode with the "storm-stilling" episode of 8,23-27 J.P. HEIL, *Jesus Walking on the Sea*, 102, suggests that the proclamation of the disciples in 14,33 is a confirming answer to the puzzling question they raise in 8,27: "What sort of man is this, that even the winds and the sea obey him?" After experiencing a similar and more powerful manifestation of his power, now they can convincingly proclaim: "Truly you are the Son of God".

In 16,16 Peter confesses that Jesus is the Christ, the Son of the living God, as a response to Jesus' question to the disciples about their understanding of his identity (16,13-16). All the three Synoptic writers report this event (Mark 8,27-29; Luke 9,18-20). While the title "the Christ" is given in all three, "the Son of the living God" is found only in the account of Matthew.

The designation "the Son of the living God" echoes the proclamation of the disciples in 14,33, where their recognition of Jesus' identity as the Son of God led them to worship him. Matthew begins his gospel stating the identity of Jesus as the Christ (1,1). Up to this point of the story this title has been mentioned six times (1,1.16.17.18; 2,4; 11,2). In parallel, Jesus has been presented also as the Son of God on different occasions (2,15; 3,17; 4,3.6; 8,29; 11,27; 14,33). In 16,16, for the first time, these two titles are used together, complementing each other.[37] Jesus is the Christ, who should be worshipped as the Son of God (14,33); similarly, he is the Son of God who has a messianic role to fulfil (see 1,21; 20,28; 26,28; 27,22).

In the OT the expression "living God"[38] often refers to the saving presence of God amidst his people (see Deut 5,26; Josh 3,10; Jer 10,10; Dan 6,20.26 etc.). This qualification emphasizes the truth of God's existence: he is the true God, not an abstract idea, not a dead idol created according to the imagination of an artist. Thus, by proclaiming Jesus as the Son of the living God, Peter also confesses his faith in the true God. Indeed, as we know from the gospel story, it is through the Son that the disciples experience the "living God" (1,23) and his salvific presence (1,21; 4,16; see Luke 1,68; 7,16) amidst them. Jesus' use of the term "my Father" in his response confirms the truth of Peter's confession.[39]

1.5 *The Confession of the Centurion and his Companions*

Whereas the first testimony to Jesus' identity as the Son is given by the Father (3,17), the final testimony is given by a Gentile centurion and his

---

[37] However, there is a hint in 1,18 where the evangelist presents Jesus Christ as the child of the God. Later in 22,42 Jesus implicitly affirms the divine Sonship of Christ by challenging the popular Jewish idea that the Christ is the son of David. Ironically, in 26,63 the high priest uses the same expression as he questions Jesus.

[38] This expression is found nowhere else in the gospels except Matt 26,63 (but cf. John 6,57).

[39] See A. MULLOOR, *Jesus' Prayer of Praise*, 48. Jesus' response to Peter draws attention to the profundity of his confession (16,17-20). He commends Peter by qualifying him as "blessed" (μακάριος), because he is chosen as a channel of revelation by the Father, who alone knows the true identity of the Son (see 11,27).

companions who witness his death (27,54). Unlike Mark (15,39) and Luke (23,47), who narrate the testimony of the centurion as a personal confession, Matthew presents it as a collective confession of the centurion and his companions. Thus he intensifies the credibility of the confession. Most probably, they were among the persons who mocked Jesus in the praetorium (27,27-31). As they were keeping watch over him (27,36), they might have heard the deriding comments and challenges of the chief priests and other people who passed by (27,40.43). Now, having witnessed the death of Jesus and the events that accompanied it, they are converted,[40] and they know for certain that he was not a fraud but truly the Son of God.[41]

The impact of these events on the soldiers seems to be similar to that of the transfiguration on the disciples. The same phrase ἐφοβήθησαν σφόδρα is used in both contexts to describe their resultant inner-experience (17,6; 27,54). Similarly, their confession corresponds to the proclamation of the disciples in 14,33. The wording of the confession in Matthew is similar to that of Mark but quite different from Luke. Besides the change in word order, the only difference between the account of Mark and Matthew is that the phrase "this one" (οὗτος) is used in Matthew in place of "this man" (οὗτος ὁ ἄνθρωπος) in Mark. Thus, the centurion and his companions in Matthew rightly respond to the theophany they witness, and they dare not identify him, the true Son of God, as just a "man".[42]

---

[40] We interpret the reaction of the centurion and his men in a positive light, assuming that their confession was an expression of their conversion. However, as D.C. Sim argues, it is possible to take their reaction as an admission of guilt and a cry of defeat. See D.C. SIM, "The Confession of the Soldiers", 418-422. Whatever the case may be, their confession confirms that Jesus died as the Son of God.

[41] Matthew's presentation of the background that led to the confession is more detailed than that of Mark and Luke. Matthew alone mentions the earthquake (σεισμός) and the successive events, like the splitting of the rocks, the opening of the tombs, and the raising of the bodies of the saints in connection with the death of Jesus (27,51-54). In the OT, earthquakes sometimes mark a theophany (Isa 29,6; Ezek 3,12; Zech 14,5); likewise the earthquakes in the present text and in 28,2 could be interpreted as signs of theophany. The passives in the description of other events (ἐσχίσθησαν, ἀνεῴχθησαν, ἠγέρθησαν) also point to a divine intervention in these happenings.

[42] The absence of the definite article before the expression "Son of God" in the present context (see also Mark 15,39) has been occasionally interpreted as a reflection of the pagan belief of the centurion and his men that they confessed him not as "the son of God" but as "a Son of God". See E.S. JOHNSON, "Is Mark 15.39 the Key to Mark's Christology?", 16; D.C. SIM, "The Confession of the Soldiers", 418-422 ; T.H. KIM, "The Anarthrous υἱὸς θεοῦ in Mark 15,39", 222-225. Several scholars have refuted this conjecture by showing that it is part of NT Greek style to omit the definite article in such cases where the verb appears after the

This testimony of the pagan soldiers to the identity of Jesus at his death brings to completion a series of testimonies that began at his birth.[43] These authentic testimonies confirm that Jesus was born as the Son of God, lived as the Son of God, and died as the Son of God. However, the greatest testimony was yet to come, and it was given again by the Father himself. It was not an oral testimony but an event which really proved that he was the Son of God and that his Sonship did not end with his death. Though he underwent the earthly phenomenon of death, the Son of God is risen (28,1-6), and he continues to be with his disciples as Emmanuel (1,23; 18,20; 28,20).[44]

2. **Through the Son towards the "Childship"**

In the preceding section we have seen how the evangelist presents in different ways the identity and authority of Jesus as the Son of God. As the Son he is endowed with all power and authority. He alone knows the Father, and he alone can reveal the Father. Only through him can one know the Father and become a child of him. Who are the people to whom the Son reveals the Father? Matthew's answer, we have seen, is the disciples. He portrays them as the privileged ones who have the Son as their master, brother and companion. Jesus reveals the Father to them and guides them in the way of the Father. By doing the will of the Father, revealed through him, the disciples can become children of the Father, and thus his brothers and sisters. We mention below some of the texts wherein the evangelist underscores the role of the Son as the mediator and formator of the disciples in this process.

2.1 *The Son Calls People to Follow him*

In the call narratives great emphasis is given to the initiative of Jesus in summoning the disciples. It is he who sees (εἶδεν) the candidates and calls them to follow him (4,18.21; 9,9).[45] Thus he introduces the people to discipleship and so to the process of becoming children of God.[46]

---

predicate noun (see also 14,33). See E.C. COLWELL, "A Definite Rule", 21; E.P. BLAIR, *Jesus in the Gospel of Matthew*, 61; P.H. BLIGH., "A Note on υἱὸς θεοῦ in Mark xv.39", 51-53; U. LUZ, *Matthew 21–28*, 569-570.

[43] We have dealt with the testimonies of only the positive agents here. In the gospel there are also instances where the adversaries of Jesus refer to his divine identity. Thus the tempter (4,3.6), the demoniacs (8,29), the high priest (26,63), the people who reviled him (27,40), the chief priests, scribes and elders (27,43) ironically acknowledge Jesus as the Son of God.

[44] See H. FRANKEMÖLLE, *Jahwebund und Kirche Christi*, 166-167.

[45] Scholars note that this calling of the disciples by Jesus was quite contrary to the contemporary practice; for example, in rabbinical circles the disciples took the initiative to find

Three different expressions are used in the call narratives to refer to the summons of Jesus. The call of Peter and Andrew is given in direct speech; Jesus tells these brothers, δεῦτε ὀπίσω μου (4,19). Jesus might have used the same formula as he called the second pair of brothers too. But the evangelist does not include it in the narrative; rather he relates it using the verb καλέω (4,21).[47] The call of Matthew, the tax collector, is described again in direct speech using the imperative ἀκολούθει μοι (9,9). Both δεῦτε ὀπίσω μου and ἀκολούθει μοι convey the same demand: "come after me" or "follow me".[48] To go after the Son would imply not only following in his footsteps but also conforming to his lifestyle.[49] Later in the gospel Jesus spells out some of the characteristics expected of the people who go after him (8,20.22; 10,38; 16,24; 19,21).[50]

The call of Jesus is given not as a mere invitation but as a strong command. It underlines the authority of the Son. All the more amazing is the

---

their masters, not vice versa. See M.H. FRANZMANN, *Follow Me*, 2; G.M. SOARES PRABHU, "Jesus in the Gospel of Matthew", 159; J. PALACHUVATTIL, *"He Saw"*, 104-105.

46 Given the fact that Matthew has not narrated the call story of each individual disciple, we may take these call narratives as typical examples for all the disciples. This also shows that not only those who were called by Jesus during his earthly ministry are his true disciples, but all those who respond to him and to his message affirmatively. In fact, in Matthew's gospel this subject is handled with great care. The risen Jesus charges the eleven with the responsibility of making the disciples of all nations (28,19-20). His promise that he will be with them till the end of the age shows that through these disciples and their future successors he will be calling disciples until the end.

47 This verb καλέω has already been used six times, five of them in reference to Jesus in the infancy narrative (1,21.23.25; 2,15.23). As W. CARTER, "Matthew 4:18-22", 65, observes, "In these five instances καλέω not only names the infant but also articulates the purpose and mission of Jesus as the agent of God's salvific presence and will." As Jesus is called to manifest God's saving presence (1,21.23), so Jesus calls the disciples to join in this salvific mission.

48 BAGD, 31.574.

49 As S. KUTHIRAKKATTEL, *The Beginning of Jesus' Ministry*, 113, remarks: "Following Jesus implies a free self-commitment, a personal attachment to Jesus which shapes the whole life of his μαθηταί. This personal attachment to Jesus extends not only to the exterior aspects of the disciples' life but also to the inner core of their life: it is indeed a participation even in his destiny."

50 Jesus' reproving command to Peter in 16,23 to get behind him (ὕπαγε ὀπίσω μου) is noteworthy. When Jesus spoke about the passion and death that he would undergo, Peter could not accept it. Forgetting the truth that he must go after Jesus, Peter tries here to overtake Jesus. Instead of listening to Jesus' words he begins to rebuke him. This is a moment of severe temptation in Peter's following. That may be the reason Jesus addresses him as Satan. To overcome this temptation Peter has to go back to his proper position. See K. STOCK, *The Call of the Disciple*, 20.

fact that the text gives us no indication of any previous meeting between Jesus and these men (see Luke 4,38-41; 5,1-11). Similarly, the people whom Jesus calls to be his disciples are not persons of extraordinary quality or religious status. Except for their profession the evangelist says nothing about their profile. In fact, in the case of the tax collector it is clear that he was from a group of low esteem in Jewish society (see 9,11-13). This again manifests the free will of the Son; he chooses whomever he wills (see 11,27).

The immediate and unconditional following of the persons called shows that they too sensed Jesus' authority and credibility. Without any question, without even a word, they leave everything behind and follow (ἀκολουθέω) him (see 19,27).[51] Thus they entrust themselves to his guidance, believing that he will lead them to the right goal.[52] In this context, Zebedee's sons' leaving their father can be interpreted as a symbolic expression of the disciples' leaving their earthly family ties in order to be the members of the family of their heavenly Father (see 8,21-22; 10,37).[53]

---

[51] Matthew consistently uses the verb ἀκολουθέω to mark the positive response of the called ones (4,20.22; 9,9; see Mark 1,20). The same word has been used also to mention the going of many other people after Jesus on different occasions without any special call from him (4,25; 8,1.10; 9,27; 12,15; 14,13; 19,2; 20,29; 20,34; 26,58; 27,55). Whether we can consider them also as disciples is a debatable question. See J.D. KINGSBURY, "The Verb *Akolouthein*", 56-73; B. PARAMBI, *The Discipleship of the Women*, 108-115, for a detailed treatment of the use of this verb in Matthew. Kingsbury makes a clear distinction between the literal and metaphorical use of this term and argues that the instances where ἀκολουθέω is used metaphorically (4,20.22; 8,19.22; 9,9; 10,38; 16,24; 19,21.27.28) alone can be considered as referring to discipleship. See also W.D. DAVIES – D.C. ALLISON, *Matthew*, II, 399. Contesting this view, U. LUZ, *Matthew 1–7*, 206, and S.C. BARTON, *Discipleship and Family Ties*, 131 argue that one must read all the passages where ἀκολουθέω refers to people's going after Jesus with a connotation of discipleship. While agreeing with Kingsbury, we may also assume that at least some of them who went literally after Jesus without a special call might have done so with a real commitment (see 27,55). One thing is evident, even though Jesus did not call them personally, he permitted them to go after him. Thus they too had the good fortune to listen to him and witness some of his miracles. Our position goes well with the view of J. NOLLAND, *Matthew*, 184-185, who, referring to the following of the crowd in 4,25, writes, "Matthew may well have chosen the language of following here (and elsewhere) to suggest that, in the attention they are paying to Jesus, the crowds are headed in the direction of that following which would make true disciples of them, but he clearly has no intention of identifying their following with that costly following to which the fisherman have been called in vv.18-22."

[52] See K. STOCK, *Jesus Künder der Seligkeit*, 26.

[53] If this is true, their coming with their mother in 20,20-23 to request seats at the right and the left of Jesus in his kingdom can be considered a moment of failure in observing the radical renunciation they made at the beginning.

The narratives of Jesus' calling the twelve in 10,1-4, his dialogue with the unnamed disciple in 8,21-22, and his exchange with the rich young man in 19,21 show that the Son continued calling people during his ministry.[54]

At the end of the gospel Jesus hands this authority "to call" on to his disciples and their future successors, promising his everlasting presence with them. Meeting his disciples at Galilee, the risen Jesus commissions them to go and make disciples (μαθητεύω) of all nations (28,19-20). For that, they are asked to baptize people in the name of the Father and of the Son and of the Holy Spirit, and teach them to observe all the commandments of Jesus. Thus, all can become children of the Father. The baptism could be understood as a symbolic act of initiation into the Father's family. They will live in this family as God's children observing the teachings of Jesus. Thus Matthew makes clear that the call to be the disciples of Jesus (the grace to become children of the Father) is given not only to a group of people who lived in a particular time and space in history, but to all people of all ages.

2.2 *The Son Acknowledges the Disciples as his Brothers and Sisters*

What is the relationship between Jesus and the people who are called to follow him? Naturally, their designation as the disciples points to a master-disciple relationship. But in Matthew a familial relationship, more than a master-disciple relationship, is emphasized. We noted in the preceding chapters of this study how Jesus by presenting God as his Father and as their Father indirectly refers to his kinship with the disciples. In addition to these Father-centred relational references, there are at least two occasions in the gospel where Jesus publicly acknowledges the disciples as his brothers and sisters (12,50; 28,10).[55]

The episode that leads to Jesus' description of his true family is given by all the three Synoptic authors (Matt 12,46-50; Mark 3,31-35; Luke 8,19-21). Matthew's view of the kinship of Jesus is distinctly different from that of Mark and Luke. In Matthew alone Jesus stretches forth his hands towards his disciples as he says, "here are my mother and my brothers" (12,49).[56] The next sentence gives the criterion by which this kinship is defined: "For whoever does the will of my Father in heaven is my brother, and sister, and

---

[54] However, the rich young man's story gives us a clue to the fact that not all responded to his call affirmatively.

[55] Jesus refers to the disciples as his brothers also in John 20,17.

[56] In Mark, Jesus says these words "looking at those who sat around him" (3,34). Luke does not mention any particular group (Luke 8,21).

mother" (12,50).[57] We may not take the words of Jesus as a compliment to the disciples on their actual lifestyle and behaviour; rather, we may interpret them as a reference to the ideal life to which they are called. Moreover, they give an assurance to the disciples that by journeying together with Jesus and by learning from him they will be able to do the will of the Father. Matthew's use of the phrase "my Father" in place of "God" in Mark and Luke seems to be deliberate. Thus he presents here a family scene comprised of the Father, the Son and the disciples.[58]

The second time it is the risen Jesus who refers to the disciples as his brothers (28,10). He meets the women, who were on their way to tell the angel's message to the disciples, and repeats the words of the angel to them but with a significant change. In place of "his disciples" (τοῖς μαθηταῖς αὐτοῦ) in the angel's message, Jesus says "my brothers" (τοῖς ἀδελφοῖς μου).[59] Here again, if the actual behaviour of the disciples is considered, they are not at all worthy to be called "my brothers" by Jesus in the present context. The women were to be sent to summon them because they all had fled from Jesus seeking their own safety (26,56.69-75).[60] We may construe Jesus' addressing the disciples as "my brothers" here as a concrete gesture of forgiveness, for which he offered his life on the cross (26,27-28). Though the disciples abandoned him, he did not abandon them; he gave his life as a ransom (20,28) and restored them to their family as the Father's children, and his brothers.[61]

---

[57] As S.C. BARTON, *Discipleship and Family Ties*, 225, puts it, "Discipleship is understood as a priority of the Kingdom of God which relativizes all other ties of allegiance and makes possible access to a new solidarity, the eschatological family of 'brothers, sisters and mothers' who do the will of God."

[58] S. GRASSO, *Gesù e i suoi fratelli*, 75, summarizes well what it means for the disciples to be counted as the brothers and sisters of Jesus: "Nel dichiararsi fratello dei discepoli, Gesù attribuisce loro un'importanza primaria in confronto ai suoi parenti carnali. I primi infatti sono diventati per lui più intimi e più vicini alla sua esperienza dei suoi stessi consanguinei. Essi non diventano fratelli per delle doti particolari di genere intellettuale o umano, né perché appartenenti a un ceto sociale elevato, o per un particolare stato di perfezione religiosa, ma soltanto perché hanno risposto alla sua chiamata."

[59] This commission to the women has no parallels in Mark and Luke. However, a similar account is found in John 20,17, the only time Jesus calls the disciples brothers in that gospel.

[60] The disciples' weakness is shown even in their meeting with the risen Jesus in Galilee. Though they worshipped him when they saw him, it was not without doubt (28,17).

[61] See J.P. MEIER, *Matthew*, 364.

This command to the disciples, sent through the women, to go to Galilee can be viewed as the reconfirmation of their call to follow Jesus.[62] Though he loved them as his brothers and lived with them as a family, they failed to give him fraternal support when he was in need of it; rather they avoided troubles by fleeing from him. Humanly speaking, they who had left him alone to suffer and die would not have felt courageous and free to come back to him after his resurrection. But Jesus does not wait to know whether they will repent and return. He takes the initiative to convene them and restore their momentarily broken fraternity. When they come together in Galilee Jesus does not even say a word about the past events. No questions, no accusations! But the disciples still waver. They still find it difficult to believe what they see before their eyes (28,17). The evangelist's comment about their doubt is quite telling in this context. Jesus seems to overlook it. Ignoring their perplexity, he entrusts them with the mission to make disciples, i.e. to initiate and guide people to become children of the Father, and thus to extend their family to the whole world and to all ages.[63]

2.3 *The Son Accompanies the Disciples in the Process*

The disciples are ordinary human beings living in the world together with the weeds who may obstruct their growth. The negative values of the world and its greed may attract them or put pressure on them to leave the way that leads to life. They may experience moments of confusion and turbulence; they may be tempted to give up the grace they have received and opt instead for the way that leads to destruction. In such a situation how can they go forward and continue their journey to the Father?

To those who are called to follow the Son, the Son himself shows the way. He is their only master and guide (23,8.10). Matthew's gospel ends with a promise of Jesus to the eleven disciples that he will be with them until the end of the ages (28,20). Thus the exalted Jesus assures them and all the future disciples that in their mission and in their journey to the Father they are not alone, the Son is always with them. This final promise of Jesus' perpetual presence with the disciples is unique to Matthew, and it echoes with the message of the angel to Joseph in 1,23: "[…] they shall name him Emmanuel,

---

[62] It is true even spatially. See the message of the angel directed to the disciples: "he is going before you (προάγει ὑμᾶς) to Galilee; there you will see him" (28,7). See K. STOCK, *The Call of the Disciple*, 23-24.

[63] See S. GRASSO, *Gesù e i suoi fratelli*, 191-194.

which means 'God with us'."[64] The disciples are the privileged ones who experience and enjoy his presence most. Being called to follow Jesus they were chosen to be with him. Though not mentioned always explicitly, it is evident, except for a single occasion (14,22-24), that the disciples were always with Jesus from the time of their call to the moment of his arrest.[65] Thus they could personally experience the lifestyle of the Son, his fulfilling the will of the Father; they could hear what he taught and witness all his miracles. Through such an intense personal accompaniment Jesus shows them the way to become children of the Father. What they have to do is to listen to his words and to act on them (7,24).[66]

All the five discourses, as we have seen above, are primarily addressed to the disciples. In addition, a number of other occasions are found in the gospel where he instructs them publicly (e.g. 4,23; 9,35; 21,23) and privately (e.g. 16,24-28; 19,23-30). Taken as a whole, we may classify these instructions under two categories: "revelatory" and "ethical".[67] Through the revelatory instructions of Jesus the disciples come to know about the Father (11,27), the mysteries of the kingdom (13,11), the identity and mission of the Son (20,28; 26,28), and the events of the end times (24-25). Jesus shows them through his ethical instructions the right behaviour required of them to become the Father's children (5,9.45) and to enter his kingdom (5,20; 7,21; 18,3; 19,23).

The Son not only shows the disciples the way of the Father through his instructions but also persuades them to live according to his words. In our study we have seen how he encourages them repeatedly to recognize their identity as the children of the Father. He commends Peter for his expression of faith (16,17); he promises the disciples recompense for their choice of following him (19,28-29); at the same time, he also reproves Peter (16,23) and all of them (20,20-29) when they stumble and go away from the way of the Father, and he rebukes them when they vacillate in their faith (6,30; 8,26; 14,31; 16,8). Thus the Son accompanies the called ones in their journey and guides them to the eternal "childship". The eyes and ears of the disciples are

---

[64] As many have noted, these two verses (1,23 and 28,20) function as an *inclusio* in the gospel of Matthew. It is the good news of this "God being with us" that we hear in the gospel.

[65] On many occasions the evangelist explicitly mentions their being with him in public (see 8,23; 9,19; 12,1; 13,10.36; 14,15; 15,12.23.32; 16,5.13.21; 17,6.24; 18,1; 19,10.13.23; 21,20; 23,1; 24,1; 26,1.8.17.20.36) and in private (see 13,10; 17,19; 20,17; 24,3). See K.H. REEVES, *The Resurrection Narrative*, 84. On two occasions Jesus takes only three of his disciples with him (17,1-14; 26,36-46).

[66] The Father himself attests to the authenticity of the Son's words and asks the disciples to listen to him in their journey (17,5).

[67] See F. FORESTI, *The Sermon on the Mount*, 88.

blessed, because they have the grace to see the Son and listen to his words which many prophets and wise men before them longed to see and hear but could not (13,16-17). If they hear his words and put them into practice, they will be like a wise man who builds his house on a rock. Such a house will survive tempest and flood however violent they are (7,24-25).

The Son, who accompanies the disciples until the end of the ages, himself will appear as the judge of the nations on the last day (7,21-23; 16,27; 25,31). On that day, he will recognize his brethren and welcome them to his Father's kingdom: "Come, O blessed of my Father, inherit the kingdom prepared for you from the foundation of the world" (25,34). Thus through the Son they too will shine forth in the kingdom of their Father as his children (13,43).

3. **The Lifestyle of the Son the Perfect Model for the Disciples**

The most credible guidance Jesus gives to the disciples on living as the children of the Father is his own life example. Through different episodes the evangelist shows how Jesus, the Son exemplifies in his own life the virtues he demands from the disciples.[68] It is enough for them to learn (μανθάνω) from him and take his yoke upon them (11,29). We mention some of these exemplary episodes below.

3.1 *The Son Triumphs over the Temptations*

Jesus has repeatedly told the disciples that it is "no easy thing" to live in this world as the children of God (see 13,18-23; 19,16-26; 26,41). From the moment of its sowing until the harvest the seed will have to face and resist different lures and threats of the enemy (13,24-30.36-43). Not even the Son of God had any immunity from such trials and temptations!

Soon after his being filled with the Spirit at the baptism, which was followed by the Father's testimony on his Sonship, Jesus had to face the tempter in the wilderness. In the temptation episode (4,1-11), we see the devil attempting different strategies to bring Jesus under his control. So sly is he that in the first two temptations he uses Jesus' identity as the Son of God itself as the trap. If he is the Son of God, why should he starve (4,3)? If he is the Son of God why can't he show it off (4,5)? In the third one he mocks at that identity asking Jesus to fall down and worship him, promising him all the

---

[68] Several scholars have noted Matthew's presentation of Jesus as exemplary for the disciples. see F.J. MATERA, *Passion Narratives*, 142-148; D.R. BAUER, *The Structure*, 57-63; D.B. HOWELL, *Matthew's Inclusive Story*, 251-259.

kingdoms of the world and their glory in exchange (4,8-9). But Jesus withstands the tempter's snares and delusions. He chases the adversary away and proves himself the true Son, showing his undivided fidelity to God and his words (4,4.7.10; see 6,24).

The test Jesus had from the devil before the beginning of his ministry was not the last one. Later in his public ministry he had to face several of them. Matthew relates different events where the Son was tested by people who did not acknowledge his identity and authority (see 12,38; 16,1; 19,3; 22,17.35). But they could never make him take their bait. On the contrary, he caught them out in their own traps and showed them that he was the Son of God, who needed no approval from human authorities (12,39; 16,4; 21,27; 22,18.22).

The devil manifests himself also through the disciples. When Jesus told the disciples for the first time about his passion and death, Peter rebuked Jesus and tried to persuade him to evade it. Jesus' interpretation of Peter's act is significant: "You are setting your mind not on divine things, but on human things" (16,23). If the disciples set their mind on human things or think according to human ways, they will not be able to understand the Son and his mission. The Son's loyalty to the Father is intact; his mind is set always on the things of the Father. Nobody, not even the man to whom he will entrust the keys of the kingdom (16,19), can deter him from it. Jesus harshly reproaches Peter calling him Satan and asks him to get behind him (16,23). Peter and his companions have to go after the Son to learn to set their mind on the things of the Father in their process of becoming sons.

The last temptation that Jesus underwent while he was on the cross was perhaps the worst one. Seeing him hanging on the cross, helpless and abandoned, his adversaries and the people passing by derided him saying, "If you are the Son of God come down from the cross" (27,39-43). Their mockery sounds similar to that of the tempter in the wilderness. Why should the Son of God die like this? If he is really the Son, can God, his Father, the Lord of heaven and earth, remain passive at the tragic plight of his Son? Jesus triumphs over their temptations by yielding up his spirit (27,50). The people who witnessed his death then realized that God had not abandoned his Son, and so they proclaimed, "Truly this one was the Son of God" (27,54). Jesus faced all these tests and trials adhering to his filial relationship with the Father, obeying him and fulfilling his will. So, nothing could shake him or pull him back from his mission.

3.2 *The Son Seeks the Glory of the Father*

Jesus taught the disciples that their life should be centred on the Father, and their lifestyle should lead others to the Father. They should never seek self-glory (6,1-6.16-18) but shine their light before people, so that seeing their good deeds people may give glory to their Father (5,16). Matthew gives us two concrete examples that show how Jesus' deeds led people to glorify God.

The first one is in the context of the healing of the paralytic where the authority of Jesus over sin and sickness is explicitly portrayed (9,2-8). The evangelist comments on the reaction of the people who witnessed the healing: "When the crowd saw it, they were afraid, and they glorified God, who had given such authority to men" (9,8). The fear (φοβέω) they experience is a positive fear, a sign of their realization of God's presence in their midst (see Gen 28,16-17; Exod 20,20).[69] Therefore, they interpret this miracle as an intervention of God through Jesus. The relative clause "who had given such authority to men", found only in Matthew (see Mark 2,12; Luke 5,26), underscores the instrumentality of Jesus.[70] It is significant that in the present context the crowd identifies Jesus as one of the "men" (see the plural τοῖς ἀνθρώποις) who are given authority by God.[71]

The second example is in 15,29-31 where Matthew gives a summary of Jesus' healing ministry. Similar to 9,8, the evangelist reports that when the crowd saw the healings, they wondered and glorified the God of Israel.[72] Here again, though it is through Jesus that they experience the healing, they see it as an act of the God of Israel; hence they glorify him.[73]

---

[69] Or as R.T. FRANCE, *Matthew*, 166, puts it, "it indicates the supernatural impact of Jesus, as in 17:6; 27:54."

[70] Against R.H. GUNDRY, *Matthew: Mixed Church*, 165 who argues that Jesus is the God whom the crowds glorify.

[71] The readers of Matthew may identify many others, even some of their contemporaries among these "men" who have received "such authority" from God. Matthew's message is plain here: anyone who has received any authority from God should exercise it as Jesus did, leading people to glorify God.

[72] From the use of the term "the God of Israel" some commentators (e.g. H. FRANKEMÖLLE, *Jahwebund und Kirche Christi*, 117; R.H. GUNDRY, *Matthew: Mixed Church*, 319; R.T. FRANCE, *Matthew*, 248) conclude that the crowd mentioned here is a Gentile crowd. Though this appears to be a good explanation, there is no evidence to substantiate it. In fact, as Davies – Allison note, this divine appellation is a conventional title which occurs in various contexts in the OT (e.g. Exod 5,1; 1Kgs 1,48; Ps 41,13; Isa 29,23) and both Jews and non-Jews use it. See W.D. DAVIES – D.C. ALLISON, *Matthew*, II, 569.

[73] Parallel with this section, there is an account of the healing of a deaf and mute man in Mark. It is noteworthy that there the people praise Jesus saying, "He has done all things well; he even makes the deaf hear and the dumb speak" (Mark 7,37).

People's marvelling at Jesus' authority and power is mentioned in several other places in the gospel (7,28; 8,27; 9,33; 13,54; 15,31; 21,20; 22,22.33). Even his fellow townspersons who rejected him were astonished at his abilities; they wondered: "Where did this man get this wisdom and these mighty deeds?" (13,54). But Jesus never used his powers for vain glory or for self-interest.[74] He even warned some of the people who received healing from him not to publicize it (8,4; 9,30; 12,16). Matthew's portrayal of Jesus goes well with that of Phil 2,6: "Though he was in the form of God, he did not count equality with God a thing to be grasped." Rather, through his obedience and humility he always sought the glory of God, his Father.

3.3 *The Son Fearlessly Proclaims the Message of the Kingdom*

The children of the Father need not and should not fear human beings (10,26.28). If they submit themselves to the threats and scourges of their adversaries, they will not be able to bear fruit (13,21). Cowardice will force them to give up their convictions and run away from troubles. But by doing so, will they save their lives? Certainly not, rather they will lose them (10,39; 16,25). Therefore, Jesus taught them to withstand the oppositions and intimidations of the adversaries boldly and endure persecutions and tribulations gladly (5,11-12; 10,18-20.22; 24,9). During his earthly ministry Jesus also had much opposition from different corners of society. But he never bent his knee before his opponents or accusers nor gave up his mission out of fear. With the full freedom of the Son of God he went ahead with proclaiming the good news of the kingdom.

The people who opposed Jesus were mainly the religious leaders (Pharisees, scribes, Sadducees, chief priests, and elders). It is important to ask why they who taught the Law of God and claimed to be men of God opposed the Son of God? Evidently, they never recognized his identity and authority as the Son of God (see 9,3.34; 12,24; 26,63-65; 27,41-43), nor did they accept his message of the kingdom (see 8,11-12; 21,31-32.43) and his lifestyle. For example, according to them, his association with the tax collectors and sinners (9,11), many of his healings (9,3; 12,10),[75] and his approval of the behaviour of his disciples (12,2; 15,2) were all proof of his disrespect for the Law of God.

---

[74] See the explanation on the temptations of Jesus above.

[75] At least in four places the evangelist reports that Jesus touched the sick people when he healed them (8,3.15; 9,29; 20,34; see 9,20; 14,36). Touching the sick, especially the lepers, was a defiling act according to the Torah (see Lev 5,3; 13,45-46).

The Son was not frightened by the refusal and antagonism of these authorities. He was fully convinced that he had come not to abolish the Law and the prophets (as it was charged against him) but to fulfil them (3,15; 5,17-20; 7,12; 22,39-40). Therefore he demanded an exceeding righteousness (5,20), more than a perfunctory or ostentatious doing of the Law (6,1-18). The will of his heavenly Father was the compass that directed his life and mission (6,10; 7,21; 12,50; 18,14; 26,42). He considered those who accepted it and lived according to it as his kindred (12,50). He praised those people who manifested a deep faith, ignoring their inferior religious or social status (8,10.13; 9,22.29; 15,28). On the other hand, he strongly criticized the authorities for their hypocrisy and neglect of the commandments of God (9,13; 12,7; 15,3.7; 22,18; 23,13-29) and denounced them as a "brood of vipers" (12,34; 23,33).

In this connection, it is possible to see the passion and crucifixion of Jesus as a natural outcome of his conflict with the religious authorities. His opponents thought that they could silence him with a threat of death (see Wis 2,12-20). Although Jesus was fully aware of the fate awaiting him, he did not try to escape from it (16,21; 17,12.22-23; 20,18-19; 26,2). He courageously underwent the tortures and death they plotted against him. They did succeed in silencing him for a while, but not for ever. The death to which they condemned him and by which they labelled him as an accursed one (Deut 21,22-23) became the "sacrifice of salvation" for the human race (20,28; 26,28).

3.4 *The Son Submits to the Authority of the Father*

In their process of becoming children of the Father, the disciples had to submit themselves completely to the authority of the Father. Here again Jesus is the ideal model for the disciples to imitate. Though the Son had all authority on heaven and earth, he was fully obedient to the Father. He never pretended to have any authority or power that was not given by the Father (see Num 20,10-12). This attitude of Jesus is perceptible throughout the gospel.

There are at least two instances in the gospel where we find the Son explicitly acknowledging his subordination to the authority of the Father (20,23; 24,36). The first one is in the context of the request of the mother for honourable positions for her sons in the kingdom (20,20-23). One thing is certain from their request: they believed that Jesus had the power to grant such positions in the kingdom. Responding to her, Jesus asks John and James whether they can drink the cup that he is to drink (20,22). When they answer him affirmatively, Jesus approves it. But he tells them that it is not for him to decide to whom to grant (δίδωμι) such honours but his Father (ὑπὸ τοῦ πατρός μου).[76] Thus Jesus corrects their misunderstanding and teaches them that it is the Father, not he, who is the supreme authority in the kingdom (see 25,34).

Similarly, to the question of the disciples about the time and signs of his second coming and of the close of the ages (24,3), Jesus gives them a detailed description of the events that will accompany the end times. However, he adds his inability to know the exact time of these events: "But of that day and hour, no one knows, not even the angels of heaven, nor the Son, but the Father only" (24,36).[77] The Father's exclusive knowledge about the end times and of the second coming of the Son shows his absolute authority over the universe and over the Son. He, who feeds the birds of the sky, clothes the lilies of the field, and even knows when a sparrow falls to the ground, decides how this universe should function and when it should come to completion. Likewise, the Father, who sent the Son into the world to redeem it, will decide when to send him again as its judge. The Son humbly acknowledges this. Whether it is now or in the future he is functioning not by his own authority but by the authority of his Father.

3.5 *The Son Surrenders to the Will of the Father*

The way to the divine "childship" is a narrow way (7,13). As forewarned often in the gospel, in the process the children may meet with many forces of opposition including persecution and death. In their joys and sufferings, the same power should guide them forward: an unceasing craving to do the will of their Father. Perhaps, Jesus' demand for doing the will of the Father can be considered the kernel of his teaching on discipleship (6,10; 7,21; 12,50; 18,14; 21,31). His was a life totally engaged in fulfilling that will. As a human person he too had moments of pain and agony, confusion and doubt. But he conformed his will to the will of the Father and surrendered unconditionally to it. We have seen above how he overcame the tests and trials with great dedication to the will of the Father.

In Gethsemane, we have an example of his transcending the existential human pain with prayer and obedience to the will of the Father. Tormented

---

[76] In the parallel Markan text (10,40) the Father is not mentioned explicitly; instead a divine passive is used.

[77] A number of manuscripts (א[1] L W f^1 33 g[1] 1 vg sy co) omit the phrase οὐδὲ ὁ υἱός (nor the Son). This may be to avoid a doctrinal embarrassment arising from the question of how the Son can be ignorant of the end times. See J.P. MEIER, *Matthew*, 290; R.T. FRANCE, *Matthew* 347.

with a deep inner crisis, he tells his disciples, "My soul is very sorrowful, even to death" (26,38). He pleads for the company of his disciples. Three times he prays to the Father to let the cup pass if it be possible (26,39.42.44). But the next moment he surrenders totally to the will of the Father saying, "Yet not as I will, but as you will" (26,39); and "[...] your will be done" (26,42; see 6,10). That was his final yes, and thereafter he did not turn back. From Gethsemane to Golgotha, when he was betrayed by one of his own, captured like a robber, abandoned by his beloved ones, dragged before the council and the rulers, mocked, scourged, and crucified, he underwent all of these as the loyal Son of the Father. There was even a moment when he felt that even the Father had abandoned him (27,46)!

4. **Conclusion**

Summarizing the above observations, we may reaffirm our thesis with a christological corroboration: in the gospel of Matthew, discipleship is viewed as a process of becoming children of God. It is through Jesus, and only through him, one can enter into, proceed with, and accomplish this process. He is the unique Son of the Father, sent into the world to guide people to the Father and to his eternal kingdom. The Father himself has given witness to the identity and authority of the Son. Jesus came to the world and lived here as the authentic Son of the Father. He showed the people the way to the Father through his words and deeds and invited them to become the Father's children. He is the Emmanuel, "God with us", and continues his mission in the world through his disciples of every age. Those who listen to his words, respond to his call, and live a life following his model are God's children in his earthly family, and they will become God's children in the heavenly family.

GENERAL CONCLUSION

1. Discipleship as a Process of Becoming Children of God

Examining all the πατήρ passages which refer to God as the Father of the disciples, we have shown in this study that in the gospel of Matthew discipleship is viewed as a process of becoming children of God.[1]

Through Jesus, his Son, God offers all human persons the possibility of becoming his children. Jesus proclaimed the good news of the advent of the kingdom of heaven through his words and deeds, and he invited people to repent and prepare for entering the kingdom. Actually, with the coming of Jesus the kingdom has begun unfolding on earth and progressing towards its final consummation (11,12; 12,28; 13,31-32.33). Those who respond positively to Jesus and his message become members of his earthly family as his disciples and receive the grace of divine "childship". However, their filial identity in the earthly stage of their life is provisional and conditional. The continuity and confirmation of their "filiality" depend on their manner of life in the world. Those who live as the authentic disciples of Jesus, listening to his words and putting them into practice, will be judged worthy of entering the heavenly kingdom as God's children. In the heavenly kingdom their filial status will be eternal and irrevocable.

In Matthew there are twenty-one passages where God is portrayed as the Father of the disciples using the appellation πατήρ. In different ways these texts and their contexts present discipleship as a process of becoming children of God. Almost all the texts highlight the disciples' present identity as the children of the Father and give them guidelines for living out that identity.

---

[1] The extensive and selective use of the term πατήρ for God in relation to the disciples in Matthew accounts for our identification of this divine appellation as the key for understanding the concept of discipleship in the gospel.

Some of the texts, either directly or indirectly, refer to their future status as the children of the Father. A synthesis of our observations is given below:

1.1 *References and Allusions to the Disciples' Present Filial Status*

Jesus' repeated use of the relational phrase "your Father", as he speaks of God to them, is the most prominent indicator of the fact that the disciples are already enjoying filial status (5,16.45.48; 6,1.4.6^2.8.14.15.18^2.26.32; 7,11; 10,20.29; 18,14). Similarly, Jesus accentuates this status by asking them to address God as "our Father" in the model prayer (6,9). In fact, their filial relationship with the Father is reflected in all the petitions of the model prayer. In 23,10, Jesus tells them explicitly that God is their only Father, and so they should not call anyone on earth their father.[2]

There are several instances in the gospel where Jesus, emphasizing the filial status of the disciples, exhorts them to be different from the Gentiles (5,47; 6,7-8.32), the tax collectors (5,46) and the scribes and Pharisees (5,20) in their lifestyle. As the children of the Father the disciples should not imitate these people. On various occasions the emphatic pronoun ὑμεῖς is used to underscore the disciples' distinctive identity and status (see 5,13.14.48; 6,9.26; 10,20.31; 23,8).

The disciples are the precious children of the Father. They are cared for and valued much more than all the creatures of the world. The examples of the birds of the air (6,26), the lilies of the field (6,30), and the sparrows (10,29.31) emphasize this privileged status of the disciples. In 7,7-11 they are encouraged to ask their Father for all their needs, and they are promised that he will give them good things, much more even than what earthly fathers give to their children.

In 5,14-16 the disciples are identified as the light of the world. Since God is the supreme Light, the disciples' being the light of the world shows that they are God's children. When people see this light in the disciples, they will recognize the nature of the Father in them and give glory to him (5,16).

1.2 *References and Allusions to the Disciples' Future Filial Status*

At least two of the texts we have studied (5,43-48; 13,36-43) refer explicitly to the future filial status of the disciples. In 5,45, Jesus presents the

---

2 It is noteworthy that in Matthew Jesus presents God as the Father to no one except his followers. This means the divine "childship", both in the earthly family and in the heavenly family, is a privilege granted exclusively to the disciples of Jesus.

disciples' becoming children of the Father (γένησθε υἱοὶ τοῦ πατρὸς ὑμῶν) as the rationale for loving their enemies and praying for their persecutors. Their Father is a perfect Father. The disciples should grow into his perfection by imitating his model (5,48); thus they will become his true children. The notion of the future divine sonship of the disciples is reflected also in the beatitude on the peacemakers, "they will be called sons of God" (5,9).

In the Parable of the Weeds (13,24-30.36-43), the wheat which withstands the destructive attempts of the weeds and produces good grain symbolizes the disciples who triumph over the temptations and threats of the enemy and grow as the authentic children of the kingdom. At the end of the age, they will be judged righteous (οἱ δίκαιοι) and be received into the kingdom of their Father where they will shine like the sun (13,43).

One can find allusions to the future filial status also in the "divine reward" passages (5,46; 6,1.4.6.18; see also 5,12; 10,41-42), the "enter the kingdom" passages (7,21; see also 5,20; 18,3; 19,24.29; 25,34) and the "inheritance" passages (5,5; 19,29; 25,34). The eschatological tone of the petitions of the "Our Father" also points to this future state that the children are eagerly looking forward to while they are in the earthly family.

1.3 *From the Earthly Family towards the Heavenly Family*

Although the disciples receive the grace of divine "childship" as they follow Jesus, their relationship with the Father and Jesus will be broken off if they do not live a life befitting this identity. Consequently, their journey towards the eternal divine "childship" will be interrupted. To help them live their filial identity in the earthly stage and become worthy of being received into their eternal home, Jesus shows them the right way that they should pursue. If they listen to him and live according to his words, they will successfully complete the process that leads them from the earthly family to the heavenly family (7,21.24-27;13,43).

The instructions Jesus gives to the disciples are not merely ethical imperatives. They are rather guidelines for relationships – the disciples' relationship with the Father, with the world and with God's other children. In other words, they invite the disciples to recognize their filial identity and to relate with the world, and with their brothers and sisters as God's children.

1.3.1 Relationship with the Father

The disciples should realize that they are God's children and that their Father loves them dearly. In him should they trust; in his paternal care should they seek refuge (6,26.32; 7,11; 10,20.31; 18,14). He knows all their needs and provides them with what is good for them (6,8.32; 7,11). So they should not worry about anything in life (6,25-34), but should seek the Father's kingdom and his righteousness (6,10.33).

If they trust in the Father they will be confident of their own worth as his children (6,26.30; 10,31). Then they will not behave like people who do not even know the Father (5,47; 6,7.32), but will manifest their filial identity in every sphere of their life (5,16) and grow as the perfect children of the perfect Father (5,48).

It is not enough that they do good and pious deeds; they must do them with the right intention (6,1-18). Their righteousness is to surpass the self-centred righteousness of the hypocrites who perform their good deeds to attract people's praise and honour (6,2.5.16; see 5,20). The children's honour comes from the Father, and they should be convinced that their Father sees them and all their good works (6,4.6.18). Through their deeds they should glorify the Father (5,16), sanctify his name (6,9) and fulfil his will (6,10; 7,21; 12,50).

Different adverse forces may try to deter them from being the Father's children (6,13; 10,16-25; 13,24-30.36-43). They can triumph over these enemies only by anchoring their life in the Father. Sometimes, when they are troubled by the world or persecuted by their enemies, they may be tempted to think that their Father has forsaken them. But they should know that nothing happens to them without his knowledge; even in their trials and persecutions, he is with them (10,20-21.29-31).

1.3.2 Relationship with the World

Naturally, the disciples' relationship with the Father will be reflected in their relationship with the world and with their brothers and sisters. Life in the world is crucial for the process. It is an opportunity given to them to live as the Father's children in the earthly family and thus to store up treasure in the heavenly family (6,20; 19,21). The quality of their lives here will be the criterion by which they will be judged at the end (7,21-23;10,41-42; 16,27; 25,31-46).

On the other hand, the world is also a field of temptation (4,1-11; 18,7). The enemy too has sown his seeds in this field (13,25). The sons of the evil one may impede the growth of the sons of the kingdom (13,19). They may entice the children with worldly riches and glory or may menace them with persecution and death (13,21-22). The children must not forget that as this world is transient, so also are its riches and sufferings (6,19). However, they cannot make any progress by ignoring the world and its challenges. Their

Father wills the redemption of the world, and they are his missionaries (9,35–11,1; 28,16-20). Without conforming to the standards of the world, the children have to function as the instruments for the world's salvation, being its salt and light and guiding people on their way to becoming the Father's children (5,13-16).

In their dealings with people they will imitate the model of their Father (5,45); they will forgive their debtors (6,12.14-15), love their enemies, and pray for their persecutors (5,44). Thus they will show to the world that they are the true children of their Father.

1.3.3 Relationship with the Other Children

In the process that leads them towards their heavenly home, the disciples have a personal and collective responsibility towards their brothers and sisters who journey together with them. They are to treat each other as the Father's children and help each other to live their filial identity in the earthly family. As the children of the Father they are all equal (23,8-10); no one should consider himself/herself superior to others; rather each one should think of himself/herself as a servant of others (20,26; 23,11-12).

The Father does not want any of his children to be lost (18,14). The strengths and weaknesses of the children are diverse. But they should not insult their brothers and sisters or judge them (5,22; 7,1-5); no one should cause scandal to the "little ones" or despise them (18,6-10). If some of them stumble during their journey, the others must not forsake them but take every possible step to win them back to their family (18,10-14. 15-20).

Forgiveness is the hallmark of the Father's family. The Father accepts and forgives the weaknesses of the children; he even goes in search of a straying child (18,12-14). But he will not forgive those who do not forgive their brothers and sisters from their heart (6,12.14-15; 18,35).

2. **Through the Son, with the Son, in the Son**

The concept of discipleship that we have explored in this study is deeply rooted in Matthew's Christology. The Sonship of Jesus is the foundation for the divine "childship" of the disciples both in the earthly and in the heavenly family. Jesus is the unique Son of the Father sent into the world (1,18.20; 2,15; 3,17; 11,25-27; 14,33; 16,16; 17,5; 27,54; 28,18-19). He is the only one who knows the Father (11,27). The Father has given to him all authority in heaven and on earth (11,27; 28,18). Only through him can one know the Father and become a child of the Father. Without him no one can enter the family of God or experience God's paternity.

Jesus invites people to become his disciples (4,18.21; 9,9; 28,19), and he thus initiates them into the Father-children relationship. He reveals the Father to those he chooses (11,27), guides them in their process, and acknowledges those who do his Father's will as his own (7,21; 12,50). As the Emmanuel, he accompanies his brothers and sisters to the Father (1,23; 18,20; 28,20). Those who journey with him already live as the children of the Father.

In Jesus the disciples experience the ideal of sonship. All that he taught them, he lived himself. He died on the cross to fulfil the Father's redemptive programme for all human persons (1,21; 20,28; 26,28). The Father authenticated him and his mission by raising him from the dead. On the last day, he will appear in the glory of his Father as the judge of the world (7,21-23; 16,27; 25,31-46). Then he will receive those who have lived, following his model, as true children into the eternal family of the Father (7,21; 13,43; 25,34).

3. **For the Disciples of all the Ages**

Matthew's gospel ends with a command of the risen Jesus to his disciples to go and make disciples (μαθητεύω) of all nations baptizing them in the name of the Father, and of the Son, and of the Holy Spirit (28,19). He also promises them that he will be with them until the end of the ages (28,20). This final command of Jesus is an open invitation for all people of all times to become his disciples and thus children of the Father. With baptism one is initiated into this process. This means that all those who receive the Christian faith are the disciples of Jesus and children of God. They will complete the process by observing the teachings of Jesus in their life (28,20). His disciples in every generation go out to the world with an invitation from their master. Those who receive them receive Jesus and the Father who sent him (10,40), thereby joining the family of God.

The texts we have studied depict an ideal picture of discipleship. But Matthew's portrayal of the actual disciples, who were fortunate to witness the life and mission of Jesus, shows that they could not always live up to that ideal in their earthly stage. They were men who often vacillated between firm faith and little faith. For example, when Jesus called them, they immediately followed him without showing any doubt (4,18-22). Leaving everything they had, they accompanied him in his mission journey; they recognized him as the Lord and proclaimed him as the Christ and the Son of the living God (16,16). But in moments of crisis, they behaved like men of little faith (8,26; 14,31; 16,8; 17,20). The same Peter who confessed Jesus as the Christ also tried to dissuade him from his salvific death (16,22); he denied his relationship with

Jesus three times (26,69-75). Two others came with their mother requesting a superior position in the kingdom (20,20-28). During his passion they left him alone to suffer and fled in search of their safety. Even after the resurrection, when Jesus appeared to them, they doubted (28,17).

Many of the future disciples of Jesus may feel an affinity with the actual disciples in their daily struggle to believe and live as the children of the Father. Portraying the actual disciples sometimes in bright and sometimes in dark colours, relating their ups and downs in faith, the evangelist consoles and encourages these future generations of disciples to go forward on their journey, accepting their weaknesses and failings but all the while trusting in the Son who accompanies them to the Father.

ABBREVIATIONS

ABD	D.N. FREEDMAN, ed., The Anchor Bible Dictionary
ABR	*Australian Biblical Review*
ACCS.NT	Ancient Christian Commentary on Scripture. New Testament
ACNT	Augsburg Commentary on the New Testament
ACW	Ancient Christian Writers
AnBib	Analecta Biblica
AncB	The Anchor Bible
ANFa	The Ante-Nicene Fathers
AThR	*Anglican Theological Review*
AThR.SS	Anglican Theological Review Supplementary Series
BAGD	W. BAUER – W.F. ARNDT – F.W. GINGRICH – F.W. DANKER, *A Greek-English Lexicon of the New Testament*
BDF	F. BLASS – A. DEBRUNNER – R.W. FUNK, A Greek Grammar of the New Testament and Other Early Christian Literature
BEThL	Bibliotheca ephemeridum theologicarum lovaniensium
Bib	*Biblica*
BiBh	*Bible Bhashyam*
BiTod	*The Bible Today*
BJRL	*Bulletin of the John Rylands University Library of Manchester*
BR	*Biblical Research*
BS	*Biblotheca Sacra*
BSRel	Biblioteca di Scienze Religiose
BTB	*Biblical Theology Bulletin*
BU	Biblische Untersuchungen
BulBR	*Bulletin for Biblical Research*

BZ	*Biblische Zeitschrift*
CB.NT	Coniectanea Biblica. New Testament Series
CBQ	*The Catholic Biblical Quarterly*
CChr.SL	Corpus Christianorum. Series Latina
CEV	Contemporary English Version
cf.	confer
ch/chs.	chapter/chapters
CivCatt	*La Civiltà Cattolica*
CNT(N)	Commentaire du Nouveau Testament
DR	*Downside Review*
e.g.	exempli gratia
EBC	The Expositor's Bible Commentary
ed.	editor/editors
EDNT	H. BALZ – G. SCHNEIDER, ed., Exegetical Dictionary of the New Testament, I-III
EHS.T	Europäische Hochschulschriften: Reihe 23, Theologie
EKK	Evangelisch-Katholischer Kommentar zum Neuen Testament
EstB	*Estudios Bíblicos*
ET	*Expository Times*
EtB	Études Bibliques
etc.	et cetera
EThL	*Ephemerides Theologicae Lovanienses*
EvTh	*Evangelische Theologie*
f.	and the following
FaCh	The Fathers of the Church
FilolNT	*Filologia Neotestamentaria*
Fs.	Festschrift
GCS	Die griechischen christlichen Schriftsteller der ersten drei Jahrhunderte
GNS	Good News Studies
HeyJ	*Heythrop Journal*
HThK	Herders theologischer Kommentar zum Neuen Testament
HThR	*Harvard Theological Review*
i.e.	id est
IBSt	*Irish Biblical Studies*
ICC	International Critical Commentary
ID.	Idem

IDB	G.A. BUTTRICK, ed., Interpreter's Dictionary of the Bible
Interp.	*Interpretation*
ISBE	G.W. BROMILEY, ed., International Standard Bible Encyclopaedia 1-IV
IVP	Inter Varsity Press
JBL	*Journal of Biblical Literature*
JES	*Journal of Ecumenical Studies*
JSNT	*Journal for the Study of the New Testament*
JSNT.S	Journal for the Study of the New Testament Supplement Series
JSOT.S	Journal for the Study of the Old Testament Supplement Series
JThS	*Journal of Theological Studies*
LeDiv	*Lectio Divina*
LOUW–NIDA	J.P. LOUW – E.A. NIDA, *Greek-English Lexicon of the New Testament Based on Semantic Domains*, I-II
LSJ	Liddle–Scott–Jones, *Greek-English Lexicon*
LThPM	Louvain Theological and Pastoral Monographs
LXX	Septuagint
MSSNTS	Monograph Series. Society for New Testament Studies
n.	footnote number
NAB	New American Bible
NAC	New American Commentary
NCBC	The New Century Bible Commentary
Neotest.	*Neotestamentica*
NIBC	New International Biblical Commentary
NIDNT	New International Dictionary of New Testament Theology
NIGTC	New International Greek Testament Commentary
NIV	New International Version
NPNF	A Select Library of the Nicene and Post-Nicene Fathers
NT	*Novum Testamentum*
NT.S	Novum Testamentum Supplements
NTC	New Testament Commentary
NTD	Das Neue Testament Deutsch
NTMes	New Testament Message

NTOA	Novum Testamentum et Orbis Antiquus
NTS	*New Testament Studies*
OBO	Orbis Biblicus et Orientalis
p.	page/pages
par.	parallel/parallels
PBC	The Pontifical Biblical Commission
PG	J. MIGNE, ed., *Patrologia Graeca*
PL	J. MIGNE, ed., *Patrologia Latina*
PSV	*Parola spirito e vita*
RB	*Revue biblique*
RdT	*Rassegna di Teologia*
RExp	*Review and Expositor*
RSV	Revised Standard Version
RTR	*Reformed Theological Review*
SBEC	Studies in the Bible and Early Christianity
SBFA	Studii Biblici Franciscani Analecta
SBL	Society of Biblical Literature
SBL.SP	*Society of Biblical Literature Seminar Papers*
SBM	Stuttgarter biblische Monographien
SBT	Studies in Biblical Theology
SEÅ	*Svensk exegetisk årsbok*
ser.	series
SJTh	*Scottish Journal of Theology*
SPIB	Scripta Pontifici Instituti Biblici
StBL	Studies in Biblical Literature
StMiss	*Studia Missionalia*
Str-B	H.L. STRACK, – P. BILLERBECK, Kommentar zum Neuen Testament aus Talmud und Midrasch, I-VI
StTh	*Studia Theologica*
TaS	Texts and Studies. Contributions to Biblical and Patristic Literature
TDNT	G. KITTEL – G. FRIEDRICH, ed., Theological Dictionary of the New Testament, I-IX
TG.ST	Tesi Gregoriana. Serie Teologia
ThH	Théologie historique
ThHK	Theologischer Handkommentar zum Neuen Testament
ThLZ	*Theologische Literaturzeitung*
ThV	*Theologische Versuche*
ThZ	*Theologische Zeitschrift*

TJ	*Trinity Journal*
TNTC	The Tyndale New Testament Commentaries
trans.	translation
TS	*Theological Studies*
TynB	*Tyndale Bulletin*
v./vv.	verse/verses
VJTR	*Vidyajyoti Journal of Theological Reflection*
WBC	Word Biblical Commentary
WMANT	Wissenschaftliche Monographien zum Alten und Neuen Testament
WUNT	Wissenschaftliche Untersuchungen zum Neuen Testament
ZNW	*Zeitschrift für die neutestamentliche Wissenschaft*
ZSTh	*Zeitschrift für systematische Theologie*
ZThK	*Zeitschrift für Theologie und Kirche*

BIBLIOGRAPHY

AGNEW, F.H., "Almsgiving, Prayer, and Fasting", *BiTod* 33, 4 (1995) 239-244.

ALBRIGHT, W.F. – MANN, C.S., *Matthew. Introduction, Translation, and Notes,* AncB 26, Garden City, NY 1971.

ALLISON, D.C, Jr., "The Structure of the Sermon on the Mount", *JBL* 106 (1987) 423-445.

———, "'The hairs of your head are all numbered'", *ET* 101 (1990) 334-336.

AUGUSTINE OF HIPPO, *De sermone Domini in monte, PL* 34, 1230-1308; English trans., *Saint Augustine. Commentary on the Sermon on the Mount with Seventeen Related Sermons*, FaCh – Writings of Saint Augustine, 3, Washington, D.C. 1951.

BAILEY, M.L., "The Parable of the Tares", *BS* 155 (1998) 266-279.

———, "The Doctrine of the Kingdom in Matthew 13", *BS* 156 (1999) 443-451.

BARR, J., "Abba Isn't 'Daddy'", *JThS* 39 (1988) 28-47.

———, "The Hebrew/Aramaic Background of 'Hypocrisy' in the Gospels", in P.R. DAVIES – R.T. WHITE, ed., *A Tribute to Geza Vermes. Essays on Jewish and Christian Literature and History*, JSOT.S 100, Sheffield 1990, 307-326.

BARTH, G., "Das Gesetzesverständnis des Evangelisten Matthäus", in G. BORNKAMM – G. BARTH – H.J. HELD, *Überlieferung und Auslegung im Matthäusevangelium*, WMANT 1, Neukirchen 1959, 54-154; English trans., "Matthew's Understanding of the Law", in G. BORNKAMM – G. BARTH – H.J. HELD, *Tradition and Interpretation in Matthew*, London 1963, 58-164.

BARTON, S.C., *Discipleship and Family Ties in Mark and Matthew*, MSSNTS 80, Cambridge 1994.

BAUER, D.R., *The Structure of Matthew's Gospel*, JSNT.S 31, Sheffield 1988, 1989².

BEARE, F.W., *The Gospel according to Matthew. A Commentary*, Oxford 1981.

BEASLEY-MURRAY, G.R., *Jesus and the Kingdom of God*, Grand Rapids 1986.

———, "Matthew 6:33: The Kingdom of God and the Ethics of Jesus", in H. MERKLEIN, ed., *Neues Testament und Ethik*, Fs. R. Schnackenburg, Freiburg 1989, 84-98.

BECK, M., "'Be Perfect as Your Heavenly Father Is Perfect' (Mt 5:48)", *VJTR* 63 (1999) 381-384.

BEHM, J., "νῆστις", *TDNT,* IV, 924-935.

BENNETT, W., "The Sons of the 'Father': The Fatherhood of God in the Synoptic Gospels", *Interp.* 4 (1950) 12-23.

BERGHUIS, K.D., "A Biblical Perspective of Fasting", *BS* 158 (2001) 86-103.

BETZ, H.D., "Eine Episode im Jüngsten Gericht (Mt 7,21-23)", *ZThK* 78 (1981) 1-30; English trans., "An Episode in the Last Judgment (Matt. 7:21-23)", in ID., *Essays on the Sermon on the Mount*, Philadelphia 1985, 125-157.

———, "Kosmogonie und Ethik in der Bergpredigt", *ZThK* 81 (1984) 139-171; English trans., "Cosmogony and Ethics in the Sermon on the Mount", in ID., *Essays on the Sermon on the Mount*, Philadelphia 1985, 89-123.

———, *The Sermon on the Mount. A Commentary on the Sermon on the Mount, Including the Sermon on the Plain (Matthew 5:3–7:27 and Luke 6,20-49)*, Hermeneia, Minneapolis 1995.

BEUTLER, J., "Ihr seid das Salz des Landes (Mt 5,13)", in C. MAYER – K. MÜLLER – G. SCHMALENBERG, ed., *Nach den Anfängen fragen*, Fs. G. Dautzenberg, Gießen 1994, 85-94.

BIEDER, W., "σκυθρωπός", *TDNT,* VII, 450-451.

BLACK, M., *An Aramaic Approach to the Gospel and Acts*, London 1946, 1979³.

BLAENTINE, S.E., *Prayer in the Hebrew Bible. The Drama of Divine-Human Dialogue*, Minneapolis 1993.

BLAIR, E.P., *Jesus in the Gospel of Matthew*, New York 1960.

BLASS, F. – DEBRUNNER, A. – FUNK, R.W., *A Greek Grammar of the New Testament and Other Early Christian Literature*, Chicago – London 1961.

BLIGH, P.H., "A Note on υἱὸς θεοῦ in Mark xv.39", *ET* 80 (1968-1969) 51-53.

BLOMBERG, C.L., *Interpreting the Parables*, Leicester 1990.

———, *Matthew*, NAC 22, Nashville 1992.

BONHOEFFER, D., *Nachfolge*, München 1937; English trans., *The Cost of Discipleship*, New York 1959, 1995².

BONNARD, P., *L'Évangile selon saint Matthieu*, CNT(N) 1, Neuchâtel 1963, 1970².

BORCHERT, G.L., "Matthew 5:48 – Perfection and the Sermon", *RExp* 89 (1992) 265-269.

BORING, M.E., "The Gospel of Matthew", in *The New Interpreter's Bible*, VIII, Nashville 1995, 89-505.

BORNKAMM, G., "Enderwartung und Kirche in Matthäusevangelium", in G. BORNKAMM – G. BARTH – H.J. HELD, *Überlieferung und Auslegung im Matthäusevangelium*, WMANT 1, Neukirchen 1959, 13-47; English trans., "End-Expectation and Church in Matthew", in G. BORNKAMM – G. BARTH – H.J. HELD, *Tradition and Interpretation in Matthew*, London 1963, 15-51.

———, "Der Aufbau der Bergpredigt", *NTS* 24 (1978) 419-432.

BRONGERS, H.A., "Fasting in Israel in Biblical and Post-Biblical Times", in *Instruction and Interpretation. Studies in Hebrew Language, Palestinian Archaeology and Biblical Exegesis*, (Papers read at the Joint British-Dutch Old Testament Conference held at Louvain, 1976) Leiden 1977, 1-21.

BROOKS, S.H., "Apocalyptic Paraenesis in Matthew 6.19-34", in J. MARCUS – M.L. SOARDS, ed., *Apocalyptic and the New Testament. Essays in Honour of J. Louis Martyn*, JSNT.S 24, Sheffield 1989, 95-112.

BROWN, J.K., *The Disciples in Narrative Perspective. The Portrayal and Function of the Matthean Disciples*, SBL Academia Biblica 9, Atlanta 2002.

BROWN, R.E., "The Pater Noster as an Eschatological Prayer", *TS* 22 (1961) 175-208; also in ID., *New Testament Essays*, Milwaukee 1965, 217-253.

BROWN, R.E., *The Gospel according to John (i–xii). Introduction, Translation and Notes*, AncB, Garden City, NY 1966.

BROWN, R.N., "Jesus and the Child as a Model of Spirituality", *IBSt* 4 (1982) 178-192.

BROWN, S., "The Mission to Israel in Matthew's Central Section", *ZNW* 69 (1978) 73-90.

BUCHANAN, G.W., *The Gospel of Matthew*, I-II, Mellen Biblical Commentary, New Testament Series 1-2, Lewiston, NY 1996.

BULTMANN, R., "ἀφίημι" *TDNT*, I, 509-512.

———, "ἔλεος", *TDNT*, II, 477-487.

BYRNE, B., "The Messiah in whose Name 'the Gentiles will Hope' (Matt 12,21): Gentile Inclusion as an Essential Element of Matthew's Christology", *ABR* 50 (2002) 55-73.

BYRSKOG, S., Jesus the Only Teacher. Didactic Authority and Transmission in Ancient Israel, Ancient Judaism and the Matthean Community, CB.NT 24, Stockholm 1994.

CADOUX, C.J., The Historic Mission of Jesus, London 1941.

CAIROLI, M., *La "Poca Fede" nel Vangelo di Matteo*, AnBib 156, Roma 2005.

CAMPBELL, K.M., "The New Jerusalem in Matthew 5.14", *SJTh* 31 (1978), 335-363.

CARSON, D.A., *Matthew 1–12.13–28*, EBC, Grand Rapids 1995.

CARTER, W., *Households and Discipleship. A Study of Matthew 19–20*, JSNT.S 103, Sheffield 1994.

———, "Challenging by Confirming, Renewing by Repeating: The Parables of 'the Reign of the Heavens' in Matthew 13 as Embedded Narratives", *SBL.SP* 34 (1995) 399-424.

———, "'Solomon in All His Glory': Intertextuality and Matthew 6,29", *JSNT* 65 (1997) 3-25.

———, "Matthew 4:18-22 and Matthean Discipleship: An Audience-Oriented Perspective", *CBQ* 59 (1997) 58-75.

———, Matthew. Storyteller, Interpreter, Evangelist, Peabody, MA 1996, 2004[2].

CASTAÑO FONSECA, A.M., Δικαιοσυνη en Mateo. Una interpretación teológica a partir de 3,15 y 21,32, TG.ST 29, Roma 1997.

CHARETTE, B., *The Theme of Recompense in Matthew's Gospel*, JSNT.S 79, Sheffield 1992.

CHARLES, J. D., "Garnishing with the 'Greater Righteousness': The Disciple's Relationship to the Law (Matthew 5:17-20)", *BulBR* 12 (2002) 1-15.

CHASE, F., *The Lord's Prayer in the Early Church*, TaS I,3, Cambridge 1891.

CHEN, D.G., *God as Father in Luke-Acts*, StBL 92, New York 2006.

CHILTON, B., "God as 'Father' in the Targumim, in Non-Canonical Literatures of Early Judaism and Primitive Christianity, and Matthew", in ID., *Judaic Approaches to the Gospels*, Atlanta, Georgia 1994, 39-73.

CHROMATIUS OF AQUILEIA, "Tractatus in Matthaeum", in R. ÉTAIX – J. LEMARIÉ, ed., *Chromatii Aquileiensis opera*, CChr.SL IXa, Turnhout 1974.

CHRYSOSTOM, J., *Commentarius in sanctum Matthaeum Evangelistam*, *PG* 57-58; English trans., *Saint Chrysostom. Homilies on the Gospel of Saint Matthew*, NPNF 1, 10, Oxford 1851, Allegheny, P.A. 1888, Grand Rapids 1983.

COLWELL, E.C., "A Definite Rule for the Use of the Article in the Greek New Testament", *JBL* 52 (1933) 12-21.

COOK, J.G., "The Sparrow's Fall in Mt 10,29b", *ZNW* 79 (1988) 138-144.

CYPRIAN OF CARTHAGE., *De Dominica Oratione*, *PL* 4, 535-562; English trans., "The Lord's Prayer", in *Saint Cyprian – Treatises*, FaCh 36, Washington, D.C 1959, 125-162.

CYRIL OF ALEXANDRIA, "Fragmenta in Matthaeum", in J. REUSS, ed., *Matthäus-Kommentare aus der griechischen Kirche*, Berlin 1957, 153-269.

D'ANGELO, M.R., "Abba and 'Father': Imperial Theology and the Jesus Traditions", *JBL* 111 (1992) 611-630.

D'SA, F.X., "'Dhavani' as a Method of Interpretation", *BiBh* 5 (1979) 276-294.

DA SPINETOLI, O., Matteo. Il vangelo della chiesa, Assisi 1971, 1983[4].

DALMAN, G., Die Worte Jesu mit Berücksichtigung des nachkanonischen jüdischen Schrifttums und der aramäischen Sprache, Leipzig 1898; English trans., The Words of Jesus Considered in the Post-Biblical Jewish Writings and the Aramaic Language, Edinburgh 1909.

DANIELL, D, ed., *Tyndale's New Testament. Translated from the Greek by William Tyndale in 1534; in a Modern Spelling Edition and with an Introduction by David Daniell,* New Haven – London 1989.

DAVIES, W.D. – ALLISON, D.C. Jr., A Critical and Exegetical Commentary on the Gospel according to Saint Matthew, I. Matthew 1–7. II. Matthew 8–18. III. Matthew 19–28, ICC, Edinburgh 1988, 1991, 1997.

DAVISON, J.E., "Anomia and the Question of an Antinomian Polemic in Matthew", *JBL* 104 (1985) 617-635.

DE RU, G., "The Conception of Reward in the Teaching of Jesus", *NT* 8 (1966) 202-222.

DEISSMANN, A., *Licht vom Osten: das Neue Testament und die neuentdeckten Texte der hellenistisch-römischen Welt*, Tübingen 1909.

DELLING, G., "βατταλογέω" TDNT, I, 597.

DERRETT, J.D.M., "The Light and the City", *ET* 103 (1991-1992) 174-175.

———, "Light on Sparrows and Hairs (Mt 10,29-31)", *EstB* 55 (1997) 341-353.

DIETZFELBINGER, C., "Die Frömmigkeitsregeln von Matt 6:1-18 als Zeugnisse frühchristlicher Geschichte", *ZNW* 75 (1984) 184-201.

DILLON, R.J., "Ravens, Lilies, and the Kingdom of God (Matthew 6:25-33/Luke 12:22-31)" *CBQ* 53 (1991) 605-627.

DONALDSON, T.L., *Jesus on the Mountain. A Study in Matthean Theology*, JSNT.S 8, Sheffield 1985.

———, "Guiding Readers – Making Disciples: Discipleship in Matthew's Narrative Strategy", in R.N. LONGENECKER, ed., *Patterns of Discipleship in the New Testament*, Grand Rapids – Cambridge 1996, 30-49.

DU PLESSIS, P.J., "Love and Perfection in Matt. 5:43-48", *Neotest.* 1 (1967) 28-34.

DUMBRELL, W.J., "The Logic of the Rule of the Law in Matthew v 1-20", *NT* 23 (1981) 1-21.

DUMAIS, M., *Le Sermon sur la Montagne. État de la recherche, Interprétation, Bibliographie*, Paris 1995.

DUPONT, J., Les Béatitudes, I. Le problème littéraire – Les deux versions du Sermon sur la montagne et des Béatitudes, Bruges 1958. II. La Bonne Nouvelle. III. Les Évangélistes, EtB, Paris 1969, 1973.

EDWARDS, R.A., "Uncertain Faith: Matthew's Portrait of the Disciples", in F.F. SEGOVIA, ed., *Discipleship in the New Testament*, Philadelphia 1985, 47-61.

———, *Matthew's Narrative Portrait of Disciples. How the Text-Connoted Reader Is Informed*, Harrisburg, PA 1997.

EVANS, C.F., *The Lord's Prayer*, London 1963,1997^2.

FABRIS, R., *Matteo. Traduzione e commento*, Commenti biblici, Roma 1982.

FALLON, M., *The Gospel according to Saint Matthew*, Kensington 1997.

FARRER, A., *St. Matthew and St. Mark*, Westminster, 1954.

FEDRIGOTTI, L.M., *An Exegetical Study of the Nuptial Symbolism in Matthew 9:15*, New York 2006.

FENTON, J.C., *Saint Matthew*, London 1963, 1977^2.

FIEDLER, M.J., "Gerechtigkeit im Matthäus-Evangelium", *ThV* 8 (1977) 63-73.

FILSON, F.V., *A Commentary on the Gospel according to St. Matthew*, London 1960.

FINKEL, A., "The Prayers of Jesus in Matthew", in A. FINKEL – L. FRIZZELL, ed., Standing Before God. Studies on Prayer in Scriptures and in Tradition with Essays in Honour of John M. Oesterreicher, New York 1981, 131-169.

FITZMYER, J., "Abba and Jesus' Relation to God", *LeDiv* 123 (1985) 15-38.

FLANNERY, A., ed., *Vatican Council II. The Conciliar and Post Conciliar Documents*, New York 1975.

FOERSTER, W., "ἐπιούσιος", *TDNT,* II, 590-599.

FORESTI, F., *Introduction to the Sermon on the Mount in the Gospel of Matthew*, Darlington 1983.

FOSTER, R., "Why on Earth Use 'Kingdom of Heaven'?: Matthew's Terminology Revisited", *NTS* 48,4 (2002) 487-499.

FOULKES, F., *A Guide to St. Matthew's Gospel*, London 2001.

FRANCE, R.T., The Gospel According to Matthew. An Introduction and Commentary, TNTC, Grand Rapids – Cambridge 1985.

FRANKEMÖLLE, H., *Jahwebund und Kirche Christi. Studien zur Form und Traditionsgeschichte des Evangeliums nach Matthäus*, Münster 1974.

———, *Matthäus. Kommentar* I-II, Düsseldorf 1994, 1997.

FRANZMANN, M.H., *Follow Me. Discipleship According to Saint Matthew*, St. Louis 1961.

FURNISH, V.P., *The Love Command in the New Testament*, London 1972.

GALLARDO, C.B., "Matthew: Good News for the Persecuted Poor", in L.E. VAAGE, ed., *Subversive Scriptures. Revolutionary Readings of the Christian Bible in Latin America*, Valley Forge, PA 1997, 173-192.

GAMBA, G.G., *Vangelo di San Matteo. La proclamazione del Regno dei Cieli: la fase della "semina" (Mt 4,17–13,52)*, BSRel 195, Roma 2006.

GARLAND, D.E., *The Intention of Matthew 23*, NT.S 52, Leiden – New York – København – Köln 1979.

GIAVINI, G., *Ma io vi dico. Esegesi e vita attorno al Discorso della Montagna*, Milano 1993.

GIESEN, H., *Christliches Handeln: Eine redaktionskritische Untersuchung zum δικαιοσύνη-Begriff in Matthäus-Evangelium*, Frankfurt am Main, 1982.

GINZEL, G.B., *Die Bergpredigt: jüdisches und christliches Glaubensdokument*, Heidelberg 1985.

GNILKA, J., *Das Matthäusevangelium*, I-II, HThK, Freiburg – Basel – Wien 1986-1988.

GOSHEN-GOTTSTEIN, A., "God the Father in Rabbinic Judaism and Christianity: Transformed Background or Common Ground?", *JES* 38,4 (2001) 470-504.

GOULDER, M., *Midrash and Lection in Matthew*, London 1974.

GRASSO, S., *Gesù e i suoi fratelli. Contributo allo studio della cristologia e dell'antropologia nel Vangelo di Matteo*, Bologna 1993.

———, *Il Vangelo di Matteo*, Roma 1995.

GREEN, M., *The Message of Matthew. The Kingdom of Heaven,* Nottingham 2000.

GREGORY OF NYSSA, *De Oratione Dominica*, *PG* 44, 1120-1193; English trans., "The Lord's Prayer", in *St. Gregory of Nyssa*, ACW 18, Westminster 1954, 21-84.

GRILLI, M., *Comunità e Missione: le direttive di Matteo. Indagine esegetica su Mt 9,35–11,1*, EHS.T 458, Frankfurt am Main 1992.

———, "Il mandato missionario. Lettura di Mt 28,16-20 in chiave comunicativa", *StMiss* 52 (2003) 23-50.

GRUNDMANN, W., *Das Evangelium nach Matthäus*, ThHK 1, Berlin 1968, 1990[7].

GUELICH, R.A., *The Sermon on the Mount. A Foundation for Understanding*, Dallas 1982.

GUNDRY, R.H., *Matthew. A Commentary on His Handbook for a Mixed Church under Persecution*, Grand Rapids 1982, 1994[2].

HAGNER, D.A., *Matthew 1–13.14–28*, WBC 33/a-b, Dallas 1993, 1995.

———, "Matthew's Parables of the Kingdom (Matthew 13,1-52)", in R.N. LONGENECKER, ed., *The Challenge of Jesus' Parables*, Grand Rapids, Michigan 2000, 102-124.

HAMERTON-KELLY, R., *God the Father. Theology and Patriarchy in the Teaching of Jesus*, Philadelphia, 1979.

HARRINGTON, D.J., *The Gospel of Matthew,* Sacra Pagina 1, Collegeville, MN 1991.

HARTIN, P.J., "Call to Be Perfect through Suffering (James 1,2-4). The Concept of Perfection in the Epistle of James and the Sermon on the Mount", *Bib* 77 (1996) 477-492.

HEIL, J.P., *Jesus Walking on the Sea. Meaning and Gospel Functions of Matt 14:22-33, Mark 6:45-52 and John 6:15b-21*, AnBib 87, Rome 1981.

HEMER, C., "ἐπιούσιος", *JSNT* 22 (1984) 81-94.

HENDRICKX, H., *The Sermon on the Mount*, London 1984.

HENDRIKSEN, W., *The Gospel of Matthew*, NTC, Edinburgh 1973, 1989[5].

HILL, D., *Greek Words with Hebrew Meanings. Studies in Soteriological Terms*, MSSNTS 5, Cambridge 1967.

———, *The Gospel of Matthew*, NCBC, London 1972.

———, "False Prophets and Charismatics: Structure and Interpretation in Matthew 7,15-23", *Bib* 57 (1976) 327-348.

———, "'Our Daily Bread' (Matt 6.11) in the History of Exegesis", *IBSt* 5 (1983) 2-10.

HOET, R., *"Omnes Autem Vos Fratres Estis". Etude du concept ecclésiologique des "frères" selon Mt 23,8-12*, Roma 1982.

HOFIUS, O., "Father", *NIDNT,* I, 614-616.

HOWARD, T.L., "The Use of Hosea 11:1 in Matthew 2:15: An Alternative Solution", *BSac* 143 (1986) 314-328.

HOWELL, D,B., *Matthew's Inclusive Story. A Study in the Narrative Rhetoric of the First Gospel*, JSNT.S 42, Sheffield 1990.

HULTGREN, A.J., *The Parables of Jesus. A Commentary*, Grand Rapids 2000.

HUTTON, W.R., "The Salt Sections", *ET* 58 (1946-47) 166-68.

JEREMIAS, J., "θύρα", *TDNT*, III, 173-180.

———, *Die Gleichnisse Jesu*, Göttingen 1958.

———, *The Prayers of Jesus,* SBT 6, London 1967.

———, *New Testament Theology*, London – New York 1971.

JOHNSON, E.S., "Is Mark 15.39 the Key to Mark's Christology?", *JSNT* 31 (1987) 3-22.

JOSEPHUS, F., *The Jewish War*, English trans. by G.A. WILLIAMSON, Aylesbury 1959.

KALLIKUZHUPPIL, J., "The Greater Righteousness", *BiBh 10* (1984) 89-105.

KAYALAPARAMBIL, T., "The Missionary Discourse in the Gospel of Matthew", *BiBh* 10 (1984) 247-256.

KEE, A., "The Question about Fasting", *NT* 11 (1969) 161-173.

KEENER, C.S., *The IVP Bible Background Commentary. New Testament*, Downers Grove, IL – Leicester 1993.

———, *Matthew*, IVP New Testament Commentary, Downers Grove, IL – Leicester 1997.

KEERANKERI, G., *The Love Commandment in Mark*, AnBib 150, Rome 2003.

———, "Matthew's Gospel and the Kingdom-Church Discourse", in A. MALINA, ed., *On His Way*, Fs. K. Stock, Katowice 2004, 102-120.

———, "Fulfilling all Righteousness: the Baptism of Jesus", in *VJTR* 69 (2005) 144-151.

KILGALLEN, J.J., *A Brief Commentary on the Gospel of Matthew*, New York 1992.

KIM, J.R., *"...perché io sono mite e umile di cuore" (Mt 11,29). Studio esegetico-teologico sull'umiltà del Messia secondo Matteo. Dimensione cristologica e risvolti ecclesiologici*, TG.ST 120, Roma 2005.

KIM, T.H., "The Anarthrous υἱὸς θεοῦ in Mark 15:39 and the Roman Imperial Cult", *Bib* 79 (1998) 221-241.

KINGSBURY, J.D., *The Parables of Jesus in Matthew 13*, London 1969.

KINGSBURY, J.D., *Matthew: Structure, Christology, Kingdom*, Minneapolis 1975, 1989².

———, "The Verb *Akoluthein* ('to Follow') as an Index of Matthew's View of his Community", *JBL* 97 (1978) 56-73.

———, *Matthew as Story*, Philadelphia 1986, 1988².

———, "The Place, Structure, and Meaning of the Sermon on the Mount within Matthew", *Interp.* 41 (1987) 131-142.

KLASSEN, W., "The Authenticity of the Command: 'Love Your Enemies'", in B.D. CHILTON – C.A. EVANS, ed., *Authenticating the Words of Jesus*, Leiden – Boston – Köln 1999, 385-407.

KOTTACKAL, J., "The Righteousness Required of the Followers of Christ", *BiBh* 10 (1984) 132-139.

KRENTZ, E., "Community and Character: Matthew's Vision of the Church", *SBL.SP* 26 (1987) 565-573.

KRETZER, A., *Die Herrschaft der Himmel und die Söhne des Reiches: Eine redaktionsgeschichtliche Untersuchung zum Basileiabegriff und Basileiaverständnis im Matthäusevangelium*, SBM 10, Würzburg 1971.

KÜMMEL, W.G., *Verheissung und Erfüllung: Untersuchungen zur eschatologischen Verkündigung Jesu*, Zürich 1951, 1956³; English trans., *Promise and Fulfilment. The Eschatological Message of Jesus*, London 1957.

KUTHIRAKKATTEL, S., *The Beginning of Jesus' Ministry according to Mark's Gospel (1,14-3,6): A Redaction Critical Study*, AnBib 123, Rome 1990.

LACHS, S.T., "On Matthew VI.12", *NT* 17 (1975) 6-8.

LAGRANGE, M.J., *Évangile selon saint Matthieu*, Paris 1923, 1948⁵.

LAMBRECHT, J., *The Sermon on the Mount. Proclamation and Exhortation*, GNS 14, Wilmington 1985.

———, *Nieuw en oud uit de schat. De parables van het Matteüsevangelie*, Leuven 1991; English trans., *Out of the Treasure. The Parables in the Gospel of Matthew*, LThPM 10, Louvain 1992.

LANDMESSER, C., *Jüngerberufung und Zuwendung zu Gott: Ein exegetischer Beitrag zum Konzept der matthäischen Soteriologie im Anschluß an Mt 9,9-13*, Tübingen 2001.

LATHAM, J.E., *The Religious Symbolism of Salt*, ThH 64, Paris 1982.

LIEBENBERG, J., *The Language of the Kingdom and Jesus. Parable, Aphorism, and Metaphor in the Sayings Material Common to the Synoptic Tradition and the Gospel of Thomas*, Berlin – New York 2001.

LINTON, O., "St. Matthew 5:43", *StTh* 18 (1964) 66-79.

LOCHMAN, J.M., *Unser Vater. Auslegung des Vaterunsers*, Gütersloh 1988.

LOUW, J.P. – NIDA, E.A., *Greek-English Lexicon of the New Testament Based on Semantic Domains*, I-II, New York, 1988, 1989[2].

LUZ, U., "Die Jünger in Matthäusevangelium", *ZNW* 62 (1971) 141-171; English trans., "The Disciples in the Gospel according to Matthew", in G. STANTON, ed., *The Interpretation of Matthew*, Philadelphia – London 1983, 98-128.

———, *Das Evangelium nach Matthäus, I-IV*, EKK 1, 1-4, Zürich – Neukirchen 1985, 1990, 1997, 2002; English trans., *Matthew 1–7 . A Continental Commentary*, Minneapolis 1989; *Matthew 8–20*, Hermeneia, Minneapolis 2001; *Matthew 21–28*, Hermeneia, Minneapolis 2005.

———, "Die Jüngerrede des Matthäus als Anfrage an die Ekklesiologie oder: Exegetische Prolegomena zu einer dynamischen Ekklesiologie", in K. KERTELGE – T. HOLTZ – C.P. MÄRZ, ed., *Christus Bezeugen*, Fs. W. Trilling, Leipzig 1989, 84-101; English trans., "Discipleship: A Matthean Manifesto for a Dynamic Ecclesiology", in U.LUZ, *Studies in Matthew*, Grand Rapids 2005, 143-164.

———, *Die Jesusgeschichte des Matthäus*, Neukirchen 1993; English trans., *The Theology of the Gospel of Matthew*, Cambridge 1995.

MAGGI, A., "Nota sull'uso di 'ΤΩΙ ΣΩΙ ΟΝΟΜΑΤΙ' e 'ΑΝΟΜΙΑ' in Mt 7,21-23", *FilolNT* 3 (1990) 145-149.

MANGATT, G., "Reflections on the Apostolic Discourse (Mt 10)", *BiBh* 6 (1980) 196-206.

———, "The Kingdom of God and Detachment (Mt 6:19-34)", *BiBh* 10 (1984) 122-131.

MANICARDI, E., "La paternità di Dio nel discorso della montagna secondo Matteo", *PSV* 39 (1999) 101-118.

———, "Dio Padre nella prospettiva del vangelo secondo Matteo", *Lateranum* 66 (2000) 81-106.

MANSON, T.W., *The Sayings of Jesus*, London 1949.

MANSON, T.W., "The Lord's Prayer", *BJRL* 38 (1955-56), 436-448.

MARCHEL, W., *Abba, Père!. La Prière du Christ et des Chrétiens*, AnBib 19, Rome 1963.

MARECEK, P., *La Preghiera di Gesù nel Vangelo di Matteo. Uno studio esegetico-teologico*, TG.ST 67, Roma 2000.

MARGUERAT, D., *Le jugement dans l'Évangile de Matthieu*, Genève 1981.

MARSHALL, I.H., "'Fear Him who Can Destroy both Soul and Body in Hell' (Mt 10:28)", *ET* 81 (1970) 276-280.

———, "Jesus – Example and Teacher of Prayer in the Synoptic Gospels", in R.N. LONGENECKER, ed., *Into God's Presence. Prayer in the New Testament*, Grand Rapids 2001, 113-131.

MARTINEZ F.G, – TIGCHELAAR, E.J.C. ed., *The Dead Sea Scrolls Study Edition*, Leiden – New York – Köln 1997.

MASSEY, I.A., *Interpreting the Sermon on the Mount in the Light of Jewish Tradition as Evidenced in the Palestinian Targums of the Pentateuch*, SBEC 25, Lewiston – Queenstown – Lampeter 1991.

MATERA, F.J., *Passion Narratives and Gospel Theologies. Interpreting the Synoptics through their Passion Stories*, New York 1986.

MEIER, J.P., *Law and History in Matthew's Gospel. A Redactional Study of Mt 5,17-48*, AnBib 27, Rome 1976.

———, *The Vision of Matthew*, New York 1979.

———, *Matthew*, NTMes 3, Wilmington 1980, 1986[5].

METZGER, B.M., *A Textual Commentary on the Greek New Testament*, Stuttgart 1971, 1994[2].

MEYNET, R., "La composition du Notre Père", *Liturgie* 119 (2002) 158-191.

MICHAELS, J.R., "Christian Prophecy and Matthew 23,8-12: A Test Exegesis", *SBL.SP* 15 (1976) 305-310.

MICHEL, O., "Der Lohngedanke in der Verkündigung Jesu", *ZSTh* 9 (1931) 47-54.

MILER, J., *Les citations d'accomplissement dans l'Évangile de Matthieu. Quand Dieu se rend présent en toute humanité*, AnBib 140, Roma 1999.

MINEAR, P.S., "The Disciples and the Crowds in the Gospel of Matthew", in M.H. SHEPHERD – E.C. HOBBS, ed., *Gospel Studies in Honour of S.E. Johnson*, AThR.SS 3 (1974) 28-44.

MINEAR, P.S., "The Salt of the Earth", *Interp.* 51 (1997) 31-41.

MITCHELL, C.C., "The Practice of Fasting in the New Testament", *BS* 147 (1990) 455-469.

MOHRLANG, R., *Matthew and Paul*, MSSNTS 48, Cambridge 1984.

MONTEFIORE, H.W., "God as Father in the Synoptic Gospels", *NTS* 3 (1956-1957) 31-46.

MORRIS, L., *The Gospel according to Matthew*, Grand Rapids, 1992.

MOULE, C.F.D., "An Unsolved Problem in the Temptation Clause in the Lord's Prayer", *RTR* 33 (1974) 65-75.

MOUNCE, R.H., *Matthew*, NIBC 1, Peabody, MA 1991.

MOWERY, R.L., "God, Lord, and Father: The Theology of the Gospel of Matthew", *BR* 33 (1988) 24-36.

———, "The Matthean References to the Kingdom", *EThL* 70 (1994) 398-405.

MULLOOR, A., *Jesus' Prayer of Praise. A Study of Mt 11:25-30 and Its Communicative Function in the First Gospel*, New Delhi 1996.

MURPHY-O'CONNOR, J., "The Prayer of Petition (Matthew 7:7-11 and par.)", *RB* 110,3 (2003) 399-416.

NEERAKKAL, C., *The Concept of "Perfect" in the Gospel of Matthew. An Exegetico-Theological Investigation*, (Excerpta ex dissertatione ad Doctoratum in Facultate Theologiae Pontificiae Universitatis Gregorianae), Roma 1991.

NEUSNER, J., *The Mishna. A New Translation*, London 1988.

NEWMAN, B.M – STEINE P.C., *A Translator's Handbook on the Gospel of Matthew*, London 1988.

NEWPORT, K.G.C., *The Sources and Sitz im Leben of Matthew 23*, JSNT.S 117, Sheffield 1995.

NGOWI, W., *Jesus' Teaching on Prayer in the Sermon on the Mount. An Exegetico-Theological Study*, (Excerpt from the Dissertation of Doctoral Thesis in Biblical Theology at the Pontifical Gregorian University), Rome 2004.

NOLLAND, J., "'In Such a Manner it is Fitting for us to Fulfil all Righteousness': Reflections on the Place of Baptism in the Gospel of Matthew", in S.E. PORTER – A.R. CROSS, ed., *Baptism, the New Testament and the Church. Historical and*

Contemporary Studies in Honour of R.E.O. White, JSNT.S 171, Sheffield 1999, 63-80.

NOLLAND, J., *The Gospel of Matthew. A Commentary on the Greek Text*, NIGTC, Grand Rapids 2005.

O'NEILL, J.C., "The Kingdom of God", *NT* 35 (1993) 130-141.

OAKLEY, I.J.W., "Hypocrisy in Matthew", *IBSt* 7 (1985) 118-138.

OLSTHOORN, M.F., *The Jewish Background and Synoptic Setting of Mt 6,25-33 and Lk 12,22-31*, SBFA 10, Jerusalem 1975.

ORIGEN, "Commentariorum in Matthaeum libri 10-17", in E. KLOSTERMANN, ed., *Origenes Werke*, X, GCS 40, Leipzig 1935; English trans., "Origen's Commentary on the Gospel of Matthew", in ANFa 10, Grand Rapids 1980[5], 411-512.

———, *De Oratione*, *PG* 11, 416-561; English trans., "Prayer", in *Origen,* ACW 19, Westminster 1954, 15-140.

OVERMAN, J.A., *Matthew's Gospel and Formative Judaism. The Social World of the Matthean Community*, Minneapolis 1990.

PALACHUVATTIL, J., *"He Saw". The Significance of Jesus' Seeing Denoted by the Verb εἶδεν in the Gospel of Mark*, TG.ST 84, Roma 2002.

PAMMENT, M., "The Kingdom of Heaven according to the First Gospel", *NTS* 27 (1980-81) 211-232.

PARAMBI, B., *The Discipleship of the Women in the Gospel according to Matthew. An Exegetical Theological Study of Matt 27:51b-56,57-61 and 28:1-10*, TG.ST 94, Roma 2003.

PARK, E.C., *The Mission Discourse in Matthew's Interpretation*, WUNT, Tübingen 1995.

PATTE, D., *The Gospel according to Matthew. A Structural Commentary on Matthew's Faith*, Philadelphia 1987.

———, *Discipleship according to the Sermon on the Mount. Four Legitimate Readings, Four Plausible Views of Discipleship, and their Relative Value*, Valley Forge, PA 1996.

———, *The Challenge of Discipleship. A Critical Study of the Sermon on the Mount as Scripture*, Harrisburg, PA 1999.

PENNA, R., "La Paternità di Dio nel Nuovo Testamento", *RdT* 40 (1999) 7-39.

PESCH, W., *Der Lohngedanke in der Lehre Jesu*, München 1955.

PETERSEN, W.L., "The Parable of the Lost Sheep in the Gospel of Thomas and the Synoptics", *NT* 23 (1981) 128-147.

PIPER, R.A., "Matt 7,7-11 par. Luke 11,9-13. Evidence of Design and Argument in the Collection of Jesus' Sayings", in J. DELOBEL, ed., *Logia. Les paroles de Jésus – The Sayings of Jesus. Mémorial Joseph Coppens*, Leuven 1982, 411-418.

PLUMMER, A, *An Exegetical Commentary on the Gospel according to Matthew*, London 1909.

THE PONTIFICAL BIBLICAL COMMISSION, *The Interpretation of the Bible in the Church*, Rome 1993.

POPKES, W., "Die Gerechtigkeitstradition im Matthäus-Evangelium", *ZNW* 80 (1989) 1-23.

PÖTTNER, M., "Metaphern der universalen Liebe (Mt 5,13a.14a)", *ThLZ* 122 (1997) 105-121.

POWELL, M.A., "Do and Keep What Moses Says (Matthew 23:2-7)", *JBL* 114 (1995) 419-435.

PREISKER, H., "μισθός κτλ", *TDNT*, IV, 695-728.

PRYZYBYLSKI, B., *Righteousness in Matthew and his World of Thought*, MSSNTS 41, Cambridge 1980.

QUELL, G. – STAUFFER, E., "ἀγαπάω", *TDNT*, I, 21-55.

von RAD, G., "Die Stadt auf dem Berge", *EvTh* 8 (1948-49) 439-447.

REEVES, K.H., *The Resurrection Narrative in Matthew. A Literary-critical Examination*, New York 1993.

REUMANN, J., *Righteousness in the New Testament*, Philadelphia 1982.

ROH,T., *Die familia dei in den synoptischen Evangelien. Eine redaktions- und sozialgeschichtliche Untersuchung zu einem urchristlichen Bildfeld,* NTOA 37, Fribourg 2001.

SABOURIN, L., "Why Is God Called 'Perfect' in Mt 5:48?", *BZ* 24 (1980) 266-268.

———, *The Gospel according to St. Matthew*, I-II, Bombay 1982.

SABUGAL, S., *El padrenuestro en la interpretación catequética antigua y moderna*, Salamanca 1982.

SALDARINI, A.J., *Matthew's Christian-Jewish Community*, Chicago – London 1994.

SÁNCHEZ NAVARRO, L., *"Venid a mí" (Mt 11,28-30). El discipulado, fundamento de la ética en Mateo*, Studia Teologica Matritensia 4, Madrid 2004.

SAND, A., *Das Gesetz und die Propheten. Untersuchungen zur Theologie des Evangeliums nach Matthäus*, Regensburg 1974.

SCHERMAN, N., *Translation, Commentary and an Overview – "Kaddish/Prayer of Sanctification"*, New York 1980, 1982².

SCHIFFMAN, L.H. – VANDERKAM, J.C. ed., *Encyclopaedia of the Dead Sea Scrolls*, I-II, Oxford 2000.

SCHLATTER, A., *Der Evangelist Matthäus: seine Sprache, sein Ziel, seine Selbständigkeit*, Stuttgart 1963.

SCHMID, J., *Das Evangelium Nach Matthäus*, Regensburg 1965.

SCHMIDT, K.L., "ἔθνος in the New Testament", *TDNT*, II, 369-372.

SCHMIDT, T.E., "Burden, Barrier, Blasphemy: Wealth in Matt 6:33, Luke 14:33 and Luke 16:15", *TJ* 9 (1988) 171-189.

SCHNACKENBURG, R., *Die sittliche Botschaft des Neuen Testamentes*, München 1954; English trans., *The Moral Teaching of the New Testament*, New York 1965.

———, "Ihr seid das Salz der Erde, das Licht der Welt", in ID., *Schriften zum Neuen Testament. Exegese in Fortschritt und Wandel*, München 1971, 177-200.

SCHNEIDER, G., *Botschaft der Bergpredigt*, Aschaffenburg 1969.

———, "Das Bildwort von der Lampe. Zur Traditiongeschichte eines Jesus-Wortes" in ID., *Jesusüberlieferung und Theologie*, NT.S 67, Leiden – New York – København – Köln 1992, 116-142.

SCHNIEWIND, J., *Das Evangelium nach Matthäus*, Göttingen 1936, 1984¹³.

SCHWARZ, G., "Matthäus vii 13a: Ein Alarmruf angesichts höchster Gefahr", *NT* 12 (1970) 229-232.

SCHWEIZER, E., *Das Evangelium nach Matthäus*, NTD 2, Göttingen 1973, 1976².

———, *Die Bergpredigt*, Göttingen 1982.

SCULLION, J.J., "Righteousness", *ABD, V*, 724-736.

SEITZ, O.J.F., "Love Your Enemies. The Historical Setting of Matthew v.43f.; Luke vi. 27f.", *NTS* 16 (1969) 39-54.

SENIOR, D., *The Gospel of Matthew,* Interpreting Biblical Texts, Nashville 1997.

———, "Between Two Worlds: Gentile and Jewish Christians in Matthew's Gospel", *CBQ* 61 (1999) 1-23.

SHEFFIELD, J., "The Father in the Gospel of Matthew", in A-J. LEVINE, ed., *A Feminist Companion to Matthew*, Sheffield 2001.

SHERIDAN, M., "Disciples and Discipleship in Matthew and Luke", *BTB* 3 (1973) 235-255.

SIBINGA, J.S., "Exploring the Composition of Matth. 5–7: The Sermon on the Mount and Some of Its 'Structures'", *FilolNT* 7 (1994) 175-195.

SIDEBOTTOM, E.M., "Reward in Matthew v.46, etc.", *ET* 67 (1955-56) 219-220.

SIM, D.C., "The 'Confession' of the Soldiers in Matthew 27:54", *HeyJ* 34 (1993) 401-424.

———, "The Gospel of Matthew and the Gentiles", *JSNT* 57 (1995) 19-48.

SIMONETTI, M., ed., *Matthew 1–13*, ACCS.NT 1a, Downers Grove 2001.

SMITH, C.W.F., "Lord's Prayer", *IDB*, III, 154-158.

SMITH, M., "Mt. 5.43: 'Hate Thine Enemy'", *HThR* 45 (1952) 71-73.

SMITH, R.H., *Matthew*, ACNT, Minneapolis 1989.

SOARES PRABHU, G.M., "Jesus in the Gospel of Matthew", *BiBh* 1 (1975) 37-54; also in S. KUTHIRAKKATTEL, ed., *A Biblical Theology for India. Collected Writings of George M. Soares Prabhu*, II, Pune 1999, 157-171.

———, *The Formula Quotations in the Infancy Narrative of Matthew. An Enquiry into the Tradition History of Mt 1–2*, AnBib 63, Rome 1976.

———, "Following Jesus in Mission. Reflections on Mission in the Gospel of Matthew", in J. KAVUNKAL – F. HRANGKHUMA, ed., *Bible and Mission in India Today*, Bombay 1993, 64-92; also in I. PADINJAREKUTTU, ed., *Biblical Themes for a Contextual Theology Today. Collected Writings of George M. Soares Prabhu*, I, Pune 1999, 26-47.

———, "The Church as Mission: A Reflection on Mt 5:13-16", *Jeevadhara* 24 (1994) 271-281.

ŠOLTÉS, P, *„Ihr seid das Salz des Landes, das Licht der Welt". Eine exegetische Untersuchung zu Mt 5,13-16 im Kontext*, EHS.T, Frankfurt am Main 2004.

SONNET, J.P., "De la généalogie au 'Faites disciples' (Mt 28,19). Le livre de la génération de Jésus", in C. FOCANT – A. WENIN, ed., *Analyse narrative et Bible. Deuxième colloque international du Rrenab,*

Louvain-La-Neuve, avril 2004, BEThL 191, Louvain 2005, 199-209.

SOUČEK, J.B., "Salz der Erde und Licht der Welt. Zur Exegese von Matth. 5,13-16", *ThZ* 19 (1963) 169-179.

SPARKS, H.F.D., "The Doctrine of the Divine Fatherhood in the Gospels", in D.E. NINEHAM, ed., *Studies in the Gospels,* Fs. R.H. Lightfoot, Oxford 1957, 241-262.

SPICQ, C., "Une allusion au Docteur de Justice in Matthieu, XXIII,10?", *RB* 66 (1959) 387-396.

STENDAHL, K., "Prayer and Forgiveness", *SEÅ* 22 (1957) 75-86.

STOCK, A., *The Method and Message of Matthew*, Collegeville 1994.

STOCK, K., *Jesus Künder der Seligkeit. Betrachtungen zum Matthäus-Evangelium*, Innsbruck – Wien 1986.

———, *Discorso della montagna Mt. 5–7. Le Beatitudini*, Roma 1988, 2002[4].

———, *I racconti pasquali dei vangeli sinottici*, Roma 1991, 2002[2].

———, "I figli sono liberi (Mt 17,26; Lc 15,11-32)", *PSV* 23 (1991) 145-161.

———, "Giusto e Ingiusto nell'insegnamento di Gesù", *PSV* 34 (1996) 137-149.

———, "Die Bergpredigt als Programm für das Reich Gottes", *StMiss* 46 (1997) 1-20.

———, "Gott, der Vater, nach dem Zeugnis Jesu", in A. ZIEGENAUS, ed., *Mein Vater – euer Vater*, Theologische Sommerakademie Dießen 1999, Buttenwiesen 2000, 9-31.

———, *Marco. Commento contestuale al secondo Vangelo*, Bibbia e Preghiera 47, Roma 2003.

———, *Vivir en la Fe la Comunión con Jesús*, Onda 2005; English trans., *The Call of the Disciple*, Roma 2005.

STRACK, H.L – BILLERBECK, P., *Kommentar zum Neuen Testament aus Talmud und Midrasch,* I-VI, München 1921-1961.

STRECKER, G., *Der Weg der Gerechtigkeit: Untersuchung zur Theologie des Matthäus*, Göttingen 1962.

———, *Die Bergpredigt. Ein exegetischer Kommentar*, Göttingen, 1984; English trans., *The Sermon on the Mount. An Exegetical Commentary*, Edinburgh 1988.

STROTMANN, A., *"Mein Vater bist du!" (Sir 51,10): zur Bedeutung der Vaterschaft Gottes in kanonischen und nichtkanonischen frühjüdischen Schriften*, Frankfurt am Main 1991.

SWETNAM, J., "Hallowed Be Thy Name", *Bib* 52 (1971) 556-563.

SYREENI, K., *The Making of the Sermon on the Mount. A Procedural Analysis of Matthew's Redactoral Activity. Part I: Methodology and Compositional Analysis*, Helsinki, 1987.

———, "Separation and Identity: Aspects of the Symbolic World of Matt 6.1-18", *NTS* 40,4 (1994) 522-541.

SZIKSZAI, S., "Anoint", *IDB*, I, 138-139.

TALBERT, C.H., *Reading the Sermon on the Mount. Character Formation and Decision Making in Matthew 5–7,* Colombia 2004.

TASKER, D.R., *Ancient Near Eastern Literature and the Hebrew Scriptures about the Fatherhood of God*, StBL 69, New York 2004.

TASKER, R.V.G., *The Gospel According to St. Matthew. An Introduction and Commentary*, TNTC, London 1961.

TEHAN, T.M – ABERNATHY, D., *An Exegetical Summary of the Sermon on the Mount*, Dallas 2003.

TERTULLIAN, *De Oratione*, *PL* 1, 1153-1165; English trans., "Prayer", in *Tertullian-Disciplinary. Moral and Ascetical Works*, FaCh 40, Washington, D.C. 1959, 153-188.

THOMAS, J.C., "The Kingdom of God in the Gospel according to Matthew", *NTS* 39 (1993) 136-146.

THOMPSON, M.E.W., *I Have Heard Your Prayer*, Peterborough 1996.

THOMPSON, M.M., *The Promise of the Father: Jesus and God in the New Testament*, Louisville 2000.

THOMPSON, W.G., *Matthew's Advice to a Divided Community, Mt. 17,22–18,35*, AnBib 44, Rome 1970.

THURSTON, B.B., "Matthew 5:43-48", *Interp.* 41 (1987) 170-173.

van TILBORG, S., *The Jewish Leaders in Matthew*, Leiden 1972.

———, *The Sermon on the Mount as an Ideological Intervention. A Reconstruction of Meaning*, Assen 1986.

TOWNSEND, J.T., "Matthew XXIII. 9", *JBL* 12 (1961) 56-59.

TRILLING, W., *Das wahre Israel*, Leipzig 1958, 1975[3].

———, *Das Evangelium nach Matthäus*, I-II, Leipzig 1962, 1965.

TRUDINGER, P., "The 'Our Father' in Matthew as Apocalyptic Eschatology", *DR* 107 (1989) 49-54.

TURNER, V., *The Ritual Process*, New York 1966, 1977².

VANNI, U., "Il 'Padre Nostro', I", *CivCatt* 144,3 (1993) 345-358.

———, *Con Gesù verso il Padre. Per una spiritualità della sequela*, Bibbia e Preghiera 41, Roma 2002.

VELLANICKAL, M., *The Divine Sonship of Christians in the Johannine Writings*, AnBib 72, Rome 1977.

———, "The Christian Righteousness (Mt 6:1-18)", *BiBh* 10 (1984) 106-121.

VERMES, G., *The Dead Sea Scrolls in English*, Sheffield 1962, 1995⁴.

VERSEPUT, D.J., "The Role and Meaning of the 'Son of God Title' in Matthew's Gospel", *NTS* 33 (1987) 532-556.

———, "The Faith of the Reader and the Narrative of Matthew 13.53–16.20", *JSNT* 46 (1992) 3-24.

VIA, D.O. Jr., *Self-Deception and Wholeness in Paul and Matthew*, Minneapolis 1990.

WALLACE, D.B., *Greek Grammar beyond the Basics. An Exegetical Syntax of the New Testament*, Grand Rapids 1996.

WALTER, N., "ἐθνικός", *EDNT*, I, 381.

WATTS, J.D.W., "God the Father", *ISBE*, II, 509-511.

WEAVER, D.J., *The Missionary Discourse in the Gospel of Matthew. A Literary-Critical Analysis*, JSNT.S 38, Sheffield 1990.

WEDER, H., *Die Gleichnisse Jesu als Metaphern. Traditions- und redaktionsgeschichtliche Analysen und Interpretationen*, Göttingen 1978.

WELLMANN, B., "'So sollt ihr beten... '. Das Vaterunser und die Frömmigkeit (Mt 6,1-18)", in D. BAUER, ed., *Die Bergpredigt entdecken. Lese- und Arbeitsbuch zur Bergpredigt*, Stuttgart 2000, 88-101.

WIEFEL, W., *Das Evangelium nach Matthäus*, ThHK, Leipzig 1998.

WILCKENS, U., "ὑποκρίνομαι κτλ", *TDNT*, VIII, 559-571.

WILKINS, M.J., *The Concept of Disciple in Matthew's Gospel. As reflected in the Use of the Term μαθητής*, NT.S 59, Leiden – New York – København – Köln 1988.

WILKINS, M.J., "Named and Unnamed Disciples in Matthew: A Literary-Theological Study", in E.H. LOVERING, ed., *Society of Biblical Literature 1991 Seminar Papers*, Atlanta 1991, 418-439.

WINTER, B.W., "The Messiah as the Tutor: The Meaning of καθηγητής in Matthew 23,10", *TynB*, 42 (1991) 152-157.

WITHERINGTON III, B. – ICE, L.M., *The Shadow of the Almighty. Father, Son, and Spirit in Biblical Perspective*, Grand Rapids 2002.

WOOD, W.S., "The Salt of the Earth", *JThS* 25 (1924) 167-72.

WOUTERS, A., *„...wer den Willen meines Vaters tut". Eine Untersuchung zum Verständnis vom Handeln im Matthäusevangelium*, BU 23, Regensburg 1992.

ZAHN, T., *Das Evangelium des Matthäus*, Leipzig 1903, 1905[2].

ZELLER, D., "God as Father in the Proclamation and in the Prayer of Jesus", *in* A. FINKEL – L. FRIZZELL, ed., *Standing Before God. Studies on Prayer in Scriptures and in Tradition with Essays in Honour of John M. Oesterreicher*, New York 1981, 117-129.

ZERWICK, M., *Graecitas Biblica*, Roma 1960[4]; English trans., *Biblical Greek Illustrated by Examples*, SPIB 114, Roma 1963, 1994[6].

———, *Analysis philologica Novi Testamenti graeci*, SPIB 107, Roma 1966[5]; English trans., ZERWICK, M. – GROSVENOR, M., *A Grammatical Analysis of the Greek New Testament*, Roma 1974, 1996[5].

ZIESLER, J.A., *The Meaning of Righteousness in Paul. A Linguistic and Theological Enquiry*, MSSNTS 20, Cambridge 1972.

ZUMSTEIN, J., *La Condition du croyant dans l'évangile selon Matthieu*, OBO 16, Fribourg – Göttingen 1977.

AUTHOR INDEX

SCRIPTURAL INDEX
(Selected)

Stampa: Aprile 2008

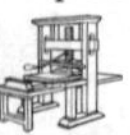

presso la tipografia
"Giovanni Olivieri" di E. Montefoschi
Roma • info@tipografiaolivieri.it